Information Warfare

Information Warfare

Daniel Ventre

First published 2007 in France by Hermes Science/Lavoisier entitled: *La guerre de l'information*
© LAVOISIER 2007
First published 2009 in Great Britain and the United States by ISTE Ltd and John Wiley & Sons, Inc.

ISTE Ltd
27-37 St George's Road
London SW19 4EU
UK

www.iste.co.uk

John Wiley & Sons, Inc.
111 River Street
Hoboken, NJ 07030
USA

www.wiley.com

© ISTE Ltd 2009

Library of Congress Cataloging-in-Publication Data

Ventre, Daniel.
  [Guerre de l'information. English]
  Information warfare / Daniel Ventre.
      p. cm.
  Includes bibliographical references and index.
  ISBN 978-1-84821-094-3
  1. Business intelligence. 2. Trade secrets. 3. Information technology--Security measures. 4. Computer security--Management. 5. Data protection. I. Title.
  HD38.7.V4713 2009
  355.3'43--dc22

                                                                      2009026202

British Library Cataloguing-in-Publication Data
A CIP record for this book is available from the British Library
ISBN 978-1-84821-094-3

Table of Contents

Abbreviations

ACINT	Acoustic Intelligence
AFDD	Air Force Doctrine Document
AFIWC	Air Force Information Warfare Center
AFPD	Air Force Policy Directive
AIIT	Army Institute of Information Technology
APCERT	Asia Pacific Computer Emergency Response Team
ASCON	Army Static Switched Communication Network
BARC	Bhabha Atomic Research Center
BFT	Blue Force Tracking
BOA	Bulle Opérationnelle Aéroterrestre ("Air and Land Operations Bubble")
C2	Command and Control
C2W	Command and Control Warfare
C3I	Command, Control, Communication, Intelligence
C4	Command, Control, Communication, Computers
C4I	Command, Control, Communication, Computers, Intelligence
C4I2SR	Command, Control, Communication, Computers, Intelligence, Information, Surveillance and Reconnaissance
C4ISR	Command, Control, Communications, Computers, Intelligence, Surveillance, and Reconnaissance
CBINT	Chemical and Biological Intelligence
CERT	Computer Emergency Response Team
CERT-In	Computer Emergency Response Team - India

CIA	Central Intelligence Agency
CMO	Civil-Military Operations
CNA	Computer Network Attacks
CNCERT/cc	China Computer Emergency Response Team/Coordination Center
CND	Computer Network Defence
CNE	Computer Network Exploitation
CNO	Computer Network Operations
COMINT	Communications Intelligence
COMSEC	Communication Security
DDoS	Distributed Denial of Service
DIA	Defense Intelligence Agency
DISA	Defense Information System Agency
DIWA	Defense Information Warfare Agency
DoD	Department of Defense
DoDAF	Department of Defense Architectural Framework
DoS	Denial of Service
DPP	Democratic Progressive Party
DPRI	Defense Policy Review Initiative
DSO	Defense Science Organisation
DSTA	Defense Science and Technology Agency
EA	Electronic Attack
EBO	Effect-Based Operations
EDB	Economic Development Board
EIW	Economic Information Warfare
ELINT	Electronic Intelligence
EMP	Electromagnetic Pulse
EP	Electronic Protection
ES	Electronic Support
EW	Electronic Warfare
FAGCI	Federal Agency of Government Communications and Information
FBI	Federal Bureau of Investigation
FIRST	Forum of Incident Response and Security Teams
FIWC	Fleet Information Warfare Center
FSB	Federal Security Bureau

GDP	Gross Domestic Product
HKCERT/cc	Hong Kong Computer Emergency Response Team/Coordination Center
HUMINT	Human Intelligence
IAD	Information Assurance Department
IBW	Intelligence Based Warfare
ICE	Integrated Control Enablers
ICT	Information and Communication Technologies
IDA	Infocomm Development Authority (of Singapore)
IED	Improvised Explosive Device
IFF	Identification Friend or Foe
IIT	Indian Institutes of Technologies
IKC2	Integrated Knowledge-based Command and Control
ILS	Integrated Logistics Support
IMINT	Image Intelligence
INDU	Indian National Defense University
INFOSEC	Information Security
IO	Information Operations
IP	Intellectual Property
IPv6	Internet Protocol version 6
ISC	Indian Science Congress
ISP	Internet Service Provider
ISR	Intelligence, Surveillance, Reconnaissance
IW-D	Information Warfare – Defense
IWSC	Information Warfare Support Center
JCS	Joint Chiefs of Staff
JDA	Japan Defense Agency
JEWEL	Joint modelling and simulation Environment for Wargaming and Experimentation Labs (Singapore)
JPCERT/cc	Japan Computer Emergency Response Team/Coordination Center
KGB	Komitet Gossoudarstvennoï Bezopasnosti
KISA	Korean Information Security Agency
KMT	Kuomintang
KrCERT/cc	Korea Computer Emergency Response Team
LIC	Low Intensity Conflict

LIWA	Land Information Warfare Activity
LTTE	Liberation Tigers of Tamil Eelam
MASINT	Measurement and Signature Intelligence
MDA	Media Development Authority
MILDEC	Military Deception
TARM	Tupak Amaru Revolutionary Movement
MyCERT	Malaysia Computer Emergency Response Team
NASA	National Aeronautics and Space Administration
NATO	North Atlantic Treaty Organization
NCW	Network Centric Warfare
NGA	National Geospatial-Intelligence Agency
NICT	New Information and Communication Technologies
NISS	National Institue of Strategic Studies
NIWA	Naval Information Warfare Activity
NSA	National Security Agency
NSCC	National Security Coordination Centre
NUCINT	Nuclear Intelligence
NUS	National University of Singapore
NGO	Non-Governmental Organization
OODA	Observation, Orientation, Decision, Action
OPSEC	Operations Security
ORNS	Operational Ready National Servicemen
OSINT	Open Source Intelligence
P2P	Peer to Peer
PAIR	Physical Action - Information - Response
PBA	Predictive Battlespace Awareness
PC	Personal Computer
PKK	Partiya Karkerên Kurdistan (Kurdistan Workers' Party)
PLA	(Chinese) People's Liberation Army
PSYOPS	Psychological Operations
PSYWAR	Psychological Warfare
RADINT	Radar Intelligence
RAHS	Risk Assessment and Horizon Scanning
RAW	Research and Analysis Wing

RINT	Radiation Intelligence
RMA	Revolution in Military Affairs
ROI	Return on Investment
SAF	Singapore Armed Forces
SBA/MBA	Singapore Broadcasting Authority/Media Development Authority
SCADA	Supervisory Control and Data Systems
SCME	Singapore Air Force Center for Military Experimentation
SIGINT	Signal Intelligence
SingCERT	Singapore Computer Emergency Response Team
SM3	Standard Missile-3
SMA	Singapore Manufacturer's Federation
SPIIRAS	St Petersburg Institute for Informatics and Automation of the Russian Academy of Science
SPRING	Standard, Productivity and Innovation Board
SVR	Sluzhba Vneshney Razvedki (Foreign Intelligence Service)
TECHINT	Technical Intelligence
TLD	Top Level Domain
TSU	Taiwan Solidarity Union
TWCERT/cc	Taiwan Computer Emergency Response Team/Coordination Center
WMD	Weapons of Mass Destruction

Introduction

While industry and society started imagining, creating and dreaming of new lifestyles for humanity with the evolution of information technologies, strategists were imagining new conflict scenarios for the 21st Century; how could we take advantage of information and information technologies to take the lead over our competitors or enemies?

The Gulf War in 1991 seemed to provide an early conclusive answer. Controlling information and its technologies is the key to victory against modern conflicts. The expression "information warfare" was recognized throughout the world as a new and major concept, becoming the object of concern for many decision makers and strategists, whether they were military or civilian.

During the 1990s, other concepts took root in these debates on the control, risks and challenges of information and new technologies, such as, for example, information operations, cyber warfare, computer network attack, network-centric war or cyber terrorism. Since then, international literature has abounded with books, articles, reports, studies, analyses and official, unofficial, serious, and even sometimes far-fetched expert comments, describing these concepts and theories ad infinitum. Today, in the military field, we sometimes prefer the expression "information operation", though we increasingly mention cyber warfare, infowar or cyber attacks; however, the basic concept remains the broader "information warfare", which includes a range of operations carried out within the information world.

Information technologies, presented as the primary vector of international growth in the 21st Century, seem also to be our worst enemy, the Achilles heel of our societies dependent on information systems because, through them and with them, our adversaries and enemies can attack us.

And attacks are widespread in cyberspace. They may vary in type (spamming, phishing, intercepting, intrusions, data leaks, site defacements and DoS[1] attacks) but they are all an attack. As for the attackers, they have long had the image of a hacker, sometimes a minor, wrongly portrayed as a prodigy of computer genius (as if one needed genius to type on a computer to attack systems), able to penetrate the computer systems of a bank or government agency alone, and even suspected of being able to launch a major and destructive attack against the networks of a nation. But attackers are not all teenagers desperate for a new game. There can be multiple profiles and motivations; attacks do not only take the form of hacker attacks.

More generally, the concern that cyber attacks can disrupt the economy of a corporation or a nation, or even affect global stability, has become the nightmare of countries dependent on information technologies. The world has become conscious that it has entered the information technology insecurity age, controlled by security vendors.

And, since it is no longer possible to do without information and information technologies, we might as well, while we're at it, do well by them and, if possible, be harmful to our enemies. How can we use information and information systems to increase our defence capabilities? How can we dominate the enemy? How can we defeat them?

Information warfare must respond to these expectations. It must provide nations that do not have the resources to reach the level of more powerful nations on a military, technological, economic and digital basis, the means to rival them. But for all that, information warfare is not the weapon of the poor, the rock that must be thrown at the giant's eye to blind him, because information warfare supposes that we have relatively significant technological means, financial means and, especially, strategies.

The expression "information warfare" has not found a single, consensual definition. The reason is undoubtedly in the terms that it is made up of. The term "warfare" is still the subject of many a debate and its definition is different whether we are a sociologist, anthropologist, economist, historian, political scientist or member of the military. As for "information", it is approached in a different way whether we are a mathematician, computer specialist, sociologist, journalist, member of the military or economist.

This book, which introduces the concept of "information warfare", is not meant to completely solve these questions of definition. Its objective is to analyze what information warfare can be, its multiple aspects and components (because

---

1. Denial of Service.

information warfare cannot be reduced only to attacks against computer networks), to identify its players, challenges and possible strategies, as well as looking at the input of some of the larger nations, where the world's economic, political and military balances are decided at the beginning of the 21st Century.

Chapter 1

The United States

The United States proved the undeniable power of their military with Desert Storm in 1991. Since then, their modern military and combat styles have served as examples to the rest of the world. Of course, the impressive volume of troops deployed to conquer Iraq explained, in part, their victory against an inadequate military. But what people have retained is the new face of war: information is now at the forefront and its "digital" nature clearly provides a new power to its users. Not only could the planet watch the launching of operations in real time, but optimized use of information and communication technologies to help troops, and the coordination and preparation of operations and the carrying out of attacks proved to be, if not the key to victory, at least a major player in not losing. The lessons drawn from this victory raised several questions: was this a new type of war? Should we call it "information age warfare" or "information warfare"? This first chapter is naturally dedicated to the United States since they have been used as a reference and as an object of observation for the rest of the world. They have also put forward a series of doctrinal texts and innovative concepts in the last 20 years.

1.1. Information warfare in the 1990s

1.1.1. *Points of view from security experts*

In 1994, in his book *Information Warfare* [SCH 94], Winn Schwartau, security expert and author of many reference publications in the field of information technologies, defined three categories of information warfare:

– personal information warfare (called Class 1 information warfare), created through attacks against data involving individuals and privacy: disclosure, corruption and intercepting of personal and confidential data (medical, banking and communications data). These attacks aimed at recreating or modifying the electronic picture of an individual by illicit means, or simply by using available open-source information, can often be simply carried out through technical solutions for standard catalog or Internet sales;

– commercial information warfare (called Class 2 information warfare) occurs through industrial espionage, broadcasting false information about competitors over the Internet. The new international order is filled with tens of thousands of ex-spies looking for work where they can offer their expertise. The United States is the target of economic and industrial espionage from Russia, from ex-members of the Eastern bloc, from Japan (which has almost destroyed the American information technology industry in Silicon Valley), and France and Germany who would not hesitate to use hackers to steal information;

– global information warfare (called Class 3 information warfare) aimed at industries, political spheres of influence, global economic forces, countries, critical and sensitive national information systems. The objective is to disrupt a country by damaging systems including energy, communications and transport. It is the act of using technology against technology, of secrets and stealing secrets, turning information against its owner, of prohibiting an enemy from using its own technologies and information. It is the ultimate form of conflict in cyberspace occurring through the global network. This class of information warfare generates chaos.

According to Winn Schwartau[1], real information warfare uses information and information systems as a weapon against its targets that are information and information systems. This definition eliminates kinetic weapons (for example bombs and bullets). Information warfare can attack people, organizations or countries (or spheres of influence) via a wide range of techniques, such as breach of confidentiality, attacks against integrity, psychological operations and misinformation.

Information warfare is therefore not limited to the military sphere: it can be carried out against civil infrastructures, constituting a new facet of war where the target can be the national economic security of an enemy. On the other hand, methods for carrying out a war are not a military monopoly. A small group of antagonists can launch an information warfare offensive remotely, while comfortably seated in front of a computer and completely anonymous. A group of hackers could choose to declare war against a country, independently from any control of state power.

---

1. [SCH 94], and for more recent approaches [SCH 02] and [SCH 05].

For Al Campen[2], U.S. Air Force colonel, one of the main criteria for defining information warfare is what is different from the past; this difference involves dependence on a vulnerable technology (information technology). Al Campen[3] limits the field of information warfare to information (data) in its digital form and to the software and hardware responsible for its creation, modification, storage, processing and distribution. From this point of view, psychological operations[4] consisting of scattering leaflets over populations are not information warfare operations; public broadcasting and electronic manipulation of television images, however, are part of information warfare. The physical destruction of telecommunications devices is not information warfare, but disrupting or paralyzing communication with the help of a virus is.

For James F. Dunningan[5], information warfare is attacking and defending the capability of transmitting information[6].

For Fred Cohen, information technology security expert and inventor of the concept of the "computer virus"[7], information warfare is a conflict in which information or information technology is the weapon, target, objective or method[8].

Martin C. Libicki[9] defines information warfare as a series of activities triggered by the need to modify information flows going to the other party, while protecting our own; such activities include physical attack, radio-electronic attack, attacks on systems and sensors, cryptography, attacks against computers, and psychological operations. His definition is not limited to military information warfare. In 1995, Libicki wondered about the nature of this new concept: was it a new form of war, a new art, or the revisited version of an older form of war? A new form of conflict that would exist because of the global information infrastructure, or an old form that would find new life with the information age? Is information warfare a field by itself? In order to attempt to define the parameters of this concept, Libicki identifies seven major components:

– command and control warfare (C2);

– intelligence warfare;

---

2. Source: [THR 96].
3. See [CAM 92] and [CAM 96].
4. This concept is addressed in more detail later in this chapter.
5. Read [DUN 96].
6. Source: [THR 96].
7. See http://all.net/contents/resume.html as well as
http://www.iwar.org.uk/cip/resources/senate/economy/cohen~1.htm
8. Source: [THR 96].
9. http://www.rand.org/about/contacts/personal/libicki/

– electronic warfare;

– psychological operations;

– hacker warfare (software attacks against information systems);

– economic information warfare (through the control of commercial information);

– cyber warfare (i.e. virtual battles).

Some aspects of information warfare are as old as time: attempting to strike at the head of the enemy (C2 war), carrying out all sorts of deceptions (deceiving, abusing and misleading the enemy), and psychological operations. On the other hand, hacker warfare and cyber warfare are completely new methods linked to the revolution of information and communications technologies.

For Larry Merritt[10], technical director for the Air Force Information Warfare Center (AFIWC), information warfare includes all actions undertaken to exploit or affect the capacity of an adversary to acquire a realistic image of the battlefield or to operate the command and control of his troops. Information warfare also includes actions undertaken for the protection of our own capabilities; electronic warfare, computer network attacks, intelligence, reconnaissance and surveillance are all defensive actions.

The "information warfare" concept creates multiple approaches which can be very different. The reason is in the nature of the terms making up the expression: what is "warfare", what is "information"? The problem in defining the semantic parameters is the cause of the different points of view on information warfare.

But regardless of the approach, information warfare seems closely linked to our new social and technical structure, to the strong dependence now linking our exchanges (our social, economic, cultural and political transactions) to information technologies. Information warfare could be a type of battle for the control of the digital space involving the whole of society. Information and information systems can be used to attack and conquer the enemy. Some would prefer to call it "information age warfare" to define the capacity to control and use the information battlefield, which then becomes an additional factor in the war, in the same way that the capacity to control air and space did in conventional wars in the industrial age.

The major point that seems to define the debate on information warfare is framed by the following questions: can the war be carried out only in the world of information? Are wars, as fought by man since the beginning of time with their streams of increasingly lethal weapons and bloody battles, on the verge of

---

10. Source: [THR 96].

disappearing? Will information technologies revolutionize societies to the point of revolutionizing the way we fight wars, i.e. imposing our political will on others only through battles in the information sphere? Or will they only be a new complementary method? Should we call it "information warfare" or "information age warfare"?

The information space, understood as a space of violence, conflict and battle completely replacing the more traditional fields of conflicts, is one of the major ideas in the development of the "information warfare" concept: "Information technology is the most relevant basis for modern warfare. It has become conceivable to fight a war solely with information, which is expressed by the term 'information warfare'[…]. Information warfare could be defined as comprising all the means of accomplishing and securing information dominance so as to support politico-military strategies by manipulating adversary information and information systems and simultaneously securing and protecting one's own information and information systems, and increasing their efficiency"[11].

1.1.1.1. *Official military documents*

It is impossible to list all the publications, reports, commentaries, analyses, opinions and notices published and expressed by experts of all fields on the subject since the beginning of the 1990s.

But in order to understand as much as possible what the United States mean by "information warfare", it is necessary to understand military doctrines which have endeavored to provide the definitions of key concepts, while keeping in mind the pragmatic needs of defense. The idea is not to theorize but to provide the military with guidelines and precise frameworks for their organization, strategies, operations and tactics.

The text that formally launched the concept of information warfare is a classified guideline of the Department of Defense, from 1992[12]. Subsequent evolutions, however, enhanced the concept before it finally found its place within the different American military doctrines.

---

11. Elisabeth Hauschild, "Modern and information warfare: A conceptual approach", in *International Security Challenges in a Changing World* (*Studies in Contemporary History and Security Policy, vol. 3*), Spillmann, K.R. & Krause, J. (Eds); see: http://www.isn.ethz.ch.
12. DoD Directive TS-3600.1, December 21, 1992, "Information Warfare".

In an instruction from January 1995[13], the Navy defined information warfare as an action taken to support the national security strategy[14] in order to reach and maintain a decisive advantage, by attacking the information infrastructure of the enemy, by using, paralyzing or influencing opposite information systems while protecting friendly information systems. For the American Navy, the term "information warfare" means that ICTs are a force multiplier authorizing more efficient operations: more efficient electronic warfare, better cryptology. The military can carry out the same operations as before but in a better way. ICTs provide improvement compared to the past. This improvement attracts more attention than the idea of radical transformation of ideologies, objectives or targets.

The Air Force document called "The Foundation of Information Warfare"[15] makes a distinction between information age warfare and information warfare: the former uses computerized weapons and the latter uses information as a weapon, an independent field.

The Army, Navy and Air Force do not share a common doctrine. This trend will be more obvious in the coming years.

1.1.2. *US Air Force doctrine: AFDD 2-5 (1998)*

In August of 1998, the US Air Force published its doctrine on information operations (Air Force Doctrine Document – AFDD 2-5 – Information Operations[16]). Examining the content of this document with a comparative analysis of the official doctrine of the Joint Chiefs of Staff (JP 3-13)[17] published the same year is interesting, as will be seen in section 1.1.3.

How is information warfare defined in this doctrine from the US Air Force? What are its components? Which concepts must be compared with the concept of information warfare?

---

13. Instruction 3430.26, Department of the Navy, Washington DC 20350-2000, OPNAVINST 3430.26, No 6, 18 January 1995.
14. The strategy consists of defining fundamental long term goals and choosing action methods and resources necessary for the achievement of these objectives. It is the part of military science involving the general behavior of the war and the defense organization of a country. It is the art of making an army evolve through operations until it is in contact with the enemy. The tactic is the application of the strategy, all the methods used to achieve a short term result. It is the art of combining all military methods to achieve goals.
15. [WOO 95].
16. http://www.ttic.mil/doctrine/jel/service_pubs/afd2_5.pdf.
17. Joint Pub 3-13. Joint Doctrine for Information Operations, 9 October 1998. Joint Chiefs of Staff. 136 pages. http://www.c4i.org/jp3_13.pdf.

1.1.2.1. *Superiority of information*

Superiority of information is the degree of dominance in the field of information providing friendly forces the possibility of collecting, controlling, using and defending information without actual opposition.[18]

Superiority of information, as considered by the Air Force, is a state of relative advantage, and not a capacity as presented in JP 3-13.

1.1.2.2. *Information operations*

This term groups actions taken to conquer, use, defend or attack information and information systems, including "information-in-warfare" and "information warfare" simultaneously. Information-in-warfare means conquering (acquiring) information and using it. Information warfare means attacking and defending.

1.1.2.3. *Information warfare*

Information warfare is made up of information operations carried out to defend our own information and our own information systems, or to attack and affect the information and information systems of an enemy. The definition introduces concepts that will not be found in the Joint Chiefs of Staff approach (JP 3-13): the concept of counter-information and its two subsets of offensive counter-information and defensive counter-information. Counter-information establishes the desired level of control over functions of information, enabling friendly forces to operate at a given moment and place, without prohibitive interference from the adversary.

Offensive counter-information group offensive operations in information warfare, carried out to control the information environment by paralyzing, deteriorating, interrupting, destroying or attempting to deceive information and information systems include:

– psychological operations (the definition adopted is the same as the one subsequently published in the JP 3-13 document);

– electronic warfare (the definition adopted is the same as the one published in the JP 3-13 document);

– military deception;

– physical attacks (the definition adopted is the same as the one in JP 3-13);

– information attack, an action taken to manipulate or destroy enemy information systems without visibly changing the physical entity in which they

---

18. Air Force Doctrine Document 2-5, August 5, 1998,
http://www.dtic.mil/doctrine/jel/service_pubs/afd2_5.pdf.

reside. This means attacking the content without leaving a visible trace on the outside. The closest term is CNA (Computer Network Attacks)[19] in JP 3-13. The JP 3-13 document includes computer destruction.

Defensive counter-information group activities carried out to protect and defend friendly information and information systems include:

– information assurance;

– operations security;

– counter-intelligence;

– psychological counter-operations;

– counter-deception;

– electronic protection.

1.1.3. *The doctrine of the Joint Chiefs of Staff committee: JP 3-13 (1998)*

Information warfare is also defined in a publication from the Joint Chiefs of Staff (JCS) on October 9, 1998, called Joint Pub 3-13 "Joint Doctrine for Information Operations (IO)"[20]. The JCS text was published after the Air Force document. This detail is important because the JCS publication is intended, theoretically at least, to apply to all departments. Since the "Goldwater-Nichols Department of Defense Reorganization" Law[21] of 1986, each department must ensure the compliance of its doctrine and procedures with the common doctrine established by the Joint Chiefs of Staff. Information operations doctrines, however, were developed concurrently.

The JCS publication provides the doctrinal basis for the conduct of information operations during joint operations.

1.1.3.1. *Superiority of information*

Acquiring "superiority of information" means being able to collect, process and distribute an uninterrupted flow of information, while using or blocking the possibilities of an opponent to do the same.

Document JP 3-13 defines superiority of information as absolute perfection, with the idea of "uninterrupted flow of information" for friendly forces, banning this flow to the enemy. The U.S. Air Force is not seeking such an absolute, considering

---

19. The abbreviation CNA will be used throughout this book.
20. http://ics.leeds.ac.uk/papers/pmt/exhibits/469/jp3_13.pdf.
21. http://www.ndu.edu/library/goldnich/99433pt1.pdf.

instead that operations in the field of information cannot be perfect. It prefers to speak of "relative advantage": opponents will try to disrupt information operations, but Air Force superiority of information will ensure that these attempts are unsuccessful.

The components of superiority of information are also different, and the common components are structured differently. For JP 3-13, there are three components: information systems, relevant information and information operations. The Air Force only has one component for superiority of information: information operations.

1.1.3.2. Information operations

Information operations are the actions taken to affect the information and information systems of the enemy, while defending our own information and information systems. There are two main sub-divisions in information operations: offensive information operations (gain) and defensive information operations (exploitation)[22]. Remember that for the Air Force, the two sub-divisions of information operations are information warfare and information-in-warfare.

For JP 3-13, the expression "offensive information operations" means actions aimed at affecting adversary decision-makers in reaching or promoting specific objectives. For the Air Force, offensive activities of information warfare are carried out to control the information environment.

The objective of offensive information operations, which can be carried out in a wide range of military operation situations, at all levels of warfare (strategic, operational and tactical) and that can have an even greater impact when carried out in times of peace or at the beginning of a conflict, is to affect enemy decision-makers or to reach specific goals. Offensive activities include, among others:

– operations security;

– military deception (deceive, trick, and set the enemy up to act against his own interests);

– psychological operations;

– electronic warfare;

– physical attack, destruction;

– special information operations;

– computer attacks.

---

22. Page vii, JP 3-13.

Defensive information operations integrate and coordinate policies, procedures, operations, resources and technologies for the defense and protection of information and information systems. They must ensure necessary protection and defense of information and information systems that joint forces depend on to carry out their operations and reach their objectives. They consist of:

– information assurance (IA);

– operations security;

– physical security;

– counter-deception;

– counter-propaganda;

– counter-intelligence;

– electronic warfare;

– special information operations.

Defensive and offensive operations are complementary and support each other. Offensive operations can support defensive operations through four processes:

– protecting the information environment;

– detecting attacks;

– restoration capabilities;

– responding to attacks.

Because of their relationship, it is important that all offensive and defensive operations components are integrated. If, theoretically, defensive and offensive are separate, in reality, they must be designed and taken as inseparable.

The report also identifies "special information operations", a category of information operations that requires detailed examination and a process of approval because of their sensitivity, their effect or impact potential, their security needs or risks to the national security of the United States.

1.1.3.3. *Information warfare*

The superiority of information diagram, according to JP 3-13, does not include information warfare, only defined as the series of operations carried out during a crisis or conflict to reach or promote specific objectives over one or more specific adversaries[23]. Information warfare therefore is only a subset of information operations: simply operations conducted in times of crisis or conflict. In times of peace, we could not speak of information warfare. But the doctrine does not define the notions of "crisis" and "conflict" either.

This definition is quite different from the Air Force's definition.

In both approaches, information warfare is an information operation. But even though JP 3-13 separates information warfare and information operations according to the time space in which they occur, the Air Force considers that we are constantly in a state of information warfare because the defensive side is always engaged. This approach (from the US Air Force) may seem more relevant considering the situation after over ten years. The United States (and many other nations) are the subject of permanent attacks launched against their information space (targeting the Pentagon and sensitive infrastructures of the country through massive and coordinated DDoS (Distributed Denial of Service) attacks in increasing intensity since 2005), imposing a state of permanent defense, a cyber security and cyber defense strategy applied to all levels of the grid, i.e. to civilian and military information infrastructures. This defense must be engaged despite the absence of specificly known enemies, in a period where peace, crisis and conflict are mixed without clear temporal boundaries.

Information operations cover peace and returning to peace periods because of their presumed deterring character, which should also apply to adversaries in times of crisis, making them hesitate in initiating actions. The ultimate objective of information operations remains to affect enemies or potential enemies, so that they put a stop to actions threatening the American national security interests. The 1998 text obviously did not take into account the terrorist threat. The question still remains today: can information operations be efficient enough to dissuade or intimidate any type of adversary? The dissuasive character seems implausible. The main quality of the information space is to provide any type of attacker the ways to bypass security and defense methods. No nation, military or police force has been able to implement totally dissuasive measures against determined players, to this day. The main reason resides in the operation of networks ensuring invisibility and thus impunity to all who want to become attackers. In 2009, it seems that the computer weapon as bypass weapon, and certainly not as a weapon of dissuasion, is an accepted fact.

1.1.4. *Components of information warfare*

It is necessary at this point to explain in more detail the fundamental concepts discussed previously, particularly those called components of information warfare

---

23. Page 23 in the document.

that we invariably find in the different doctrines which are formulated in the United States, but also all over the world. They are Psychological Operations (PSYOPS), Electronic Warfare, military deception, Operations Security (OPSEC), Information Assurance (IA) and Computer Network Attacks (CNA).

1.1.4.1. *Psychological operations*

The sub-title of this section could be "The importance of psychology in battles between individuals or groups of individuals". PSYOPS emerged way before the digital age and will probably outlive it. They can be summarized as the use of communication to influence behavior.

Communication is the process by which an individual influences another person, involving the spectrum of human actions (speaking, writing, etc.). Theories of communication (particularly those of Melvin L. Defleur for whom communication is the group of methods making it possible to exert social control, allocate roles and coordinate efforts) provide more detail. Communication is a tool for relations, not only for individuals between each other, but also for individuals with their historical perspectives. Communication consists of:

– controlling the media to control received and broadcast information; filtering real information, real but partially presented information (scaling of facts), creating and broadcasting false information. The presence of the media in the field during conflicts, or close to a conflict, makes it possible for PSYOPS to take action contributing to the success of military operations, as long as the media can be controlled;

– manipulating minds through information;

– using the emotional impact of words, images, speeches or sounds;

– launching "positive propaganda" operations intended for our own camp, and "intoxication" operations aimed at the enemy.

Psychological operations by misinformation, intoxication, deception, banning and propaganda[24] are incredibly important in a period of conflict because they contribute to the success of military operations, help in dominating the opponent, are used to attempt to dissuade the enemy from pursuing the fight, get him to surrender weapons and to surrender himself, help in preserving the morale of our own troops, and also help in getting and maintaining support from the population and national and international public opinion.

Psychological operations also attempt to reach thoughts, opinions, beliefs and emotions in order to influence behaviors, attitudes and affect national interests.

---

24. For more information on the term "propaganda", refer to [CHO 02].

Potential psychological operation applications have led to the idea of the "noosphere", a field in which dominance of ideas, instead of dominance over land or populations, would be predominant.

The implementation of psychological operations presumes a deep knowledge of theories of communication and information, psychology of individuals, their behaviors and cultures. Nobody can pretend to really understand the direct or indirect impacts of these operations today.

1.1.4.2. *Electronic warfare*

Electronic warfare priorities are denial of service (jamming, mimicry, physical attack), deception (that can be directed at automated systems or people) and exploitation (intercepting/listening, obtaining any information with operational value from the enemy's use of his electronic systems).

The goal of electronic warfare is to control the electromagnetic spectrum.

The American doctrine[25] defines electronic warfare as any military action using directed electromagnetic energy to control the electromagnetic spectrum or to attack the enemy. The three main sub-divisions of electronic warfare are:

– Electronic Attack (EA) aimed at attacking people, equipment and installations with the purpose of deteriorating, neutralizing and destroying enemy combat capabilities by jamming, electromagnetic deception, the use of lasers and particle beam weapons. Attacking communications can reach different objectives: access contents, detect and destroy system nodes, jam communications to disrupt the adversary, destroy the opponent's equipment with the help of high power microwaves and send instructions instead of enemy commands (deception). Deception is one of the major tools of electronic attacks. Deceiving the enemy by manipulating his perception in such a way that the relevance of his judgment and his capability of acquiring targets are deteriorated. Physical destruction is another important facet of electronic attack. Destruction or neutralization by jamming sensors and opposite communications is called soft kill; physical destruction is qualified as hard kill;

– Electronic Protection (EP) includes systems design resistant to jamming by any kind of attack. Cryptography (also called Comsec – Communications Security) is an element of electronic warfare;

– the objective of Electronic Warfare Support (ES) is to search, intercept, identify and locate sources of electromagnetic energy in order to recognize

---

25. Joint Pub 1-02 document.

immediate threats. Electronic support provides necessary intelligence and the identification of threats for efficient attack and protection. Electronic support includes Sigint (signals intelligence) which is made up of Comint (Communications Intelligence, a collection of enemy communications such as the contents of messages and traffic data) and Elint (Electronic Intelligence, which captures enemy radar signals and other non-communicating electromagnetic energy sources). Before attacking the communications of an enemy, their network of communications must be mapped out; this is the role of SIGINT that will consist of extracting information from signal masses and from network traffic. Reception equipment today is able to pick up almost all signals transmitted, locate transmitters with precision and feed databases with the signals collected. Data collected must be analyzed. We must especially be able to select the traffic because trying to collect, process and analyze everything is not reasonable.

Electronic weapon systems are made up of sensors (radars, infrared, and sonars), communication lines (transporting data from sensors to command and control (C2) centers) and output devices (lasers, jammers, EMP).

These systems are part of the composition of C2 networks which transmit and receive data, voice and images. Communications must be secure between army commanders and political leaders, for example, so that messages and orders are not corrupted, intercepted or blocked. There are many methods threatening this security: cryptanalysis, sabotage, subversion of personnel, robbery of material, deception, jamming (such as jamming signals transmitted from a plane to the missile it just launched), physical destruction of networks and communication equipment, interception of unsecured communications (particularly if the communication uses methods such as public or radio telecommunication networks which can be the subject of interception), intercepting orders and replacing them with others, or using voice morphing techniques to substitute commands.

With the help of this series of methods, the military develops attack and defense strategies, which are generally a mix of possibilities.

1.1.4.3. *Military deception*

"Deception" is a series of measures designed to "deceive the enemy by manipulating, deteriorating or falsifying evidence to trigger a reaction that is detrimental to his interests"[26].

For the American military, deception is aimed at enemy decision-makers, by affecting their information collection and analysis process and with dissemination systems. This deception requires an in-depth knowledge of the enemy and his

---

26. Joint Pub 1-02 document.

decision-making processes. Anticipation is one of the keys. Command must imagine the way in which they think the enemy would act at critical times in the battle. These desired actions become the objective of deception operations. Military deception focuses on the desired behavior, and not only on deceiving the mind. Camp B must get Camp A command to form an inappropriate opinion of the capabilities and intentions of the troops in camp B, so that they make decisions contrary to their interests. Military deception operations depend on intelligence operations to identify the correct targets of the deception. We must be able to create a credible story and evaluate the efficiency of the deception plan and, to have the best chance of success for such an operation, a very small number of people may need to be kept informed, to reduce the risk of an information leak. But this type of operation may also have a disruptive effect among our own camp[27].

1.1.4.4. *Operations security*

Operations security (OPSEC) is a methodology intended to keep an adversary from accessing "critical" information involving his camp and allies, i.e. information necessary to correctly evaluate the capabilities and intentions of the target.

The concept of OPSEC can be analyzed in the light of the doctrine in the official document titled "Operations Security – Joint Publication 3-13.3", from 29 June 2006, which modifies the previous text from 24 January 1997, referenced 3-54[28].

This new doctrinal text establishes the rules that the American military must follow in their activities and operations. It is divided into three major chapters discussing general aspects (definitions, context), operation security processes and operation security planning, consecutively. Appendices help in the practical understanding of the illustrated concepts.

The proposed definition highlights the main characteristic of OPSECs being one of the information operations. It is a process that:

– identifies critical information in order to determine whether allied actions can be observed by enemy intelligence systems;

– determines if the information obtained by adversaries could be interpreted in such a way that would be useful to them;

---

27. For more information on the American approach, please refer to document JP 3-58, *Joint Doctrine for Military Deception*. Joint Chiefs of Staff. 31 May 1996. 61 pages. http://www.dtic.mil/doctrine/jel/new_pubs/jp3_58.pdf.
28. Joint-Pub 3-54, *Joint Doctrine for Operations Security*. 24 January 1997. Joint Chiefs of Staff, USA. 79 pages. http://www.iwar.org.uk/rma/resources/opsec/JP3_54.pdf.

– executes selected measures eliminating or reducing the possibility for the enemy to use critical allied information[29].

Security programs protect classified information. OPSEC identifies, controls and protects generally non-classified information that is associated with, or can be linked to, sensitive operations or activities.

On our side, we have:

– classified information, protected by security programs;

– non-classified information but which can be linked to sensitive activities or operations, then qualified as "critical" and thus must be identified and protected by OPSEC;

– "indicators", which are a class of information associated to an activity in a significant way;

– a military that is visible to the public and enemy intelligence, in times of peace, training, drills or operations. Non-classified information, when correlated with other non-classified information, can become classified or reveal a sensitive operation.

And in the enemy camp, we find information intelligence, acquisition and exploitation systems that we have to protect against.

The OPSEC process consists of five distinct actions:

– the identification of critical information, i.e. information that is crucial to the enemy, making it possible to categorize information to only protect what is qualified as "vital";

– the analysis of threats via intelligence, counter-intelligence and open information research and analysis to identify probable enemies. We must find the answer to the following questions: who is the enemy? What goals does the enemy have? What actions could the enemy take? What information does the enemy already have? What intelligence capabilities does the enemy have?

– the analysis of vulnerabilities via the investigation of each aspect of a planned operation to identify OPSEC indicators that could reveal critical information. The objective of OPSEC is to reduce the vulnerability of American or coalition forces with regard to the exploitation of critical information by the enemy. OPSEC applies to all military activities during operations. The following questions must be answered: which indicators of critical information that is unknown by the enemy

---

29. JP 3-13.3 document, page vii.

will be created by allied activities? Which indicators can the enemy collect? Which indicators will the enemy be able to use against allied forces?

– the evaluation of risk by the analysis of vulnerabilities identified in the previous phase, and identification of possible OPSEC measures for each vulnerability. Possible measures include secrecy, concealment, camouflage, deception, intentional diversion in relation to habits, and direct strikes against enemy intelligence systems. Technical measures (see Appendix C) consist of not giving operations information in unsecure email messages, preparing for CNAs, placing vital operational information on disk, using cryptography to protect voice, data and video communications, controlling radio communication transmissions, using systems with low probability of interception and secure phone lines. Finally, we need to monitor the possible interaction of OPSEC measures; measuring OPSEC may create an indicator (concealing equipment that was not protected before may reveal the preparation of military action);

– the application of appropriate OPSEC measures by command, who must determine if the gain in security exceeds cost in resources. Then, during their execution, the enemy's reaction must be observed to determine its efficiency.

The range of the spectrum involved by OPSEC implies a large number of players: army commands, Defense Intelligence Agency (DIA), National Security Agency (NSA), the OPSEC interagency and different Department of Defense (DoD) agencies.

The major problem lies in how to delimit the moving perimeter of "critical information". Information will become "critical" according to context; one piece of information that is ordinary today can become critical because of the emergence of new events. Yesterday's ally can become today's enemy for example. Information can be critical according to the context in which it is used, whether for counter-terrorism, hostilities, military intervention or diplomatic negotiations. Anything that is the product of the armed forces could be perceived as potentially critical. This is revealed by the bans or restrictions on military personnel being able to freely express themselves through newsgroups, chatrooms or other discussion tools and information sharing.

Annex A from JP 3-13 draws the limits of this perimeter by listing examples of "critical" information; information involving military capacities, target selection, logistic capacities, intentions, active forces and reserves, and timing of operations.

1.1.4.5. *Information assurance*

This concept groups the measures that protect and defend information and information systems by ensuring their availability, their integrity, their capacity to be authenticated, their confidentiality and their non repudiation. These measures include the restoration of information systems by incorporating protection, detection and methods of reaction[30].

For the military[31], "information assurance" is an information operation that protects and defends information systems by ensuring their availability, integrity, authentication, confidentiality and non repudiation. This security presumes the restoration of information systems with the incorporation of methods of protection, detection and reaction.

Information assurance consists of the protection and defense of information and information systems against unauthorized access and modification of stored, processed and transmitted information, and against denial of service for authorized users. Information assurance also includes the measures necessary to detect, describe and counter such threats. Information assurance is made up of computer security and communications security, also called INFOSEC[32].

"Communication security" (COMSEC) is protection resulting from all measures taken to ban access to valuable information for unauthorized people or mislead unauthorized people in their interpretation resulting from the possession and study of information[33]. Communication security includes security by cryptography, security of transmissions and physical security of communication and information methods.

1.1.4.6. *Computer network attacks*

Definitions are provided in the doctrinal text JP 3-13, pages I-9 to I-11, GL-4 to GL-10.

Document JP 3-13 from 1998 defines computer network attacks (CNA) as operations intended to disrupt, prohibit access to, deteriorate, destroy and steal information contained in computers, carried by computer networks, or targeting computers and networks. CNAs include all forms of attacks carried out against or by computers and computer networks.

The method of attack characterizing CNAs is data flow. An electronic attack such as the use of electromagnetic forces does not fall under the CNA category but is part of electronic attacks. For example, jamming a radar is an electronic attack, not a CNA. Propagating a computer virus is a CNA, not an electronic

---

30. National Information Assurance (IA) Glossary. Instruction No. 4009, revised version. June 2006. 86 pages. Committee on National Security Systems (CNSS), USA. http://www.cnss.gov/Assets/pdf/cnssi_4009.pdf.
31. JP 3-13 from 1998.
32. JP 3-13 from 1998.
33. JP 3-13 from 1998.

attack. There are many ways to develop such a computer attack: access to systems, controlling systems, destruction and distortion of data (through viruses, worms and Trojan horses), and data interception.

We also speak of cyberwar to describe these forms of aggression.

1.2. Information warfare in the 2000s

1.2.1. *Dictionary of the Department of Defense*

The dictionary of the US Department of Defense of 2001[34] uses the definition adopted by the 1998 JP 3-13 for information warfare: a methodology of information operations.

Information operations are the actions that can be taken to distort the information and information systems of the enemy, while protecting our own information and information systems. Information operations are implemented in times of peace, crisis or conflict. Those implemented only in times of crisis or conflict constitute information warfare.

In the 22 March 2007 version of the dictionary[35] the expression "information warfare" practically disappeared. We find it only in the list of abbreviations and acronyms, such as AFIWC (Air Force Information Warfare Center), FIWC (Fleet Information Warfare Center), IW-D (Defensive Information Warfare), IWSC (Information Warfare Support Center), LIWA (Land Information Warfare Activity), NIWA (Naval Information Warfare Activity) and TWI (Office for Information Warfare Support – DIA/Defense Intelligence Agency).

1.2.2. *US Air Force: AFDD 2-5 (2005) and AFPD 10-7 (2006)*

On 11 January 2005, document AFDD 2-5 "Information Operations" was published[36]. There again, as in 1998, the Air Force document was published before the document from the JCS.

---

34. Joint Publication 1-02. *Department of Defense Dictionary of Military and Associated Terms*, 782 pages, 12 April 2001. The document as amended at 17 March 2009 is available at http://www.dtic.mil/doctrine/jel/new_pubs/jp1_02.pdf.
35. Joint Publication 1-02 from 12 April 2001, revised 22 March 2007.
36. http://www.iwar.org.uk/iwar/resources/usaf/afdd2-5-2005.pdf.

The first major point to note on reading this document is that the expression "information warfare" is no longer used. Only the concept of information operations is still present, and the idea of their implementation at any time: peace, war or when returning to peace. Can the time of peace/war distinction no longer be relevant?

The acquisition and maintenance of "superiority of information" are critical tasks for commands and vital elements for kinetic and non-kinetic effect-based operations. Superiority of information is the degree of dominance in the field of information providing allied forces with the possibility of collecting, controlling, using and defending information without efficient opposition.

Information operations, carried out by the military in times of peace, war and returning to peace, are now:

– influencing operations to amplify the effects of traditional military operations, as well as for influencing in a different way than by just using force. The goal is to affect the perceptions and behaviors of leaders, groups and whole populations. These operations are psychological operations (PSYOPS), military deceptions (MILDEC), operations security (OPSEC), counter-intelligence measures (i.e. protecting against espionage, sabotage and assassinations), counter-propaganda operations and public affairs operations;

– electronic warfare operations: attacking, defending, supporting. This is the planning, use and evaluation of military methods to obtain desired effects through the electromagnetic spectrum, to support operational objectives;

– network warfare operations: attack (NetA), defend (NetD) and support (NS). This is the planning, use and evaluation of military methods to obtain desired effects through analog and digital interconnected networks in the battle space. These operations group the series of actions previously called computer network attacks (CNA). It is a war carried out through networks: destroying, disrupting and usurping information and information systems, and protecting against these attacks).

Information operations are the integrated use of these three capabilities, in collaboration with "integrated control enablers" (ICEs), to influence, disrupt, corrupt and usurp the human and automated decision process of the enemy while protecting our own.

The doctrine no longer speaks of "information-in-warfare" but of "integrated control enablers" (ICEs). These ICEs are not information operations but group methods of acquisition and exploitation; information operations only group defense and attack methods. ICEs must provide all available information.

ICEs include Intelligence, Surveillance, Reconnaissance (ISR) systems, network operations (NetOps – grouping systems, network management and information security), predictive battlespace awareness (PBA), and precision navigation.

Even though we no longer speak of information-in-warfare, the characteristics of war in the information age are described, as more emphasis is now placed on influencing political and military leaders, as well as populations, to solve conflicts. Information technologies have increased the methods of directly influencing populations and their leaders. ICTs have distributed the process of collection, storage, dissemination and processing of information. The US Air Force must use this technology as a powerful lever to acquire superiority of information and to be able to operate the cycle of decision (OODA loop) quicker than the opponent. This is what is called "decision superiority": being able to Observe, Orient, Decide and Act (the OODA loop) more quickly and efficiently than the enemy.

The AFPD 10-7(Air Force Policy Directive) document called "Information Operations"[37] of 6 September 2006 proposes a conversion chart of terminologies used by the US Air Force and JCS in the 2006 doctrines, revealing compatibility of terms used in both approaches.

ICE	IO
Acquisition and exploitation	Defend and attack

Table 1.1. *Distinction between Integrated Control Enablers (ICE) and Information Operations (IO)*

1.2.3. *The doctrine of the Joint Chiefs of Staff committee: JP 3-13 (2006)*

On 13 February 2006, JCS published the new version of the doctrinal document JP 3-13 called "Information Operations"[38].

The text eliminates the expression "information warfare" from its vocabulary. It also abandons the expressions "offensive information operations" and "defensive information operations".

The five fundamental operations of information operations are: 1) psychological operations; 2) military deception; 3) operations security; 4) electronic warfare; and

---

37. http://www.fas.org/irp/doddir/usaf/afpd10-7.pdf.
38. http://www.ttic.mil/doctrine/jel/service_pubs/afd2_5.pdf.

5) computer network operations (including the now traditional attack, exploitation and defense operations: Computer Network Exploitation (CNE) and Computer Network Defense (CND), CNA. Computer network attacks consist of paralyzing, interrupting, delaying and destroying information and/or information systems. Exploitation consists of the collection, monitoring and falsification of information. Defensive operations consist of protecting, detecting, restoring and responding.

To support these five basic methods, intelligence actions collect, analyze and provide information on the environment as well as on physical attacks, information assurance, counter-intelligence and physical security.

In the doctrine, the international dimension of operations is now taking a more significant place. Through lessons and experience learned in the past by the American military, the doctrine introduces terms such as "tribe", "family", "culture", "religion" and "alliances", absent from the 1998 version. Psychological, cultural and cognitive dimensions now occupy a central place.

Also of interest in this document is the representation of the information environment proposed by the military. Three different aspects, or dimensions, constitute the space in which the military must evolve and information operations must be carried out: a physical dimension, made up of command and control systems, infrastructures, networks and computers; an information dimension, where information is collected, processed, stored, broadcast, displayed and protected (the space of information content and flow); finally, a cognitive dimension which includes the thoughts of decision-makers and target audience: it is the space of perception, visualization, decision and thinking, and it is this dimension where battles and campaigns can be won or lost. Factors influencing the cognitive dimension are emotions, state of mind, experience, spatial awareness, public opinion, perceptions, media and rumors.

Annex B of JP 3-13 is extremely interesting because it proposes a table identifying the possible conflicts between the different actions of information operations. An attack by computer networks could be in conflict with a psychological operation if that attack prohibited the enemy from receiving the message addressed to him in the context of a psychological operation. Or a CNA type attack could be in conflict with a military deception operation when, by absence of coordination between the two, the result would be attacking the wrong target. Or when, by absence of coordination, a physical attack and a software attack are launched at the same time toward the same target. This would be wasting time and ammunition.

1.3. Other important concepts and reflections

The very lively debate that has developed in the United States in the last 20 years involving the military, security experts, academics and other institutional and industry players have made it possible to produce a series of reflections on conflicts in the informational sphere or in the information age.

In the rest of this first chapter, some of the major themes will be discussed to either clarify concepts previously mentioned, or to introduce new ones that will be useful in the rest of the book.

1.3.1. *Cyberspace and superiority of information*

In a very general way, cyberspace is made up of computers, communication systems, networks, satellites, communication infrastructures and transport systems using information in its digital form (in cars, trains, airplanes, elevators, etc.), sound, voice, text and image data that circulates and is processed, systems that can be controlled remotely via a network, all control systems operating energy supplies, digital watches, video cameras, robots, as well as weapons, missiles, GPS systems, all technologies and communication tools (Wi-Fi, laser, modems, satellites, local networks, cell phones, fiber optic, computers, storage supports, fixed or mobile equipment, etc.).

This world of interconnections and interdependence, where information circulates from one medium to another and is processed, duplicated and stored, where tools communicate, where information technology becomes ubiquitous, constitutes the world of information, the information environment and cyberspace.

This environment, however, is reserved for a small group of the global population: those who can afford to pay for it. The distinction between those who can and those who cannot is fundamental because it divides the world in two. The digital divide progressively diminishes in very wealthy and developing countries where access to information technologies is increasingly possible. But it persists in the gaps between wealthy and poor countries. The wealthiest countries on the planet are largely the beneficiaries of cyberspace.

The idea is mainly to acquire control of this sphere, an operation defined by the expression "info-dominance", because this control would be one of the major assets directing or deciding the outcome of crises, battles or conflicts. We often incorrectly present info-dominance as the ultimate goal of the great war powers (mainly the United States actually), thus confusing methods and objectives. Even though the fight for domination of the information sphere transforms information into a target, into a new, possibly virtual, front line to attack and defend, info-dominance still remains a method at the service of higher objectives: victory and political objectives. Info-dominance must not be an end in itself, but a step, a transition, an object of conquest, in times of peace or war, which once captured can contribute to paving the way to success.

The advantage of having information about an opponent is called "superiority of information". Superiority of information makes it possible to:

– obtain and process the best information;

– use this information more efficiently;

– see first, understand first, act first.

Superiority of information presumes:

– a capacity to collect, process and broadcast an uninterrupted data flow;

– being in a proactive situation. Being permanently in a state of reaction to operations carried out by the enemy prohibits information dominance.

The objective of superiority of information is to:

– affect the perceptions, attitudes, decisions and actions of the enemy;

– exploit capabilities by preventing the enemy from doing the same, as much as possible.

Superiority of information is characterized by:

– the central role that command must play, that must be able to direct operations, efficiently mobilizing methods, information systems and procedures. Information systems are a decision support tool;

– the series of methods that must be implemented: human, material and organizational methods;

– speed. Decisions must be taken quickly. Superiority of information confers the capacity of deciding and acting faster than the adversary. The objective is to lead the opponent at a pace at which he can no longer follow, that is detrimental to him, in order to keep him from being proactive. But the speed must not be detrimental to our own operations. Speed and obsession with "real time" are traps or illusions that command systems must be careful not to get into;

– the ephemera of the position of superiority. Nothing is definitive. The enemy also wants to have superiority of information. The situation permanently evolves; superiority is therefore transitory. Constant efforts must be made to retain this position;

– losing superiority of information means losing the initiative. From being proactive, we become reactive;

– aiming at the right objectives to acquire it:

- the enemy. We must understand his actions, prevent his access to, and exploitation of, his enemy's information, influence his perception, actions, his leaders, deteriorate and destroy his decision processes;

- non-combatants. We must influence them so that they support our camp and offer no resistance;

- our own camp. We must protect our own decision processes, information, information systems and provide correct information to commands.

To reach superiority of information we must act on ISR (intelligence – surveillance – reconnaissance), on information management (IM) and on information operations (IO). When the effects produced by ISR, IO and IM synchronization are greater than those of the enemy, superiority of information is then acquired.

In a situation of superiority of information, perception is close to reality. For the enemy, perception is different from reality.

The American military formalized the concept of superiority of information through their doctrines:

– in July 1996, the *Joint Vision 2010* (JV 2010)[39] was published, a founding text that provides a conceptual framework for American forces for the coming years;

– in May 1997, the Joint Warfighting Center published "Concept for Future Joint Operations. Expanding Joint Vision 2010". The report used the definition of superiority of information proposed in JV 2010: the capacity of collecting, processing and distributing an uninterrupted flow of information, while exploiting or paralyzing the capacity of the enemy to do the same;

– document Joint Pub. 3-13 from October 1998 recognizes the concept of superiority of information and its three components:

- activities that increase the capabilities of allied information systems, including the process of friendly decision support;

---

39. Downloadable from the website http://www.dtic.mil/jv2010/jvpub.htm.

- intelligence and other activities linked to information providing information on friendly forces, enemies, or potential enemies in a timely, fair, precise and relevant manner;
- offensive and defensive information operations.

Information dominance appears as the capacity of revising strategies on the basis of a systematic analysis of the enemy and the capacity of identifying his vulnerabilities and center of gravity.

Info-dominance is achieved by transforming knowledge into capacity, identifying centers of gravity. The proliferation of information technologies has created the impression that information itself is a center of gravity. The objective of info-dominance is to have greater understanding, not total understanding.

Dominating information also means dominating the media and information in terms of news. Lessons from the past should serve as examples and be the basis for developing new theories and strategies in the field of communication. "From the perspective of the U.S. Military, television coverage of the Vietnam War had a detrimental impact on the conduct of that war; policies on television coverage of future conflicts should be revised so as to not repeat past mistakes".[40]

1.3.2. *The "value" of information*

Information is a series of facts, data and instructions available in any medium, in any format. It is the meaning that man gives data through known conventions used in their representation. The same information can convey different messages and send mixed signals to recipients and users of this information, including the intelligence community[41].

Information has always had a major role in human societies. But today, information has a new and dominating status, stimulating almost all aspects of social life and modern war. The importance of information in strategy, tactics and operations has long been emphasized in the context of conflicts, notably by the Chinese, Sun Tzu: "If you know your enemy, you should not fear the outcome of a battle". Information is a strategic resource and weapon. Information also has value.

---

40. *Television coverage of the Vietnam War and its implications for future conflicts; Preamble;* 6 April 1984. Command and Staff College, U.S. Marine Corps. http://www.globalsecurity.org/military/library/report/1984/HCD.htm.
41. JP 3-13, 1998 version.

Information, information systems and information-based processes used by the military must be the subject of protection proportional to the value of the information and associated risks. The value of information can change, however, according to objectives in times of peace, crisis, conflict or post-conflict, as well as during the different phases of an operation. This link between information and security value makes any information a potential object to protect. Information may have no value today but tomorrow it will have value if the context changes. In that case, what must be protected? And when can we define that information must be "protected"?

In order to have value, to be processed, analyzed and help in a decision, information must not have been subject to distortion or carry risks. Criteria for quality include:

– precision and accuracy; the information reflects the situation;

– opportunity; the information has not been surpassed by events;

– usefulness; the information is easily understood and displayed in a format that makes sense immediately;

– completeness; the information must contain all the necessary elements;

– precision; a level of detail is required;

– assurance; we must be certain that the information is not corrupt, fake, deteriorated and that it is accurate.

Several categories of information can be distinguished:

– information that is required, where needs are clearly identified by commanders; facts, evaluations and hypotheses;

– information that is important but the need has not been specifically expressed by commanders (implicit needs);

– information that commanders need but do not possess;

– information that the commander does not have and knows nothing about;

– information that is not useful, that commanders do not need to know but that they are given. Too much information of this nature can saturate the decision process. The information must therefore be filtered, which is the role of a good information management system.

Information can also be classified into:

– facts: the information that we want to learn from an accurate and confirmed source;

– evaluations and hypotheses: this is the information that we want to know but that we cannot have with certainty.

Finally, all this information must be managed. This is the role reserved to information management systems (IM) responsible for providing relevant information to the right person, at the right time, in a usable form, in order to facilitate understanding and decision making (see document FM 6-0). Information management must ensure information circulation through the different communication networks, add meaning to information, rely on information systems (equipment and infrastructures that collect, process, store, display and broadcast information, and are an integral part of C2 systems), and ensure reliable and relevant information. Four rules must be retained:

– information that does not arrive on time and unusable information have the same effect as an absence of information;

– incomplete or inaccurate information is more important than the absence of total information;

– not relevant, inaccurate and imprecise information is worse than a total absence of information;

– relevant information must be precise, appropriate, useful and usable, complete and reliable. But relevant information at moment T can lose its quality at T+1. Relevant information is perishable.

A conflict (information warfare) confers three important characteristics to information:

– it is desirable: it is the information that we must acquire (databases, satellite images, confidential information, access codes and knowledge);

– it is vulnerable; software, databases, information systems, memory, sites, networks, all information vectors/supports, are vulnerable, can be victims of attacks, distorted, deteriorated, damaged, or even victims of their own deficiencies. In fact, the information itself is vulnerable;

– it is frightening: viruses, rumors, anything where propagation is favorable to one camp and harmful to the other. For example, instead of the sometimes dangerous lie that can come back to bite its users, we prefer truth, more efficient, but filtered, sorted in order to only broadcast information that can have a positive impact on our troops and public opinion, and doing the opposite with the adversary's public opinion.

Efficient information is information with a value that is based on its distribution and not its truthfulness. Information is efficient if it finds listeners, receivers and believers adopting the proposed point of view.

1.3.3. *Information system*

An "information system" is a group of infrastructures, organizations, people and components that collect, process, store, transmit, display, broadcast and act on information. Information systems also include information-based processes[42].

An information system is made up of integrated doctrines, procedures, organizational structures, equipment, methods and communication systems designed to help in the execution of C2 during military operations, by collecting, processing, analyzing, archiving and broadcasting information[43]. Seven components form the basic functions of information systems:

– sensors to capture data;

– processors that filter and organize data into information;

– receivers: who uses them? They can be automated weapon systems, decision support systems or decision makers themselves;

– databases, scheduling and research for stored information, regularly updated and secured against corruption or theft;

– transmitters for information distribution;

– rules defining operations and system structures;

– synergy, the most important component, ensuring that the system operates better than the sum of each of its parts, for real added value.

Information warfare consists of attacking these components and defending ours.

"Information-based processes" are the "processes that collect, analyze and distribute information in any medium or form"[44]. These processes can be present in all facets of military operations (combat, combat support, etc.) and in the elements of national power. They are included in all systems and components requiring facts, data and instructions, from strategic reconnaissance systems to important enemy decision makers, etc.

---

42. JP 3-13, 1998 version.
43. Information Operations and the Conduct of Land Warfare. *Military Review*, September–November 1998, vol. 78, no. 5, pp. 4–17.
44. JP 3-13 1998 version.

1.3.4. *Command and control warfare: C2W*

The command and control (C2) role is to "exert authority and direction by designated command on forces connected to it, in the accomplishment of a mission"[45]. C2 must plan, direct, coordinate and control forces and operations in the accomplishment of the mission.

Communications systems, surveillance systems and computer networks constitute C2 systems, enabling commanders to have a global vision of the battlefield and exert their authority on the methods under their control to reach their objectives. C2 systems are based on the security of communications systems. The objective of C2 systems is to promote a united effort, with centralized direction and decentralized command execution.

"Command and control warfare" (C2W) is the integrated use of OPSEC, military deception, PSYOPS, electronic warfare (EW) and physical destruction, mutually supported by intelligence, to deny information, to influence, degrade, or destroy adversary command and control capabilities, while protecting friendly command and control capabilities against such actions. Command and control warfare is an application of information operations in military operations. C2W is both offensive and defensive.

The OODA loop is a paradigm useful in the analysis of C2-type decision-making and activity planning. The C2W concept represents offensive information operations serving to disrupt the OODA loop of the enemy[46].

Generally, the concept ties in offensive and defensive information operations. In a note in January 1995, the Marine Corps defined C2W as any action taken by military commanders to carry out the practical effects of information warfare on the battlefield[47]. This approach includes actions blocking the enemy C2 while protecting our own C2. C2W integrates the physical destruction of the enemy's C2 targets, EW, military deception, PSYOPS and OPSEC.

The C2 process can be perceived as a fundamental universal human activity and would constitute, according to some authors [SHA 98], the battlefield of information warfare. The object of information warfare in C2 is to make the allied decision process more efficient, and enemy decision process more difficult and uncertain. C2 warfare consists of monitoring the enemy and our own troops and resources, planning and re-planning EW scenarios, evaluating alert signals and

---

45. JP 3-13 1998 version.
46. For a definition of the OODA loop, see section 1.3.7.
47. Instruction 3430.26. Department of the Navy. Washington DC 20350-2000.
OPNAVINST 3430.26, No. 6, 18 January 1995.

evaluating damages resulting from attacks, controlling the situation of a specific conflict, choosing methods of operation, facilitating execution, evaluation and control while maintaining military methods, by reconstituting and redirecting forces, and finally negotiating with the enemy to end the conflict. C2 functions are enabled by communications and intelligence systems. C3I (command, control, communication and intelligence) is the most essential component of information warfare.

A doctrinal text on C2W is used as a reference: JP 3-13-1 "Joint Doctrine for Command and Control Warfare (C2W)".

1.3.5. *Effect-Based Operations (EBOs)*

To see accurately in order to touch accurately, to see well, better, faster, while remaining invisible to the enemy; it is the combination of these factors that made it possible for the U.S. Air Force to become a decisive instrument.

Because of the influence of Boyd[48] and the theory of emerging systems, the Air Force developed a method based on a systems approach that emphasizes the effects of attacks on the enemy. It is no longer enough to destroy enemy forces, instead we must win by aiming at and hitting targets liable to have the most impact (through chain reactions), like enemy troops, the organization, the decision-making process and logistics. In this way, "small" attacks, i.e. precision hits, can have very strong effects on a whole system. The reason is the dynamics inherent to large systems, amplifying the results of an attack. In economics, we would speak of a good Return on Investment (ROI).

Although the great powers developed the principle of Effect-Based Operations (EBOs), the Iraqis, for example, also used it as their own and organized it so that they could put in practice the principle of EBO with small guerrilla cells. These cells are practically undetectable and very difficult to neutralize.

A viral computer attack can also be interesting as an EBO. Launching an attack can be simple, and the attack might not be severe enough destroy; indeed, it might not be intended to destroy but rather to cause secondary damages in series (paralyzing a computer system, for example, which paralyzes the operations of a company, blocking its economic activity and having consequences on relations with partners and clients). But an uncontrolled viral attack can sometimes shoot yourself in the foot; the military would speak of "blue against blue" or "friendly fire".

---

48. John R. Boyd (3 September 1976). *Destruction and Creation*. 8 pages. http://www.goalsys.com/books/documents/DESTRUCTION_AND_CREATION.pdf.

1.3.6. *Information-in-warfare*

It is important to differentiate "information warfare", "information-in-warfare" and "warfare in the information age". For Martin Libicki[49], the expression "information-in-warfare" simply makes no sense; all wars use information![50]

In the expression "information-in-warfare", information is simply considered as a force multiplier to have better control of a modern war, what Alvin and Heidi Toffler [TOF 80; TOF 93A] call war in the industrial age. Information is perceived as support for ground, air, sea and space warfare, and for special forces.

W. Schwartau[51] also considers that information-in-warfare is used to make conventional weapons more efficient (as a power intensifier).

Information-in-warfare is often the levering force in the success of battles and campaigns, but battles are still necessary to impose our will on the enemy.

"Information warfare" is war in the field of information, thus differs from this approach. According to Toffler and Schwartau, information warfare makes it possible to impose our will on the enemy by controlling, manipulating, or by prohibiting access to information. This vision is somewhat similar to the Soviet theory of "reflexive control". Between these two extreme concepts, the most common approach is information-based warfare. It is possible to integrate military disciplines to manipulate enemy perceptions at tactical, operational and strategic levels. This type of warfare requires changes in an organization.

1.3.7. *The OODA loop*

Colonel John Richard Boyd (1927–1997), pilot in the U.S. Air Force, proposed a model for the decision cycle, based on his experience in combat. The concept that he proposed is known as the "OODA loop".

This concept is an abstraction describing the sequence of events as they must occur in any military battle:

– O = Observation. The enemy must be observed to gain information;

– O = Orientation. The attacker must put himself in the context, in situation;

---

49. See [LBC 96] and [LBC 07] from this author.
50. Refer to the analysis from Martin C. Libicki on the Rand Corporation website: http://www.rand.org/pubs/monograph_reports/MR1016/MR1016.chap15.pdf.
51. See [SCH94] and [SCH95].

– D = Decision. The attacker must then decide; and finally…

– A = Action. The attacker must act.

From a practical standpoint, what confers the advantage over the enemy in a battle is the capacity to always be one step ahead of the enemy, to impose the pace of operations, maintaining initiative, forcing the enemy into a reactive state by prohibiting any initiative, any preemptive capacity.

We must always be ahead in this loop in relation to our enemy; the one who goes around the loop faster has an operational advantage leading him to victory.

Superiority of information enables us to get round the loop faster. Network centric warfare systems also help us take advantage of this loop. Accelerating the loop means accelerating its four elements:

– O – O – D: these phases are centered on information. We must obtain the information, distribute it, analyze it and understand it. The network operation accelerates phases O – O and facilitates phase D;

– phase A (Action) is centered on movement.

This concept of a loop is used in the military field but was also used in other fields (such as, for example, in economics and finance) where the capacity for quick decision making must confer a decisive advantage over an adversary/competitor.

In the early 1990s, planning combat objectives required approximately 24 hours. Today, we can consider reaction times of approximately 30 minutes.

1.3.8. *Fourth generation warfare*

According to William S. Lind *et al.* [LIN 89], the modern era comprises three generations of military development:

– the first reflects "the tactics of line and column" which "were developed partially in response to technological factors – the line maximized firepower" (e.g. during the Napoleonic wars);

– the second reflects tactics "based on fire and movement, and they remained essentially linear…Massed firepower replaced massed manpower. Second generation tactics remained the basis of U.S. doctrine until the 1980s";

– the third generation "was also a response to the increase in battlefield firepower" but the driving force of change "was primarily ideas". During World

War I the Germans developed new tactics (in 1918), "based on maneuver rather than attrition". This third generation of warfare was of non-linear conflicts (e.g. World War II's Blitzkrieg).

The most important drivers of change from one generation to another are technology and ideas. At the end of the 1980s, it seemed to be "time for a fourth generation to appear". Lind *et al.* identified the main characteristics of this new generation of war: "What will the fourth generation be?:

− "the fourth generation battlefield is likely to include the whole of the enemy's society";

− "increased importance for actions by very small groups of combatants," "small, highly maneuverable, agile forces will tend to dominate";

− "decreasing dependence on centralized logistics";

− "a goal of collapsing the enemy internally rather than physically destroying him";

− "targets will include such things as the population's support for the war and the enemy's culture";

− "the distinction between war and peace will be blurred to vanishing point";

− "no definable battlefields or fronts";

− "the distinction between "civilian" and "military" may disappear";

− "leaders will have to be masters of both the art of war and technology";

− "logic bombs and computer viruses, including latent viruses, may be used to disrupt civilian as well as military operations";

− "adversaries will be adept at manipulating the media to alter domestic and world opinion";

− "the West no longer dominates the world. A fourth generation may emerge from non-Western cultural traditions, such as Islamic or Asiatic traditions";

− "the genesis of an idea-based fourth generation may be visible in terrorism".

Of course, the fourth wave war as described here is not new in all its components, but it is different from the previous waves in the use and application of technologies and the economy which, with their level of integration, enable global operations. The fourth generation of war is characterized by:

− the extreme vulnerability of our societies and economies, more inter-dependent and open than they ever were;

– the importance of the media and the risk of their manipulation;

– the networking of all players;

– the disappearance of all kinds of boundaries (peace–war, military–non military, etc.). This idea is widely shared within the major powers. "This kind of war means that all means will be in readiness, that information will be omnipresent, and the battlefield will be everywhere. It means that all weapons and technology can be superimposed at will, it means that all the boundaries lying between the two worlds of war and non-war, of military and non-military, will be totally destroyed, and it also means that many of the current principles of combat will be modified, and even that the rules of war may need to be rewritten;"[53]

– the importance of the psychological dimensions of operations: "The task now is not to inflict losses in men and material but to thwart an enemy's plans, demoralize it, undermine its worldview, and destroy its intrinsic values".[54]

And can we now ask what the fifth generation will be? Which technologies (biotechnologies? nuclear technologies? nanotechnologies?) or ideas will be strong enough to drive the next changes in war? Will the tactics of lines and columns never return?

1.3.9. *Noosphere*

The concept of "noosphere" was invented by Theilard de Chardin in 1947[55]. It represents the "envelope of thinking substance" added to the biosphere, i.e. the environment of representations produced by our brains. The concept was reused by J. Arquilla and D. Ronfeldt in 1999 [ARQ 99].

1.3.10. *RMA*

The acronym RMA stands for "Revolution in Military Affairs".

Does the transformation that global armed forces go through only involve new technologies or does it also lead to deeper conceptual or doctrinal changes?

---

53. [QIA 99] page 12.
54. For the development of such ideas, see also BEREZKIN, G. A., Lessons from the war in Iraq, *Military Thought*, No. 12, 2003, pp. 139–183.
55. Pierre Teilhard de Chardin (1947). Une interprétation biologique plausible de l'histoire humaine: La formation de la Noosphère, in *La revue des questions scientifiques*, No. 563, 20 January 1947, Soc. Scientifique de Bruxelles, Union Catholique des scientifiques français, Louvain, Paris. *See also* Pierre Teilhard de Chardin (1956). *Le phénomène humain*, Le Seuil, Paris.

Early in the 1980s, a part of the Red Army led by Marshall Nikolai Orgakov wondered about the transformation of war. He predicted that the rapid changes in information technologies and high-tech weapons such as the ones used by NATO would lead to radical changes in the way to conduct a war. Orgakov spoke of a "technological military revolution". His predictions turned out to be true with the United States' victories in the Gulf War (1991) and Kosovo (1999).

Different points of view on RMA divide the comments on it as a concept:

– RMA supporters maintain that the transformation of weapons, military technology, organization and doctrines greatly reinforce the efficiency of the military;

– those from the school of asymmetric conflicts focus on the importance of asymmetrical conflicts such as guerilla and counter-terrorism. They maintain that the major threats in the post cold war period remain unconventional forces. The United States, in 1990–1991, demonstrated the technological superiority of conventional Western forces. Adversaries have no choice but to attack the weak elements of their Western enemies, who are technologically more advanced, by using terrorism, weapons of mass destruction (WMD) and, more probably, bypass strategies and tactics. There really was a technological revolution, and the introduction of these revolutionary technologies considerably reinforced the military, giving them a new superiority in weapons and forcing adversaries to choose new solutions;

– sceptics doubt that current military progress represents a revolutionary change. They speak of evolution instead of revolution. If there must be revolution in military affairs, it will be done through a revolution of doctrine, since the technological revolution is not able to trigger this fundamental revolution. Sceptics prefer to speak of "transformation" instead of "revolution" in military affairs.

But the question has been raised and remains, involving the possibility of there being a revolution in military affairs. There are two opposite points of view:

– New Information and Communication Technologies (NICTs) constitute a technological revolution. Their introduction in the military puts everything into question: organization, tactics, strategies and doctrines. A revolution in the field of information is at the basis of a real revolution in military affairs;

– NICTs are undeniably a technological revolution but their introduction in the military is perceived merely as the introduction of new methods, which will not revolutionize the military mind. NICTs are then considered as a simple force multiplier, i.e. adding methods to the ones already in place, adding methods in a familiar environment for the military, forcing them to adapt to defined models such as speed, precision and lethality. This (simplistic?) vision is not synonymous with a profound change in military outlook.

One response, with a play on words, could be that there is clearly a revolution in military affairs (the introduction of new technologies) but there is no revolution of the military affairs.

Regardless of the doctrinal considerations of the military toward the introduction of NICTs within their core, and the more-or-less advanced development of war tactics and strategies of information, the introduction of these technologies had an obvious impact on the military all over the world:

– the militaries of wealthy and industrialized countries have thrown themselves into a race for high-tech, software-based, weapons. The technology continues to evolve, and keeping up-to-date with developments forces significant investments to acquire them and for R&D. Importing foreign technologies may seem like a good alternative, but remains expensive;

– the most powerful NICTs are mostly developed by the private sector, and what's more, these developments are not *a priori* meant for the military. Developing and strengthening cooperation between private industries and the military sector has become today, in 2009, one of the most relevant issues of national security and defence policies not only in the USA but also all over the industrialized world: first, because information technologies can be dual, and work with civilian as well as military applications; and second because, if the military wants to acquire superiority of information, it must not settle for off-the-shelf products, black boxes that will be integrated with current systems. Whoever has technological control can claim control of informational space.

1.3.11. *C4ISR*

C4ISR (Command, Control, Communications, Computers, Intelligence, Surveillance and Reconnaissance) systems are the networking computer resources which make communication possible between target acquisition systems and weapons systems.

They provide support for network centric warfare (NCW), a way to fight a war by exploiting the capabilities of information systems and networks. They make it possible to coordinate and execute complex, joint operations with precision, accuracy and speed. C4ISR systems are a series of military functions for coordinating operations. C4ISR represents the infrastructure or the procedures used. These systems are implemented through an architecture called DODAF (DoD Architectural Framework) that must link the different military wings of a country together, and the military with allied forces (joint or coalition forces). France does not use the term C4ISR but instead uses *bulle opérationnelle aéroterrestre* (BOA) which, in English, translates as "air and land operations bubble".

1.3.12. *Network Centric Warfare (NCW)*

Network Centric Warfare (NCW) was defined by Cebrowski in 1998. The concept was placed at the core of the Transformation Program applied to the American military initiated by Donald Rumsfeld.

The principle is based on geographically dispersed units with real time information, interconnecting and collaborating with each other, accessing, sharing and protecting information. Information and communication technologies help in making small units function in networks, interconnecting them and giving them ways to communicate and coordinate. This form of organization can be compared to a swarm of bees.

This theory also brings up the principle of adopting civilian technologies and introducing dual technologies by the military. The introduction of networking techniques in combat systems is the military equivalent to the digitization, computerization and networking of civilian systems which took place from the middle of the 1980s; i.e. it is a radical and profound change, a major evolution.

Networking has several objectives, constraints and characteristics:

– it must accelerate the cycles of engagement;

– it must accelerate the operations pace by accelerating the O–O (Observation–Orientation) phases of the OODA loop;

– it must be done with wireless technologies which constitute the core of the NCW architecture, because platforms, units and people are mobile;

– combat platforms must be digitized to be able to transmit information from one platform to the other.

Technical problems generally dominate the debate on network centric warfare to the detriment of doctrinal or strategic aspects:

– how can we secure communications to avoid the information from being intercepted? This is the role of cryptography. We must also make sure that transmissions are undetectable;

– communications must be robust and must be resistant to jamming and to weather conditions;

– the more secure and robust a transmission must be, the more throughput intensive it becomes. Transmissions must, however, remain quick;

– messages and signals must be correctly routed;

– communication between platforms must be ensured through total interoperability of the multiple protocols used by the different aviation, marine and ground forces communication systems.

1.3.13. *ISR: intelligence, surveillance, reconnaissance*

ISR is fundamental in the process of acquisition of superiority of information. In order to be efficient, ISR must be integrated. There are a large number of data sources, and common and coordinated mechanisms must therefore be in place. The role of ISR is to produce intelligence on the enemy and the environment.

Intelligence is the product of the collection, processing, integration, analysis, evaluation and interpretation of available information involving foreign countries. It is the knowledge that we have of an adversary, obtained from observation, research, analysis and understanding. Analysis is the fusion of information and intelligence from each discipline within ISR. It is distributed and is collaborative. Intelligence must be shared, from the national to the tactical level. It provides a critical support for all operations, obviously including information operations. It helps in the planning, decision and identification of targets.

Reconnaissance is the collection of information and makes it possible to validate current intelligence or predictions. Reconnaissance is a mission carried out to obtain information on the activities and resources of an enemy or a potential enemy, as well as on the weather, hydrographic and geographic conditions of a specific area through visual observations or other detection methods. It is incorporated in the conduct of all operations, including information operations. It makes it possible to collect information that cannot be accessed through other methods. Reconnaissance units are also sent on missions before operations, but generally do not fight. However, an aggressive reconnaissance can mislead the enemy, make him believe that operations are launched and thus show his hand too soon.

Surveillance is the systematic observation of the airspace, ground and submarine/underground space, people and things, through visual, oral, electronic and photographic methods.

1.3.14. *Cyberwar*

Cyberwar includes computer-assisted warfare and computer network attacks (CNA). It corresponds to the notion of networks applied to military warfare. The concept was notably developed by John Arquilla and David Ronfeldt [ARQ 93]. As with netwar, the notion of hierarchy disappears, and power migrates from nation-state toward private players.[56]

1.3.15. *Netwar*

Netwar means network warfare. "Cyberwar" is the military version of network warfare; "netwar" is the version of network warfare in non-military society. This argument is defended by John Arquilla and David Ronfeldt (Rand Corporation) [ARQ 01].

This theory implies a new organizational structure of the opposing parties and gives an advantage to organizations that operate in the network mode (structured in units, dispersed and coordinating their common actions through networks). Arquilla and Ronfeldt define netwar as warfare in the information age:

– the parties are organizations spread as individuals and in small groups;

– the mode of contact is remote communication to coordinate activities and conduct operations. Parties are therefore interconnected;

– the structure is distributed; there is no hierarchy and no centralization.

This type of warfare through networks adapts to amorphous groupings such as terrorist organizations, and it is the type of warfare that, for example, "hacktivists" carry out, activists or international hacker groups acting as one group but often made up of individuals spread over several geographical territories.

Authors	Concepts
John Arquilla, David Ronfeldt	Netwar (2001), Cyberwar (1993)
Cebrowski, Rumsfeld	Network centric warfare – NCW (1998)
John Boyd	OODA loop

Table 1.2. *Authors and concepts*

---

56. Also see [ARQ 97] and [ARQ 00] from the same authors.

1.3.16. *Spin doctoring*

Spin doctoring is an act of propaganda or psychological warfare, an important factor in information warfare, where the precision of information sometimes becomes as important as weapons precision.

"Spin doctors" are communications specialists, responsible for "selling" the war to public opinion.

1.3.17. *Intelligence*

The different forms of intelligence have variable efficiency levels according to objectives. We generally distinguish eight sources of intelligence:

– HUMINT: human intelligence. This type of intelligence uses scouts and informers. It is information that is collected from and provided by human sources;

– SIGINT: is intelligence collected by technological methods (wave interception). The largest intelligence agency of this type is the American National Security Agency (NSA). SIGINT is a generic term grouping;

– COMINT (Communications Intelligence): intelligence from the interception of telecommunications and electromagnetic communications, by other than those to whom these communications are addressed. Interceptions and processing of unencrypted written communications, printed information and propaganda messages are excluded from this definition;

– ELINT (Electronic Intelligence) is intelligence from the interception of electromagnetic transmissions and non-communications, by other than those to whom the transmissions are addressed;

– IMINT (Image Intelligence) is supplied by satellites, drones and spy planes photographing the globe. It is intelligence by imaging acquired through photography, radar, electro-optic, infrared and temperature sensors, which can be based on the ground, on ships, in airplanes and in space;

– OSINT: is intelligence from the analysis of data and open source information, available in the global information environment;

– TECHINT: is intelligence involving foreign technological developments;

– MASINT: Measurement and Signature Intelligence. MASINT is scientific and technical intelligence obtained by the qualitative analysis of technical data associated to sources, transmitters or receivers. The role of MASINT consists of analyzing data from different measuring and sensor sources, and then returning a synthesized, multi-sensor fusion. MASINT can merge radar (RADINT: radar intelligence), acoustic (ACINT: acoustic intelligence), nuclear (NUCINT: nuclear intelligence), radio frequency (RF), electro-optic (ELECTRO-OPTINT), laser (LASINT), unintentional radiation (RINT: unintentional Radiation Intelligence), chemical and biological (CBINT: chemical and biological intelligence) intelligence and infrared data. In practice, MASINT must make it possible, for example, to identify vehicles, detect underground constructions, detect threats and guide smart weapons.

NSA is known, most often in a controversial way, for its SIGINT activities[57]: for providing information that the government can use to make important decisions and protect the rights of American citizens (with respect to the fourth amendment of the Constitution). At a national level, other agencies are responsible for other forms of complementary intelligence: the CIA (Central Intelligence Agency)[58] and DIA (Defense Intelligence Agency)[59] are responsible for HUMINT, the NGA (National Geospatial Intelligence Agency)[60] for IMINT, and MASINT is the responsibility of the DIA.

1.3.18. *Information operations*

Information operations are the actions taken to affect the decision processes, information and information systems of the enemy, while defending our own information and information systems.

Commands use information operations to attack the decision processes, information and information systems of the enemy. Information operations are used to reach the C2 capabilities of the adversary; prevent his correct use of C2s, destroy, deteriorate, interrupt, deceive, exploit and influence them. In order to reach this goal, we must attempt to influence the perception that the enemy has of the situation. The objectives of information operations are to produce a disparity in the mind of enemy commands between reality and the perception they have, and to disrupt their capacity to exercise the C2. Information operations also affect the perception and attitudes of those located in the zone of operations: populations and civilian leaders.

Information operations can be offensive and defensive. Offensive information operations are the integrated use of methods and specific activities, supported by intelligence, to affect enemy decision-makers, or influence others. The desired

---

57. http://www.nsa.gov/sigint/.
58. http://www.nsa.gov/sigint/.
59. http://www.nsa.gov/sigint/.
60. http://www.nima.mil/portal/site/nga01/.

effect is to destroy, deteriorate, disrupt, deceive, exploit and influence enemy functions. The ultimate targets are the leaders and human decision processes of the adversary or third parties found in the zone of operations.

Defensive information operations consist of the integration and coordination of policies and procedures, operations, personnel and technologies to protect and defend our own information and information systems. Defensive information operations ensure access to information (timely, precise, relevant and usable) while preventing the enemy from exploiting our information and ISs.

What activities make up information operations?

– military deception. Measures to deceive, mislead the enemy through manipulation, deterioration and tampering. The object is to influence the understanding that the enemy may have of the situation and make him act against his own interests;

– counter-deception. These are the efforts to prohibit, neutralize or decrease the effects of hostile deception. Counter-deception supports offensive information operations by reducing the harmful effects of enemy deception;

– operations security prevents the enemy from accessing critical information that is vital to the success of military operations;

– physical security. Physical security protects from unauthorized access to installations, equipment and documents and safeguards and protects information and information systems;

– electronic warfare is a military action involving the use of electromagnetic energy and directed energy to control the electromagnetic spectrum or to attack the enemy. It includes:

- electronic attack, to deteriorate, neutralize and destroy the enemy's electronic combat methods. These actions can include lethal attacks (missiles, directed energy weapons) and non-lethal attacks such as communications jamming;

- electronic protection, protecting the electromagnetic spectrum of our camp, protecting against electronic attacks (by radio silence and anti-jamming);

- electronic warfare support. To detect, identify, locate and exploit enemy signal transmitters, contributing to the understanding of the situation, the identification of targets and the evaluation of damages;

– information assurance protects and defends information systems. Threats are physical destruction, denial of service and malfunction. Assurance provides a greater degree of confidence in the possession of the following characteristics by information and information systems: availability, integrity, authentication, confidentiality, non-repudiation;

– physical destruction applies the force of the combat against targets with a connection to information operations. Targets include information systems, electronic warfare systems and control centers;

– psychological operations are planned operations influencing behavior and actions of a foreign audience by circulating chosen information and precise indicators. Psychological operations are integrated to operations security, military deception, physical destruction and electronic warfare to create a perception of the reality supporting the objectives of allied forces;

– counter-propaganda includes activities directed at an enemy leading to psychological operations against our camp. Preventive actions can be carried out consisting of increasing awareness, informing troops and population of the possibility and forms that hostile propaganda can take;

– counter-intelligence consists of identifying threats to security and knowing how to counter them. The threats are espionage, subversion and terrorism;

– Computer Network Attacks (CNA) are operations intended to interrupt or block operations, deteriorating and destroying information residing in computers or networks. Attacks can also target computers and networks themselves;

– Computer Network Defense (CND) consists of defending computers and other components interconnected in telecommunications networks against enemy CNAs. They include access controls, detection of malicious codes and intrusions;

– public affairs operations communicate information to critical audiences to influence their understanding and their perception of military operations. They influence populations by broadcasting information through the media;

– civil–military operations (CMO) apply civil affairs to military operations. These are activities that military commanders must conduct to establish, develop and influence relations between civilian authorities, government or the private sector and military forces. War no longer involves only the military. Links with civilian society are now very strong.

1.4. Loss of information control

Having control of information does not spare the wealthier nations from significant setbacks. On 28 March 2003, the U.S. Air Force were given the mission of destroying elements of an Iraqi battery and rocket launcher to the north of Basra. There were different targets on the ground. Pilots received confirmation that there were no allied ground troops in the zone and launched their attack. They were quickly informed by ground troops that they had triggered a blue on blue incident. The pilots shot at the British, resulting in one dead and four wounded. The conversation was taped and a video (which is possibly a fake)[61] was quickly found on the Internet (notably on YouTube, with the title "Friendly fire – US Kills Brits in Iraq – Leaked video" or "The friendly-fire death of a British soldier in Iraq"). The event was widely covered in the media. Several articles were published on the Internet[62], as well as the dialog transcription between the two American pilots identified as Popov 35 and Popov 36, the latter being the shooter in question. Ground troops communicating with pilots were identified as "Manila Hotel", "Manila34", "Lightning34", "Sky Chief" and "Costa58"[63].

The tape broadcast over the Internet lasted 15'24'' (starting at 1336.30 GMT and ending at 1351.54 GMT). Aircrafts (A-10s) were at an altitude of 3,500 m. We should say that A-10s are not sophisticated fighter aircraft; they are, in fact, quite simple, designed for covering ground forces.

At 1336.57 GMT, Popov 36 reported that he thought he saw orange panels on the roof of the vehicles detected. This mark is usually installed on roofs of allied vehicles so they do not get confused with others. This identification requirement has long been a constant in the military (uniforms and colors made it possible to distinguish the different troops from afar. When commanders were in a high position to observe the battle they needed clear indications to locate troop positioning and movement. When soldiers are in battle they need distinctive signals so they don't shoot each other). Information technologies have now made this necessity redundant: an automated weapon system can detect if a person in the line of fire is a target or not, by detecting (for example) a signal sent back by that person's equipment[64].

At 1337.16 GMT Popov 35 reiterated Popov 36's report and received a confirmation from Manila Hotel: "Affirmative. No allied troops". An exchange between the two pilots detecting the targets followed.

At 1338.49 GMT Popov 36 detected the vehicles and said "it looks like they have orange panels on the roof", Popov 35 then responded "I've been told that there is nobody to the North".

---

61. The possibility of seeing fake videos remains great, over the Internet as well as in the media in general. We will not question here whether the video was a fake or real; we merely want to show that soldiers can find themselves in this or a similar scenario, and especially show that communication problems can occur in these environments.
62. http://www.tothecenter.com/news.php?readmore=961,
http://www.guardian.co.uk/Iraq/Story/0,2006879,00.html.
63. http://www.guardian.co.uk/Iraq/Story/0,2006914,00.html.
64. For more details on systems in development, see http://www.checkpoint-online.ch/Check Point/Materiel/Mat0039-DangerFeuAmi.html.

At 1339.09 GMT, for the third time in no more than two minutes, the pilots indicated having seen orange on the roof of the vehicles. But, based on confirmations received, they formed another idea of what they were seeing on the ground: rocket launchers.

At 1342.09 GMT, Popov 36 fired, certain he was destroying rocket launchers. This was the attack in which the British soldier died. There were further firings at 1343.47 GMT.

At 1344.12 GMT, coming from LIGHTNING 34, "[...] there are friendly troops in the zone[...]". Why did the information arrive two minutes after firing?

At 1344.39 GMT the pilots then requested information on the situation on the ground, which came back at 1347.09 GMT from Manila 34: "we have a first assessment showing one dead and one wounded".

We have here a combat situation during which one side fires on its own camp. This type of incident, friendly fire, has always existed during wars. Other incidents were recorded in Afghanistan (40 deaths attributed to friendly fire[65]) and in Iraq. Studies attempt to evaluate the percentage of losses by friendly fire; between 12 and 15% of losses in all 20th Century wars. Will information technologies make it possible to decrease these numbers? What should we think about the 24% suggested for the Gulf War (1991) of 1991,[66] Even though that war was the advent of precision weapons!

What can seem surprising here is that, despite the so-called control of all dimensions of the combat, significant flaws remain. A number of consecutive errors led to bad, or even fatal, decision making:

– an intelligence flaw;

– the decision to shoot/not to shoot was not taken according to indications from the pilots and the doubt they expressed. Their first vision, which should have sounded alarms by creating doubt, was not confirmed by ground observation. It seems that the vision of the pilots was not taken into consideration in the decision. Their vision was then submitted to the influence of false information (there are no friendly troops in the zone). On this basis, the pilots formed a new vision that became conviction. Nothing, no mechanical or technical methods, or any procedure, make it possible for us to know what it was like in the pilots' shoes. Tactical decision support systems under stress seem nonexistent, inoperative. As the OODA loop accelerates, it seems that very little, if any, place is given to doubt, to

---

65. http://www.checkpoint-online.ch/CheckPoint/Materiel/Mat0039-DangerFeuAmi.html.
66. ibid.

questioning of information (although wrong to begin with), and disrupting the whole process;

– a problem of coordination/cooperation between American and British forces, on the ground and in the air, perhaps? Was there a failure of communication systems (GPS, radio)? Did the British convoy not announce its position?

– a failure or absence of a follow-up position or identification system in combat (IFF – identification friend or foe equipment – or still BFT – Blue Force Tracking have turned out to be inoperative in the present configuration).

Control of information is not only based on the dazzling increase of calculation capabilities, the multiplication of sensors and the increase in forces of physical destruction. The OODA loop accelerates, but in the heat of the action, there is no room for doubt to accelerate.

The decision to shoot relies here on the false information that there were no allied troops in the zone. Could we imagine the action being cancelled based on the doubts raised by the pilots?

The absence of information control by the authorities is also obvious when we see in how little time the video was released to the public. We must not forget that, beyond the fact that it had an impact on troop morale, friendly fire also has a political impact because it undermines the support of public opinion. For the public, friendly fire is the symbol of senseless death in war.

Blue against blue incidents, or friendly fire, are not specific to wars in the information age. Estimates of American losses (deaths) by the Pentagon in percentages[67], are:

– 16% during World War II;

– 14% in the Vietnam War;

– 23% in the Desert Storm operation (the much-talked-about precision fire!);

– 13% in the Afghanistan invasion.

Along the same lines of the "control of information/interpretation of information" problem, we can observe the controversy surrounding "The Apache Killing Video" (online on YouTube), or the video titled "Bombing Mistake" (2003 – Iraq) where we see an American aircraft bomb American troops mistaken for the enemy.

---

67. Figures taken from http://www.answers.com/topic/friendly-fire.

"The Apache Killing Video" was first broadcast on ABC TV to show how Americans treat insurgents. In the video, we see men going in and out of a truck seemingly transporting weapons in the night. We can distinguish forms and silhouettes and the scene is filmed by infrared camera from an Apache helicopter. The scene ends with the killing of Iraqi "insurgents", by firing from the helicopter. The video quickly raised questions: how could we be certain that the individuals filmed are really insurgents exchanging weapons, and not simply countrymen? The quality of the images does not make it possible to definitively lift doubt. One of the vehicles seen is a farm tractor. We then see a person picking up one or more long objects from the car. For the American military, the objects are missile launchers. It is impossible to dismiss the possibility that the objects may be simple farm tools or irrigation piping. The field of hypothesis is wide open.

What did Americans base their decision to open fire on? What was their perception of the scene? In doubt, are they given orders to fire? Was there an update of information from intelligence services?

The helicopter fires even though it is not threatened. Nothing in the men's attitude indicates a possible "attack" against the helicopter.

The helicopter dominates the situation; the men do not seem scared and do not make a hostile gesture.

What is, then, the reality of the situation? Was the information controlled by the helicopter pilots (compliance between information received from intelligence, C2 instructions, and correct interpretation of visual information received from their sensors)? Why and how did the video get to the Internet, to journalists? Is there not a process of suppressing sensitive information from the American military?

There are many who see this act as an assassination, a war crime according to the Geneva convention, article 3-1:1 of which states that persons not taking an active part in the hostilities, including members of the armed forces that have put down their weapons and those not able to fight [...] will be treated humanely in all circumstances, with no distinction based on race, color, religion, faith, sex, [...].

These events demonstrate the gap that still exists between complete control of information and the actual capacities of the best equipped military. The idea of a zero death war must also be forever erased from our minds. Zero deaths for whom? The Americans wished to shield their troops, but certainly not those of the enemy. It is illusory, and naïve, to believe in the possibility of a zero death war when we deploy troops, and especially weapon systems, on the scale of what has been done in the more recent wars. "Zero death" is dead. There are precise target shootings. There is collateral damage (enemy civilian), errors (firing against our own camp), the impossibility of controlling all movements and all human decisions in real time in the heat of action. Is there today a flawless automated decision system, able to distinguish an enemy target from an ally, able to decide to shoot, even to shoot alone, with an error margin close to 0%? No. Man is, and will remain, at the core of the process of the OODA loop. And man's intervention is extremely complex to model and to control. The combat situation, or simply the context of war, even if there is no direct threat on the life of a man, influences his behavior, his psychology. Why did the helicopter pilot make the decision to fire? Was he certain he was faced with a target, i.e. an enemy representing immediate danger? What, in the scene that he could not directly see, except through a screen, sensors and data processing systems, influenced his reasoning to the point where he thought "I must shoot"? Was it the immediate situation, or the immediate situation taken from all the images built prior to the situation, his conscious or subconscious modeled in a more general context of the war? In this environment, the soldier is perpetually surrounded by threats, real or shaped (by propaganda internal to the military, by the influence of other soldiers or by the media), including the threat from his own camp (remember the percentage of losses attributed to friendly fire in the Gulf War (1991): 24% or approximately 1 death in four)[68].

The soldier does not see the scene as we do, sitting safely in front of our computer. The error we make when trying to rectify this type of incident is our belief in the existence of computer systems, making the soldier out to be a 21st Century cyber warrior with a precise and infallible aim. The United States are working toward that goal but the dream is still beyond reach. Even if technology enables us to fire long range without seeing or being seen because of the existence of information technology in weapon systems, it seems painfully obvious that everything is still not possible. Research into the field of man-machine and man-man interaction via machines, and into interaction in a problem scenario and cognitive systems, is a priority. We must understand how man thinks and acts according to his environment if technology wants to be able to offer him the tools to assist him, or even replace him, in making decisions and taking action.

It takes a long time for man to make decisions in a situation of war, in stressful situations or in emergencies – all disturbing contexts. The presence of information can be valuable in making decisions. But the multiplication of data sources, and the increase in the volume of information that could be contradictory, will not necessarily alleviate man's stress nor diminish the number of errors. In 1998, the USS Vincennes shot down an Iranian jetliner, mistaking the Airbus A-300 for an F-14 fighter, killing 290 people. Will

_____

68. http://www.checkpoint-online.ch/CheckPoint/Materiel/Mat0039-DangerFeuAmi.html.

information and communication technologies make these tragic errors of decision impossible in the future?

1.5. American concerns

The DISA (Defense Information System Agency) was victim to 250,000 cyber attacks between 1991 and 1993. The Wright Patterson Air Force Base is a victim of 30,000 to 40,000 attacks every month[69].

According to the Pentagon, in 1996, American military websites were the subject of 250,000 intrusion attempts every year[70] and for every 50 attempts, only one is detected and reported to Defense authorities. According to the CSIS report in December 2008, Department of Defense systems are scanned hundreds of thousands of times a day![71]

The DISA revealed that only 6% of all hacker attacks are detected and that only 10% of that 6% are made public.

The United States is the target of an impressive number of aggressions in cyberspace. But there is a threat, hovering in the background, of an attack that would be more powerful than the others and would greatly and efficiently affect sensitive and vital sites and systems. Large scale simulation exercises are regularly carried out: CyberStorm I in 2006, Cyber Shock in February 2006, Strong Angel III civilian-military test in San Diego, CyberStorm II in 2008, etc.

What concerns the United States is not really the perpetual aggressions to which it resists pretty well (despite a few scandals revealed following the loss of sensitive data, after millions of records containing personal information about military personnel were stolen), and despite the attacks launched against the Pentagon, which is the favorite target for all hackers on the planet, not just those from foreign espionage services. What really concerns all US security and defense departments is the fatal and unstoppable attack that they call cyber Pearl Harbor (or digital, or electronic, Pearl Harbor). This unfortunate name was brought back to the "cybernetic" forefront in the 1990s and we still find it in the declarations of the security authorities in 2009. Experts in all fields venture the prediction of an imminent catastrophe, a Digital D-Day[72], launched by hostile powers and which, by

---

69. Figures are taken from [TOF 93B].
70. http://www.cnn.com/US/9605/23/internet.spying/index.html.
71. Page 12 of the report. CSIS report - Commission on Cybersecurity, for the 44th President of the United States. http://www.csis.org/tech/cyber/.
72. http://www.businessweek.com/1998/35/b3593077.htm.

one unpredictable attack, would cause such damage to the nation's network infrastructures that it would bring the United States to its knees: in a flash, no more telecommunications, networks, nothing. A hole. White. Black. A void. Nobody could communicate anymore, information would no longer get through and during this time, enemy troops could take the opportunity to deliver the final blow by launching an attack, their troops rendered undetectable and no longer risking a counter attack since the victim's radars and satellites would be silenced. The digital Pearl Harbor is a Blitzkrieg led via computer networks paralyzing the opponent. It is winning the war before it even starts.

Recently, the image of Pearl Harbor has reemerged, in its space war version. As an example, the expression *Space Pearl Harbor* can be found in Kevin Pollpeter's "The Chinese vision of space military operations" [POL 05]. Pollpeter writes that the American military is too dependent on space, and it is possible that China could conduct a "space Pearl Harbor" against the United States in order to gain mastery in space[73].

In the United States, the awareness of threats to national security started over 10 years ago, well before the 9-11 attacks. We can cite significant lines from alarmist literature from the 1990s: "While the details are classified and cannot be discussed here, we have evidence that a number of countries around the world are developing the doctrine, strategies, and tools to conduct information attacks".[74] "The spectre of terrorists sneaking into computers all over the United States and wreaking havoc has a lot of people worried these days, including President Clinton [...] It is our clear view that a cyberthreat can disrupt the provision of services and disrupt our society, disable our society even more so than can a well-placed bomb [...] Experts in the field admit no known terrorist group has the know-how currently to wage cyberattacks"[75].

The feeling of threat is vague and already linked to international terrorism. What is most striking in these lines is the visionary, perceptive character of predictions. But what is surprising is their almost inevitable character. Terrorism was a national threat before 2001, and yet nothing prevented the 9-11 attacks.

The United States had a premonition about information technology attacks when the countries observed were only in the development of their capability stages. Since

---

73. Citation from the website http://www.spacedebate.org/citation/2461#2635.
74. *Foreign information warfare programs and capabilities*. Speech by John M. Deutch, Director of Central Intelligence. 25 June 1996. https://www.cia.gov/news-information/speeches-testimony/1996/dci_testimony_062596.html.
75. *U.S. to prepare for cyberterrorism attacks, but is it necessary?* by Brian Barger, posted on the CNN Interactive website, 16 July 1996: http://edition.cnn.com/US/9607/16/cyber.terrorism/index.html.

then, these countries seem to have acquired the capabilities and started to use them, to implement aggressive operations, at least at the intelligence level through continuous attacks against (notably American) security and defense servers. If the United States saw the danger coming, they could not do much to avoid it. Regardless of the life size test revealing the flaws and security weakness of information systems of the country's vital structures, regardless of the fact that the control and security of cyberspace is the responsibility of the US Air Force or other players, regardless of the fact that security is in the hands of a single authority and that each department sets up security structures, regardless of determined political statements from the consecutive presidents in office, regardless of the multi-year projects followed by their amazing budgets, no matter what the country does, nothing seems to stop the movement that has begun.

The question then becomes "what level of threat is acceptable"? We could add "and when the major attack happens, will the country – and the rest of the world – be able to cope with it"? It is somewhat as if dreams of absolute superiority of information at a global level showed the limits of their ambitions, as if the victory of the conflict of 1991 was only an isolated episode, as if the massive investments in the development of informational space control systems turned out to be inoperative in view of players who today understand how to find the weak points of the ultra-powerful opponent by using the same weapons, and especially by making circumventing that power the efficient method of attack. The informational space cannot be secured. It can therefore not be controlled. And like a thumb to the nose, a computer virus was introduced at the end of 2008 in the international space station, as if to demonstrate that there is no confined or monitored space, no territory, be it on the ground, at sea or in space can pretend to be out of reach.

Chapter 2

China

Since the beginning of the 1990s, China has been analyzing the concept of information warfare with great interest. Over time, and based on observations and simulations, military strategists have formulated a new warfare doctrine and theories on information warfare. Marked by their cultural characteristics, these theories are compliant with Chinese thinking, and aspire to offer solutions to reach medium- and long-term political objectives set by the government, and face the immediate threats perceived by the country. China is sensitive to the risks of national security attacks that terrorism and cybercrime represent, as well as to insurrection and attempts against political and social destabilization, in short, to anything that could disrupt or question its economic development.

Although for the last 15 years it has been the army alone that has made a conceptual definition of "information warfare", cyberspace in its entirety is implied when the military and civilian spheres cross in "total war", "out of bounds war" and "people's war" theories. Civilian cyberspace is strictly regulated by the authorities but is used, as a weapon or a target, in fighting a war, in a form of information warfare other than military war, but which can, nevertheless, contribute to the political objectives of power. It could be a war in the form of network attacks: virus, worms, site defacement and psychological operations.

Although the Chinese regulation policy is denounced by international organizations defending individual rights, the United States is more concerned by the Chinese strategy of quickly modernizing its armies (with a revolution in military affairs, computerization and information warfare methods) and its acquiring of state-of-the-art technologies and know-how by any means. What can the major global power fear from the emergence of China?

This chapter first introduces the major steps of the development, implementation and application of the concept of information warfare in China. A second section presents the American point of view on Chinese information warfare, as well as on the military concepts involved (accelerated modernization, RMA and computerization). The third section discusses the relations between Beijing and Taipei – sources of the most important tensions in the region – and the way these tensions are expressed in the field of information warfare.

2.1. The concept of "information warfare": a genesis

The resounding success of the American military during the First Gulf War, the famous "Desert Storm" campaign, quickly showed the obvious superiority that information control gives the military. The concept of "information warfare" became obvious to China in this context, and China then committed itself to a profound theoretical reflection, involving significant ideological studies resulting in abundant literature on the subject. Reading through the work of the most important and most frequently quoted authors, we can trace the genesis of the "information warfare" concept in the Chinese world.

But first, we must explain the four major characteristics influencing the Chinese theory:

– definitions, theories and doctrines of information warfare are dominated by the military, who are completely responsible for developing and implementing the revolution of military affairs and modernization of the armies. They are the ones who give information warfare its specifically Chinese traits;

– the vision of the military was influenced by Russian doctrine;

– the analysis undertaken by the Chinese military is the result of observing American doctrine and practice;

– Chinese military theories are not based on recent experience.

In the first half of the 1990s, the objective given by Chinese strategists for information warfare was to control information flows. This approach is different from the one in the United States which favours attack and destruction.

2.1.1. General Wang Pufeng: one of the pioneers

In 1995, General Wang Pufeng [WAN 95] emerged as the father of the Chinese information warfare doctrine. He was impressed by the superiority of the Americans, acquired in part by satellite reconnaissance systems during the Gulf

War, which made it possible to locate strategic sites, enemy positions and attack Iraqi C2 systems with precision. In light of lessons from the American success, he defined information warfare as:

– the product of the information age;

– the use of information technologies on the battlefield;

– networkization of the battlefield (in Chinese "wangluohua"), opening up the era of a new battlefield made up of computers. The battlefield is no longer seen the same way. It has become multidimensional, the dimensions being integrated; we no longer speak of front lines and rear areas. The idea was put forward of deep strike and of warfare beyond the horizon against C2 systems perceived as vital points, the center of gravity of the enemy;

– a war where the objective is no longer the conquest of territories or the destruction of enemy troops, but the destruction of the enemy's will to resist;

– a war serving objectives and strategies by preparing the intervention of troops and assisting them. Information warfare is not the only mode of confrontation of modern wars;

– a fight for the control of information, bringing a new energy to the battlefield with the capability of using the information. This information dominance (in Chinese "zhixinxiquan") is defined as the capacity to defend our own information while exploiting and attacking the information infrastructure of the enemy. Do and prevent from doing, affect without being affected. This idea is not new; it is the foundation of any confrontation: destroy without being destroyed, kill without being wounded. What is new, though, is that the target is also a weapon: information. But the question now becomes finding out how to reach this superiority of information. With digital superiority or with new tactics and strategies?

– a war with, at its core, information technologies making it possible to combine strategic, electronic, missile and intelligence wars for a complete war;

– a war that can influence or decide victory or defeat;

– a concept that implies and justifies quick informationization of armies (in Chinese "xinxihua"). This informationization must enable the Chinese army to gain in speed, mobility, agility and capabilities to deeply attack in a battle without front lines, modifying the traditional war methods. The area of combat widens, its speed increases, there is greater precision of attack, traditional conceptions of time and space are modified. What matters now is not fire power so much as the capacity to see and know before the enemy, to act more quickly and to strike more precisely.

These considerations are certainly in line with the American vision (info-dominance, depth, revolution in military affairs). But General Wang Pufeng's reflection was not limited to replicating the theories and admiring American capabilities. While attempting to see how the concepts and principles could be integrated in a Chinese context, he brought up the possible rebirth of the concept of "people's war", possible by integrating civilian and military specialists with the same goal. This integration is made easier by the development of information systems and telecommunications networks in Chinese society. Remember that, in 1991, President Jiang Zhemin requested that China develop common telecommunications systems for both military and civilian use, in order to be able to respond to the needs of the country in times of peace and war. This common architecture was the only solution to ensure that military and civilian information systems be developed at the same speed, mutually benefiting their respective technological advances. The capabilities offered by the information age could expand the theory of "people's war" dear to Mao Zedong. This concept, unknown in the West, makes each citizen a combatant. With the concept of people's war, the forces at the service of information warfare could count on several million individuals. The simple civilian, from his home, with a simple computer connected to networks could serve the interests of the nation by attacking (hacking) enemy targets, civilian or military. Information technology, networks, electronic and telecommunications experts could become the new heroes in this new form of battle. This vision contributes to the revolution of the Chinese military world and to the specifically "Chinese" evolution of the "information warfare" concept. The traditional battlefield no longer exists, war can be everywhere; it becomes everybody's business. An article published in August 2000, in the Hong Kong Zhongguo Tonnxun She magazine, uses the concept of people's war, calling for mobilization and preparation for a "modern people's war". China must develop the means to create and enable a network people's war, i.e. collect information, process it, carry out online offensives and organize online defense. And, although the army is still responsible for the development of information warfare theories, their application can no longer be the business of the military in this perspective on the "people's war".

2.1.2. *Colonel Wang Baocun*

The vision offered by Colonel Wang Baocun [WAN 97], published in 1997, takes the form of an inventory of information warfare characteristics. It:

- – can be carried out in times of peace, crisis and war;
- – consists in offensive and defensive operations;
- – is expressed at four levels: national, strategic, operational and tactical;

– its major components are C2, intelligence, electronic, psychological, cyberspace, hacker, economical, strategic and precision wars;

– is characterized by complexity, limited goals, short duration, reduced damage, widening of the battlefield, reduced combat troops, transparency, fighting for superiority of information and finally, integration;

– includes the principles of C2 decapitation, blindness, transparency and speed of response.

Information warfare appears as an unconventional complementary strategic weapon that must be used early in a conflict. It is distinct from the informationized war which may become a new form of war in itself in the future[1].

2.1.3. *Colonels Qiao Liang and Wang Xiangsui: out of bounds war*

In the middle of the 1980s, China started to develop a new generation of combat forces. But in 1991, with the Gulf War, Chinese army strategists recognized the gap between Chinese and American potential.

The Iraqi army, equipped with Soviet and Chinese weaponry, in many ways similar to the Chinese army at the time, was defeated in 42 days, collapsing under American fire power, the speed of intervention and the efficiency and superiority of high-tech equipment. Any Chinese victory seemed highly improbable during a possible armed conflict against the United States. Quick modernization of the army and defense systems was in order. The Gulf War also raised awareness for the necessity of obtaining control of information, and information and communication systems, in order to act more quickly and efficiently than the opponent. Reflections on the reform of the Chinese army had to be totally reorganized in light of Gulf War lessons: the performance of the American military in the Desert Storm campaign confirmed the greater power of the United States. One of the keys to this quick victory was the control of information warfare. For some, the Gulf War became a model for future wars, but for others it was no more than a field of experimentation expecting very different wars in the future with the Desert Storm campaign as a foundation. The common point in all approaches was the obviously crucial role now played by new technologies. The way was opened up for a multitude of articles, conferences and reports on the theme of the introduction of information technologies in armies, on the role of information and information technologies in the course of war, on what the army should be in the information age, and on information warfare.

---

1. For other reflections on information warfare from the same period (1995–1999), see [LEI 98], [SUN 95] and [SHE 99].

During the following years, other wars served as examples and were used to feed reflections: the Kosovo conflict (Allied Forces operations, 1999) once more fought by opposing countries with very unequal power, supplied material for Chinese strategists, confirming conclusions from the Gulf War. In this conflict, the Serbian resistance impressed the Chinese. The concept of asymmetric war, where victory over a technologically superior enemy was possible, became obvious.

China then became particularly interested in the concept of information warfare, its role in the strategy and development of asymmetric war solutions.

This is the context in which colonels Qiao Liang and Wang Xiangsui published a book in 1999 that has become a standard reference: *Unrestricted Warfare* [QIA 99]. The book is made up of their reflections on strategy[2], and reveals in part, contemporary Chinese thinking. It is also a reflection on the dominant military power of this century, the United States. And finally, it is a reflection on China's place in a world that was deeply troubled during the last decade of the last century. The text has two parts: the first involves "the new form of war"; the second discusses "the new art of war". Summarizing the book in a few lines, or even a few pages, is not an easy task as it is so rich in ideas and original points of view for Western readers; here, however, we retain only the major themes.

2.1.3.1. *A series of observations on the modern world*

Major changes occurred in the world during the last decade of the 20th Century which seem to have oriented our civilization in a different direction.

There were political and military disruptions: the Gulf War changed the face of the world, followed by several wars in Kosovo and Bosnia. The fall of the Soviet Union modified the balance. There were social, technological and economic upheavals: the Internet massively entered modern societies to revolutionize them; new risks emerged; and monopolistic companies started to dominate the global economy; finally, there was the Asian financial crisis. World balances changed, revolutionized. Consequently, we must adapt the way in which we view the world and the way we fight wars.

2.1.3.2. *Governments no longer battle each other the same way*

For all its importance past and present, the Gulf War must not become a myth: "this war was not a masterpiece of military art, but [...] a luxurious salon of high-tech weapons".

---

2. Available at http://www.terrorism.com/documents/TRC-Analysis/unrestricted.pdf.

Qiao Liang and Wang Xiangsui suggest that it is vital to take a step back from the victory and the demonstration of American power. The United States won because of the wide imbalance between the forces. If this war was important, even though the victory was followed by a series of failures, it is mostly because it profoundly changed the way to fight a war. The military is no longer alone on the scene anymore; conflicts have become more complex. We no longer fight wars as before, using only armed methods:

"War will have to be revived in another form and in another arena [...] the financial attack [...], the terrorist attack [...], the attempt [...], chaos [...], over the Internet [...] represent a half war, an almost war, a sub-war, in short the embryonic form of a new type of war".

Destruction is probably no longer the most appropriate solution to win a war: "technical progress [...] offers many new possibilities of conquering. And this all makes us think that the best way to be victorious is to control and not to kill".

The authors qualify as "soft" weapons these new weapons satisfying a new war ethic (preserving human lives), "computer weapons are the most obvious example of soft weapons". Man wants to move away from the reality of trench wars, battlefields, hand-to-hand combat, slaughter, the slaughterhouse, wars where man is only cannon fodder, general killings, with its announced grand finale, the nuclear war liable to erase humanity from the Earth: "what is the purpose of conquering an enemy if that means risking destroying the world?".

In this new global order, governments no longer only fight through armed conflicts to reconfigure balances. There is a whole range of hostile acts: attacks in the economic, religious, financial, political, ecological and technological fields.

Traditional war as we know it no longer exists. If war changed, it is because it has experienced "the transformation of modern technology and the market system". Wars are now made up of different forms of non warlike actions taken alone, giving new conflicts a profile that they could not have before. This form of modern war, the authors call it "out of bounds war", means that there are many weapons and techniques, that the "battlefield will be everywhere" and that there will no longer be boundaries between war and peace. The way to fight a war changes because the soldier moves away from the traditional battlefield, from fire and blood. At least that is what he is trying to do: fighting a war from afar. It changes because civilian society interferes in military affairs. As proof, remember the hacker trying to get into military information systems. A financier or a speculator can attack a country by means other than traditional weapons. Non-military personnel can carry out hostile actions against governments. The non-military war is carried out by religious, ideological or political organizations that do not respect any law, for an unlimited war with unlimited means: "the major warmongers are no longer only sovereign States [...]. Sects [...], the mafia [...], terrorist organizations [...], drug cartels [...], hackers [...] can become military or non military warmongers" and their attacks "can be considered war actions intended to force another state to satisfy its own interests and requirements". The army is no longer the only guarantor of national security; "the military pillar alone is far from being able to support the security vault of the modern national building". "The battlefield is now here and the enemy is online", "it is permanent war". Modern war tactics are adding and combining different war tactics: military tactics (nuclear, traditional, biochemical, ecological, spatial, electronic and terrorist wars), supra military (diplomatic, network, intelligence, psychological, technological, contraband, drug or even virtual wars), non military (financial, commercial, regulatory, media, ideological wars and war for resources). The Gulf War of 1991 was a traditional, diplomatic, sanction, psychological and intelligence war. The dominant weapons used in these new wars are no longer single weapons but an "integration of systems", and they are part of larger systems. The out of bounds war consists in finding the solution to a problem in a wider field than the problem itself.

2.1.3.3. *Reflection on the importance of technique*

Modern society is dominated by technique. But there are so many new techniques in the world in which we live in that none can pretend to give its name to the era, as we could, for example, with the age of electrification, or the age of steam. No technique dominates. To speak of "the information age" is not satisfying, because there are also nuclear technologies, biotechnologies and nanotechnologies. Which technology can dominate or include all the others? There doesn't seem to be any. But we can obviously not deny the importance of information technology that has a stimulating, binding and integrating power. That is how it is revolutionary.

The common characteristic of modern technologies is integration. The permanent novelty does not really come from the invention of new techniques as much as from the association, combination and integration of existing techniques amongst each other. Integration is the key to social progress, at least as much as the invention of new techniques. "These desires to use the magic of high-technology to work some alchemy on traditional weapons so that they are completely remade have ultimately fallen into the high-tech trap involving the endless waste of limited funds and an arms race."[3] We are in the age of integration of techniques, of extremely expensive techniques. "Based on weight, the B-2, which [costs] $13–$15 billion each, is some three times more expensive than its equivalent weight in gold."[4]

---

3. *Unrestricted Warfare*, page 23. [QIA 99]
4. *Unrestricted Warfare*, page 24. [QIA 99]

"Technology is the Totem of Modern Man", and novelty has become a cult. The obsession for new technology and general fusion of techniques is the main characteristic of our era and of course the field of war, like others, is affected by this phenomenon.

If we believe the reflections of the two authors on the relative importance of technologies taken separately, and the added value of integration, information technology alone cannot guide the revolution in military affairs. Integration can also go beyond the integration of techniques to expand to the integration of the military, its doctrine, commands and strategies. The key to success, to novelty and difference resides in the way we combine techniques, structures and organizations.

2.1.3.4. *Dependence on technique*

Speaking of "American devils", who "are not necessarily the only leaders in everything", Qiao Liang and Wang Xiangsui think that "they are slaves to technology in their thinking". Which would imply that the Chinese are not?

Again according to the two authors, Americans are not able to develop a thinking on a new concept of weaponry, but only on new design weaponry (i.e. new weapons). By "new concept of weaponry", we mean being able to consider as a weapon all the different ways that exceed the military field. Anything that can benefit the world can harm it. Everything can become a weapon: "a single market crash... a single invasion by a computer virus, a simple rumor... all these actions can be put in the category of new weapon design". "The new design of weaponry results in weapons closely linked to the life of civilian populations".

2.1.3.5. *On information warfare*

War feeds new techniques and new techniques feed war. But today "a war can no longer be represented by the name of the weapons used", because no single weapon can launch a revolution in military affairs.

In the past, a weapons revolution led to a revolution in military affairs. The appearance of brass, iron, the arrow or of aircraft has each time considerably modified the military. Today, wars are fought with weapons systems; therefore no weapon can represent a war. We use wide technical concepts to replace them. We now speak of "information warfare" and "high-tech war".

Information warfare is not the same as computer warfare. Information warfare is the "war where information technology is used to obtain or destroy information". Computer warfare combines all forms of warfare "enhanced and accompanied by information technology".

"The Out of Bounds War – the Art of the Asymmetric War between Terrorism and Globalization" actually says very little about information warfare, reducing it to intelligence warfare. But these few words contain so many actions: collecting information with ISR systems; giving a central place to intelligence, espionage by networks; using open source knowledge available over the Internet; and intercepting communications. "Destroying information" is an action that is just as wide and can include the destruction of information by network attacks, the destruction of ISR methods and the interruption of observation satellites, mixing physical and logical attacks.

2.1.4. *General Dai Qingmin and Wang Baocun*

In the April 2000 publication of the "China Military Science" magazine, making its mark for its series of articles on information warfare, General Dai Qingmin [DAI 00], who was the commander of the information warfare center in Wuhan, attempted to define information by moving away from the American model.

He is a supporter of preemptive attacks, in taking the initiative and achieving superiority of information. In this attitude, he is in contradiction with the official strictly defensive strategy (active defense) of the Chinese army which officially confirms the purely defensive character of its politics and does not define itself as a militarily attacking country. It does not declare war or aggressions but engages in a war only to defend national sovereignty and territorial integrity. It only attacks after having been attacked. Cyberspace, military or civilian violation is, for China, as important as a violation of national sovereignty. It does not take initiative, it reacts. This active defense doctrine is widened today to the concept of legitimate defense and preemptive attack, in reaction to a threat to national sovereignty. China has, however, often been the initiator (from our Western point of view?) and strives to define all wars conducted by the army as strictly "defensive" wars. In matters of defense, General Dai Qingmin suggested the Serbian model (Kosovo war), an active defense model (positive defense) that made it possible to defeat the Americans, but not the Iraqi one which he considers as passive (a negative defense). The Serbian defense consisted of implementing different measures such as concealment of planes and armored vehicles, the dispersion of troops in the population, methods to avoid reconnaissance tools, decoys to attract missiles, use of the Internet to broadcast information on NATO attacks and DoS type attempted attacks against NATO sites.

His article, "Innovating and developing views of information operations", defines information operations as a series of operations carried out in an information environment in place of a battlefield, using military knowledge, and using information as a direct operational target and using electronic warfare and computer network warfare as the main form. The strategy can be different based on the technological conditions influencing it. In information operations, traditional strategies can find their place and new ones emerge. But the most important thing is the capacity of the strategy to compensate for technological gaps. China [DAI 00] is convinced that strategy can conquer technologically superior enemies. It is used to asymmetric wars, having fought and won by strategy, over past centuries, against enemies who were militarily and technologically superior to it (fighting against Japanese invaders, and against the Kuomintang). In the context of information warfare, in terms of strategy, we mean, for example, sabotage of enemy information systems, weakening of the enemy's informational strike capabilities, dispersion of enemy forces, propagation of false information and launching surprise attacks against information systems. The strategy proposed by Dai Qingmin [DAI 00] is based on electronic warfare, physical destruction, computer network attacks (jamming, sabotage of enemy information systems and weakening of the enemy's capabilities to launch information warfare), dispersion of enemy forces by concentrating our own forces, diverting enemy reconnaissance efforts, giving a false impression to the enemy and launching a surprise information attack, blinding and deafening an enemy with false information, disrupting enemy reasoning, making an enemy believe that what is true is false and vice versa, leading an enemy to make a false assumption and carry out the wrong action. Superiority of information must be reached by any means and information operations must be considered from an active offensive point of view.

Another major point in its development is the importance given to integration. Not integration in strictly military operations so much as integration of military and civilian forces, the participation of civilians in the war effort, using the ideas of "people's war" expressed a few years earlier by Wang Pufeng [WAN 95].

In the same April 2000 publication of the "China Military Science" review, Wang Baocun [WAN 00] published an article titled "The current revolution in military affairs and its impact on the Asia-Pacific region". Information warfare is presented as a form of combat action attacking the information and information systems of the enemy, while protecting our own information and information systems. The content of information warfare is military security, military deception, physical attack, electronic warfare, psychological warfare and netwar. The vital goal of information warfare is to acquire dominance of information and retain it. This definition is obviously greatly influenced by the American model.

2.1.5. *General Niu Li, Colonel Li Jiangzhou and Major Xu Dehui*

A third article, and just as important, was published in the April 2000 military review by Niu Li, Li Jiangzhou and Xu Dehui [NIU 00]. The authors address information warfare in the sense of "methods and processes designed and used for commanders and commanding forces to seize information supremacy on the basis of clever methods, making it possible to win information warfare at a relatively low cost".

The originality of the definition consists in approaching information warfare with the help of terminologies ("methods", "processes") from industry instead of from the military environment. In addition, guarantee of success is not only due to superiority of information, but also to the capacity of doing more with less than what others (mainly implying the United States) can afford to do. Intelligence and strategy must make them able to decrease the gap caused by technological disparity. This concern is central in the Chinese policy because the gap with the United States in terms of methods remains huge, even though the country embarked on a frantic race for the modernization of its armies. As in Chinese military environments, the idea is to offset this weakness by efficiently using the methods available. This specific context guides the choices available to information warfare strategists. They must create a multi-dimensional threat and force the enemy to make cognitive errors. In order to do this, they must attack cognitive and belief systems to guide commanders' thoughts, get them to make mistakes, create strong psychological pressure using intimidation by demonstrating its capacities, using the effect of surprise mainly by creating a contrived reality, using deception, deceiving the enemy by pretending to follow his choices, developing information warfare weapons and viruses to block information flow, and using all information warfare means available to conserve information supremacy. All the ingredients for psychological warfare (psychological operations, deception), hacker warfare (viruses) and network computer warfare are there. Focusing on "psychological" stratagems can be a dangerous choice in a real situation, because it mainly relies on the capacity to control the enemy's behavior and lead him to make errors in judgment which could be detrimental and fatal[5].

2.1.6. *2004 white book on national defense*

The information department of the Council of the State of China published its white book on the country's national defense on 27 December 2004. The document is structured in ten chapters and focuses on the national defense policy, the revolution in military affairs (RMA), budgets allocated to defense, system of military service, reserve and mobilization forces, challenges for science, technology and industry servicing national defense, the relationship between armed forces and the population, cooperation in terms of international security and, finally, disarmament and non proliferation policy.

---

5. As a complement to the analysis of the Chinese vision of information warfare, please refer to [YOS 01].

The report does not directly discuss information warfare strategy. It is, however, important for the fact that it presents the Chinese project in terms of defense, i.e. in the context in which the doctrine of information warfare is liable to be developed in a theoretical and pragmatic point of view.

China reaffirms the strictly peaceful character of its efforts to develop. It wishes to build a prosperous and peaceful society. China will never have expansionist ambitions and will never strive for predominant power (in reference to the United States, obviously). Its national defense policy is strictly defensive and protects national sovereignty. There cannot be modernization and economic growth without strong security. National defense and economic developments are thus linked and must be coordinated.

National security must also take into account modifications of the international environment. Large balances of power are changing internationally, characterized by a greater interdependence between governments.

Regionally, China is concerned about the role of the United States reinforcing its presence, of Japan, which is militarizing, of the Korean peninsula representing a nuclear threat, of Taiwan which seems to be claiming its independence and its government encouraging the population to have a hostile attitude toward China, and, finally, concerned about other threats including terrorism, separatism and extremism.

The armed forces have the power to stop the Taiwanese movement of independence, which would separate the country in two.

The RMA will be based on army mechanization and informatization. The development of information capabilities will be one of the three pillars of the RMA, with the development of fire power and mobility. In this way, naval, air and ground forces will have state-of-the-art technological methods as informatization is at the heart of this process. It must deploy military information systems, an information infrastructure, introduce ICT equipment in all operations and computerize weapon systems. As with Western military, the Chinese army will need new recruits, with a good level of education and able to use the new technologies. ICTs make it possible to intensify the integration of the different armed forces (ground, marine, air) to carry out joint campaigns and increase the efficiency of commands.

The document reminds us that the Chinese army puts a lot of emphasis on ideology and culture. Its influences are Marxism-Leninism, Mao Zedong's thoughts, and Deng Xiaoping's theories.

The army is opening up to civilian society. Industries and private high-tech companies can now participate in the military product market. The army is aware of the advantages of acquiring off-the-shelf products, of benefiting from state-of-the-art technologies now being produced by the private sector, clearly involving information and telecommunications technologies.

The national economy must be mobilized with the army. Mobilization of the economy agrees with the concept of people's war: soldiers and people are the foundation of victory. One of the characteristics of this national economy must be its capacity to go from a state of peace to a state of war, to go from production in peacetime to wartime production. ICTs will make it possible to create a national mobilization platform for a national economy to increase the speed, coordination and efficiency of this transformation, if it ever became necessary.

2.1.7. *Sun Tzu and information warfare*

Modern theories on information warfare are greatly influenced by Chinese military art and its ancient traditions. Since the beginning of the 1980s, we have witnessed in China a revival of strategic culture, re-establishing the tradition of military writing.

With the help of the concept of information warfare, *The art of war: The 36 stratagems*[6], which is a compilation of ancient Chinese texts, can find a field of new applications. The "thirty-six stratagems" is an interesting and anonymous work, uncovered around 300 years ago. The book focuses on military strategies, making deception an art in itself in helping to reach military objectives. Of course, it is possible to interpret this text, as with others, as what we want to hear. But to try and link information warfare applications to stratagems applying to ground troops and troops on horseback is taking the easy way out; it is being naive and especially blind to the following question: if the authors had to face mobile and communicating armies, which can strike beyond the horizon, would they have imagined the same stratagems? It is important to be able to go beyond these ancient texts.

The same can be said for the theories developed in "The art of war" by Sun Tzu[7], the oldest military treatise in the world. Anonymous attacks by networks and systems vulnerable to the multiple forms of CNA give a modernized view of

---

6. English and French translations of the 36 Stratagems are available at http://afpc.asso.fr/ wengu/wg/wengu.php?l=36ji A Chinese version is available at http://www.cc-only.com/36ji.htm.
7. Many translations of this book are available. Of note are [GRI 06] and the translation made from the Chinese by Lionel Giles, available at http://www.gutenberg.org/etext/132.

stratagems. Many of these strategies (how to deceive the vigilance of an enemy, how to beat a stronger enemy, how to choose the battlefield and the moment, how to weaken and destabilize an enemy) and principles raised by Sun Tzu (all wars are based on deception, when ready to attack we must not seem to be) can be transposed to several contexts where strategy dominates. The information and communications technologies world has long been using them.

Even though information is a constant in society, regardless of the time period and thus regardless of conflicts, the relation that man has with information, its circulation, contents, the way to process it and the importance it has in society cannot be the same all the time and everywhere. And yet, some do not hesitate to appropriate and recycle short sentences that sound like truisms, divine formulas or magical recipes for everything, ignoring differences in era, culture and context.

If the 21st Century Chinese can understand Sun Tzu because they share the same cultural heritage (though is that sufficient reason?), the gap separating us, as Westerners, from the possible depths of the spirit of this strategist is huge. This has not deterred Sun Tzu supporters, however, who see in his warlike literature the keys to the door of the Chinese soul of yesterday, today and tomorrow. Opening these doors would guarantee our understanding of how the Chinese think and act, and reveal their economic, political and military strategy.

There is no doubt that the writings of Sun Tzu are important. Chinese military strategists study them. Other ancient authors are studied in military schools. Chinese military deception is based on a thousand years' experience. For example, Sun-Tzu, Sun Pin, Wu Ch'i and Shang Yang are all authors taught in the Chinese army.

But in the West, a revived Sun Tzu is used for management, commercial management and career management classes – anything that could be related to strategy to some degree.

We must be very careful of how we interpret the writings of this strategist. In fact, why would modern Chinese apply literally the concepts of Sun Tzu? Would French armies of the 21st Century apply the army strategies of Louis XIV? How can the war precepts attributed to Sun Tzu make it possible to decipher the present, or even the future? Could we predict the future of Egypt by analyzing hieroglyphs from the pyramids? Why should the past be the bearer of all modernity?

The greatest misconception about Sun Tzu is to consider that he could be one of the first fundamental thinkers about information warfare. He is, instead, an information-in-warfare thinker. Sun Tzu's texts show that information has long been one of the major components of war. But establishing too many connections between Sun Tzu and information warfare is very risky and artificial.

Why does Sun Tzu seem so important, then? The Chinese military places great importance on knowledge, the way of thinking becomes more important than the way of doing, the strategy more important than the methods. Confrontation of commands (C2 wars) implies understanding the information supply, its control and use. Knowledge is the major strategic resource, more important than weapons. And for Sun Tzu, the greatest victory is the battle won without fighting, and this is where the link between the past and modern war lies. This ambitious goal first involves a strategy that took a long time to develop. He implies that commands are able to carry out what the Chinese call an "acupuncture war", i.e. attacking the core of the enemy's defense, which today are the networks' key points and the centers of gravity that C2s represent. The expression "acupuncture war" (we also speak of "paralysis war") appeared in a publication from the national defense university of the Chinese army in 1997 called "On Commanding Warfighting Under High-Tech Conditions". This type of war must paralyze the enemy by attacking the weak points of command, control, communications and information by analogy with the attack of acupuncture points in a kung fu fight. It is a form of asymmetric war with its foundation going back to Sun Tzu. Information warfare is an essential tool for the modern "no contact" war. The Chinese viewed the Kosovo war as a model of a no contact war.

Without rejecting Sun Tzu and the anonymous author of the thirty-six stratagems, but also without remaining attached to legend and history, the most certain way to understand contemporary Chinese thinking, to analyze orientations and trends and to establish scenarios of possible futures, is to read the writings of our own time. This means first translating, then analyzing. The effort of translating is huge, but without this effort, it would be impossible to achieve this work of intelligence vital to better understanding the other.

2.1.8. *How to implement the theories*

2.1.8.1. *Army training centers and simulation exercises*

The best strategies in the world are useless without competent people to implement them, so the Chinese are working toward the development of contingents of experts in all the disciplines involved in information warfare.

Several army training centers (Zhengzhou, the information warfare center of Wuhan, Changsha) have been teaching the military about information warfare since the middle of the 1990s.

Since 1997, the media has reported several information warfare drills[8] carried out by the armed forces, proof of a gradual shift from theory to practice. The first information warfare battle drill for the Chinese army occurred in October 1997 in Shenyang. The goal was to counter a computer attack that would paralyze its systems. In 1998, a larger scale drill was conducted, involving several military regions in the country, coordinated by Beijing. Since then, military information warfare drills continue to be carried out and are becoming more complex with time[9]: defensive drills, clash of commands, launching of attacks against enemy C4Is (command, control, communication, computers, intelligence), while ensuring the defense of the country's information systems (CNA and CND). China has adopted the attack techniques of hackers in its military drills such as virus attacks and blocking of information. In order to carry out these drills, the army collaborates with research institutes, including the civilian sector, in the development of confrontation simulation systems, defensive and offensive applications using networks, multimedia and virtual reality. The military academy of Wuhan has emerged as one of the major information warfare research centers in China. In 1998, the academy created the first experimentation and simulation center for information warfare in the country.

In April, 2004, the army's infowar group, under Beijing's military command, launched a series of drills called "red Forces against blue Forces", and the results showed that the Chinese army could conquer a Western military. We should not attach more importance to these results than they already have because the gap separating the drill simulation to reality is huge. These successes in simulation do not prove anything; China does not have a theater of operations to test its actual capacities.

2.1.8.2. *Forming specialists in defense*

One of the major components of the army is the militia force made up of approximately ten million non-military personnel. It constitutes rapid reaction detachments, infantry detachments, and detachments of specialists in fields such as communications, reconnaissance and information; all units rely on the use of leading edge technologies. Specific training is organized, specialized detachments are formed and training centers are created.

Under the responsibility of the army, special reserve units[10] were created in several provinces: Hubei (Echeng district), Fujian (Xiamen city), Shanxi (Datong city, Xian) and Shanghai. They have specific information warfare missions. Active in many cities, these units are specialized and become "centers of excellence" in

---

8. http://news.xinhuanet.com/mil/2003-06/12/content_916888.htm.
9. http://www.iwar.org.uk/pipermail/infocon/2003-July/000429.html.
10. http://news.xinhuanet.com/mil/2003-06/12/content_916888.htm.

telecommunications, networks, electronic warfare, intelligence and psychological warfare. For example, reserve forces in the city of Shanghai specialize in wireless telecommunications networks and cryptography. These "local" skills can be spread out and coordinated to form a "network fighter" corps capable of defending China, its telecommunications, command and information networks and to reach the vulnerabilities of foreign information systems. In Xian, the military invents strategies involving the different ideas of ideological texts. There are many information warfare drills conducted by information warfare divisions [TLT01] focusing their efforts on developing information weapons of war, reconnaissance operations, distortion of data, application of deception, organization of information defense and the implementation of network espionage networks.

In the field of network security[11], high level dedicated training, providing a solid theoretical basis and developing strategic capabilities, is implemented based on and reinforcing excellence research centers, such as the Network Security Research Center at the Chinese University of Sciences and Technologies, which, since the beginning of the 1970s has trained some of the best cryptography specialists. China places the security of information systems at the same level as sovereignty and national security. The security of information systems is not only a question of technique, law, policy or corporate economic protection; it is all of that: a global question, with a common vision of the military, civilians, public and private, corporations and individuals.

2.1.8.3. *Should a specialized army corps be created?*

To really reinforce the Chinese army's potential, to make it a force able to fight and win in the new dimension of information, strategists call for the creation of an independent "net force" (separated from the air, marine and ground forces) able to carry out the new high-tech battles of the future.

This approach comes down to the fact that war in cyberspace is not a simple additional skill that all the army corps must acquire, but a new army component for a new form in itself. The role of this branch of the army would be to protect sovereignty (cyberspace) and to get involved in conflicts. It would use technologies able to launch attacks on the Internet, using software to paralyze information, block it, falsify it, taking command of enemy operations through identity falsification and attack technologies coupled with defensive capacities to avoid enemy attacks.

---

11. The article with this information is available in Chinese at the following address: http://infosec.ustc.edu.cn/detail.php?siteid=1671&tplset=deptc2&pid=1671&catalogid=1673 &postid=7077.

2.1.8.4. Real attacks?

In the province of Hubei a special training base was built to train 500 people simultaneously. On 4 September 2003, the Taipei Times newspaper ran a report headed "Cabinet says Computers under Attack"[12] denouncing a systematic information warfare campaign (Trojan horse attacks) launched by the Chinese authorities against private Taiwanese companies to attempt to penetrate government databases (the National Police Department, National Defense Ministry, Central Election Commission and Central Bank of China): the attacks were made by an army of hackers based in the provinces of Hubei and Fujian. The article ended with a recommendation: it is better not to buy/use software developed in China because it may contain Trojan horses.

2.2. The American perspective on Chinese information warfare, modernization and informatization of the PLA

China perceives the strategic flexibility advocated by the United States as a wish to reinforce the American position in the Asia Pacific region, against Beijing's ambitions and claims over Taiwan.

The growth of Japanese military capacities, the increase of its fire power, added to the reinforcement of its relations with the United States in terms of security, makes Beijing believe that China has become the object or target of a multilateral strategy led by the Americans in this part of the world. The Americans have reinforced their military presence close to China. In 2006 the USA planned to increase the number of American ships, aircraft carriers and submarines in the Pacific. The island of Guam was used as a station for American operations in the Pacific. Consequently, China modernized its army[13].

Unless, of course, it is the other way around: Americans reinforcing their position in view of the military emergence of China. The result, though, is the same: a tense situation and a race to weaponry.

This modernization is precisely what concerns Americans; they do not seem to understand the underlying motivation or worry about their own predominant power. The emergence of China into the ranks of global economic and military powers worries the United States. China is watched by America, and these observations are the subject of numerous reports, at least as revealing of what America thinks as they are of the situation in China.

---

12. http://www.taipeitimes.com/News/front/archives/2003/09/04/2003066387.
13. Richard A. Bitzinger, *China adapts to US defense transformation*, 11 October 2006.

From reading a selection of these reports, we list the major problems that have recently attracted the attention of American authorities. These reports are:

– the Annual Congress Report "The Military Power of the People's Republic of China". Chinese military policy is the subject of specific observation from the Americans. In 2000, the "National Defense Authorization Act for Fiscal Year 2000" law was voted (Law No. 106-65) requiring from the Defense secretary an annual report on the military power of the People's Republic of China (Section 1202 of the law). The report must analyze the evolutions of military technological development, (military, security) strategies, operations concepts and organization of armies. The reports from 2003 to 2008 were analyzed;

– the Annual Congress Report "US–China Economic and Security Review Commission's Report". The mission of the commission consists in reporting to Congress implications on national security of bilateral commerce and economic relations between the U.S. and the People's Republic of China. Reports from 2005 and 2006 were analyzed.

2.2.1. *Interpretation problems*

The first problem encountered in this analysis and in any effort to understand Chinese concepts by Westerners is the cultural difference, the difference of views[14].

How can we understand a strategy, how can we figure out what words and concepts hide if we do not have the same references, the same key words? The problem is particularly crucial in terms of strategy, which, as we know, is not a simple technique that can be reduced to universal equations, but an art. And is there anything more subjective, more profoundly established in the individual, society and culture than art?

2.2.2. *The impenetrability of China*

China is criticized for its lack of transparency, its impenetrability, its culture of secrecy, where no one can figure out real intentions, involving Taiwan or what role China really intends to play on the international scene.

This impenetrability is a source of fear, misunderstandings and risks of errors in judgment, assessment and bad decisions: "the outside world has little knowledge of Chinese motivations […]. Chinese impenetrability […] will continue to make others

---

14. To better understand Chinese thinking, please refer to [CHE 07].

consider the possible scenarios of conflict and to act accordingly". The impenetrability factors are:

– the policy of deception and misinformation that emanates from Beijing. This policy is associated with the traditional military notion of "shi", which uses intelligence to surprise the enemy through radical political changes and unexpected attacks. In order for this policy to succeed, priority must be given to espionage and in keeping others from collecting information on China. A war must actually be fought to collect information;

– China limits contacts from foreign countries with its armies, and particularly the United States who is even pushed away from joint drills that China engages in with Russia, for example. Contacts were strictly limited following the 2001 incidents on the island of Hainan. Only in 2006 links were re-established, albeit half-heartedly, between the American and Chinese armies. But the Americans estimate that these relations are unbalanced in favor of China and that care must be taken so that the American military does not divulge too much of its capacities, technologies and know-how. The United States should also reinforce its intelligence capacities;

– the consecutive reports are a reminder that there are still many unknowns on the reality of China's financial investment in this transformation. The reports denounce or confirm China's impenetrability which publishes nothing, divulges nothing involving its strategies and does not reveal real numbers or intentions.

The Americans cannot identify the real motivation behind this race to high-tech weaponry and this transformation of Chinese armies. They think the outside world has little understanding of Chinese motivations, of decision processes and key methods supporting the modernization of the Chinese army. This lack of transparency leads to legitimate questions, as the Defense Secretary Donald Rumsfeld asked in 2005. What is the purpose of these increasing investments? The major aspects of Chinese army modernization, its goals, objectives and plans are not transparent[15]. We should certainly not pretend to believe that the Americans have no clue about China's objectives. What if the answer was as simple as so that the United States is not the only master of the world, dominating all arenas (ground, air, sea, information)? Or simply because China wants to have a credible army, worthy of China's ambitions? American questioning seems somewhat inappropriate. China, as well as the rest of the world, would be entitled to return the question back on the Americans.

---

15. 2006 Annual Report – China Military Power.

2.2.3. *Information warfare*

2.2.3.1. *The Chinese version may only be a copy of the American version*

The vision that Americans have of Chinese information warfare is obviously not only expressed through official reports to Congress.

We can cite the view expressed by James Mulvenon [MU 98]. According to him, the Chinese approach to the concept of information warfare is a simple copy of the American model with a few minor changes, because China is unable to move away from it in an original way. The fact that China has been closely examining American experiments since the First Gulf War, but has no operational or pragmatic experience itself would partially explain this "reproduction". Mulvenon identifies the following similarities:

– the information age is described by the Chinese as the third important period in the history of humanity, following the farming era and industrial revolution. This approach is not original since it uses Alvin and Heidi Toffler's theory [TOF 80] to the letter with their famous "The Third Wave";

– the objective of information warfare is to "protect oneself and control the enemy";

– China uses the theme of info-dominance;

– China uses exactly the same pillars of information warfare defined by the US Air Force, that is to say electronic warfare, tactical deception, strategic dissuasion, propaganda warfare, psychological warfare, network computer warfare and C2 warfare;

– similarities in the idea of integrating the five dimensions of war (air, ground, sea, space, electromagnetic spectrum), principles used in the report "Joint Vision: 2010".

Mulvenon also identifies a few differences:

– for the Chinese, information warfare is a strictly military affair, whereas Westerners accept that information warfare, cyberwar, or netwar (between civilian players and governments) can all be carried out;

– the Chinese resituate their discussions in their own ideological context: the Maoist guerilla strategy, the influence of the Sun Zu doctrine;

– many Chinese writings do not present information warfare as a power intensifier on the battlefield, but as an unconventional weapon of war. Information warfare is perceived as a weapon of preemption.

2.2.3.2. What would the objectives of Chinese information warfare be?

For the Chinese, information warfare must be used to destroy or interrupt the enemy's capacity to receive and process data. Information warfare could be used by the Chinese in a preemptive way.

The objectives of information warfare would be to destroy the opposing command system, shorten the duration of the war, minimize human losses on both sides, reinforce the efficiency of operations, reduce the effects on civilian populations and win support from the international community.

2.2.3.3. Capacity reinforcement of information warfare

The different reports show all the efforts, investments and progress achieved by the Chinese army in terms of information warfare capacity. They particularly identify the creation of special units. According to the Department of Defense, China has developed specialized units of information warfare and viruses to paralyze enemy systems.

The army has created information warfare units (this assertion is used by the 2007 annual report) to develop viruses to attack enemy information systems/networks, and develop tactics and measures to protect its own systems and networks. These information warfare units in the army and reserve may have been under development since at least 2000. In 2005, the Chinese army started to introduce offensive CNOs in its drills (strikes against enemy networks).

These units, made up of military personnel and civilians, could not only support the troops in their attacks, but could also carry out hacker attacks, all sorts of cyberwars against a military opponent and commercial information systems, and help in the defense of Chinese networks. Drills are conducted to integrate the information warfare units in regular military operations. This information echoes articles published in the Chinese press.

2.2.3.4. What would Chinese targets be?

In the annual report to Congress "US–China Economic and Security Review Commission's Report 2006", information warfare is a series of unconventional military methods.

China wants to exploit vulnerabilities caused by the United States' dependence on technologies. It wants to acquire C4ISR systems and be able to paralyze those of the adversary (a C4ISR architecture makes it possible to coordinate forces in all four dimensions – air, ground, space and sea – to locate, follow and aim at the enemy). Information warfare targets are military and civilian without distinction.

The United States is vulnerable to attacks, as demonstrated by the Titan Rain operation. In August and September 2006, attacks against the information systems of the Bureau of Industry and Security of the Department of Commerce led to the replacement of hundreds of computers and to the blocking of Internet access for close to a month.

China's objectives, which do not justify the transformation of its armies with budgets allocated to defense in exponential growth, can hide medium- and long-term strategies that Americans seem to have a hard time predicting. Among the strategies considered, wars conducted in the information sphere must not be ignored.

2.2.3.5. *What information warfare attack is China preparing?*

Attacks would target enemy C2s, communication systems and the transmission of precision weapon information, which are the first instruments of the modern American war.

China wants to acquire and exploit knowledge created by others and must fight a war for the acquisition of information. To reach this objective, intelligence is a major tool and China has institutionalized the practice:

– there are 2–3,000 spy companies (real or assumed) in operation in the United States;[16]

– Chinese students and residents can transmit information to China;

– economic intelligence is used.

With the use of asymmetric weapons, China would want to deteriorate enemy C4ISRs and use anti-satellite weapons, CNAs, the introduction of viruses and massive hacking. Consecutive reports highlight that China has the necessary capabilities to attack C4ISRs. CNAs are an inexpensive and efficient way to fight against a stronger enemy; they are considered long range weapons. The Chinese would favor attacks against weak points, the most vulnerable and accessible networks used to exchange unclassified information, instead of first attacking highly protected secure networks. China has considerably expanded its information operations during the last few years, reaching such a level that it is clearly designed to attack American systems.

---

16. Read the articles: *3,500 Chinese spy companies identified in Canada and the USA*, 8 August 2003, Asian Pacific News service, http://www.primetimecrime.com/APNS /20030808chinesespy.htm and *More claims of Chinese spying emerge*, 6 July 2005, Australian Broadcasting Corporation, TV Program Transcript, Reporter Tony Jones, http://www.abc.net.au/lateline/content/2005/s1408571.htm.

The Annual Report to Congress "The Military Power of the People's Republic of China 2007" emphasized the conceptual knowledge of information warfare by the Chinese and quotes a text published in the Liberation Army Daily in November 2006: "the mechanism to take control of the enemy in a war under informatization[17] conditions finds its strongest expression in our capacity or not to use several methods to obtain and ensure efficient circulation of information, our capacity or not to fully use permeability, sharing property and connection of information to achieve organic fusion of materials, energy and information in order to create a combined combat force, and in our capacity or not to use efficient methods to weaken superiority of information of the enemy and the operations efficiency of enemy computer equipment".

CNOs include CNA, CND and CNE and are an integral part of the policy of modernization of Chinese armies. The army considers CNOs as particularly critical for taking the initiative and acquiring electromagnetic dominance as soon as possible in a conflict, and as a power intensifier. We have no knowledge of Chinese CNO doctrine, but Chinese thinkers speak of "Integrated network electronic warfare", highlighting the integrated use of electronic warfare, CNOs, and limited kinetic strikes against C4 nodes to interrupt the enemy's information system networks on the battlefield[18].

2.2.3.6. *The acquisition of information warfare technologies*

The Chinese army invests in electronic counter measures, defense against electronic attacks and CNO (CNA, CND, CNE) methods to dominate the electromagnetic spectrum early in any conflict. Chinese thinkers speak of an "integrated electronic warfare network" to call for the use of electronic warfare, CNOs and kinetic strikes to destroy the information systems of the battlefield.

China continues its foreign acquisition of (notably dual) technology investments, useful to the development of computerized network centric forces: software, integrated circuits, computers, electronics, semi-conductors, telecommunications, and information security systems.

The Americans denounce the efforts of China to acquire, legally or not, dual technologies through commercial exchanges and agreements, or even joint ventures, particularly with software and integrated circuit manufacturers, at the heart of the requirements to fight network centric warfare and information warfare.

China grants large investments to acquire asymmetric military capacities (cyber warfare and electronic warfare capabilities).

---

17. See [WAN 99] and [XG 99].
18. For more information on the digital battlefield, refer to [YUA 99].

But China is not settling for acquiring, it also provides weapons to sensitive countries like Iran, Burma and Sudan. This development at any cost, despite international rules, is what concerns the Americans.

2.2.3.7. *The role of nationalist hackers or hacktivists*

The report to Congress "Annual Report on the Military Power of the People's Republic of China 2003" recalls the dangers inherent to nationalist hacking (hacktivism) in periods of tension or crisis. The increasing presence of China over the Internet and the application of the people's war principle to network warfare constitute serious threats for American networks that may be the target of massive attacks.

In light of the current and future potential of Chinese internet users, the relative proportion of attackers is reason for concern. The role of the Chinese government must be significant. Would it support hacktivism or would it not? Although the report does not further discuss these hacktivists, the media provides numerous examples.

Recently, incidents and political events perceived as threats to Chinese integrity and national sovereignty, and the identification of major adversaries, triggered massive cyber attacks from hackers wanting to defend the interests of China:

– bombing of the embassy of China by NATO forces in Belgrade on 8 May 1999 led to a series of attacks (DoS, massive email transmissions, viruses and intrusions) against American sites. We are speaking here of a Chinese–American cyberwar. The Chinese Liberation Army newspaper, on 27 July 1999 wrote that a network battle was being fought between China and the United States;

– battles in the form of duels between hackers (site defacements, data stealing, viruses) were launched following a speech from the President of Taiwan, Teng-Hui Li in August 1999, declaring the "two States" principle;

– in 2001, the United States was the victim of a legitimate attack against its official websites as a protest for the death of a Chinese pilot, Wang Wei, during a collision with an American spy plane near the Chinese coast on April 1st. Chinese hackers, including Honker Union of China (HUC) or Chinese Red Guest Network Security Technology Alliance, organized massive cyber attack campaigns during the month of April; close to 1,200 sites were affected by DoS attacks including the White House and the US Air Force[19]. Did the Chinese government sanction those attacks? Were these attacks condemned publicly? During these battles via the

---

19. For more information of the Chinese attack campaign of April 2001, you can view a series of articles at http://strategique.free.fr/archives/textes/ca/archives_ca_14.htm.

intermediary of computers, the Americans were clearly not out done because a group of hackers called PoizonBox is thought to have defaced 100 Chinese websites;

– from 2003, the exiled Tibetan government in India has been accusing groups based in Beijing of intruding on its official sites and spying. Hackers send emails containing Trojan horses with legitimate-sounding addresses to make them seem more authentic;

– in 2003, the Taiwanese government accused Chinese military hackers of launching several attacks against its information systems. But were they military or hacktivists?

– hundreds of South Korean government computers were infected during the last months of 2003 by viruses capable of stealing passwords and other sensitive information. According to KISA (Korean Information Security Agency), during the first six months of 2004, a total of 10,628 hacking cases were recorded, which is 30 times higher than in the same period in 2003;

– in April 2005, Japan was faced with strong anti-Japanese sentiment, translated by violent street manifestations in Beijing and Shanghai, with some military personnel even calling for war. The tensions were accompanied by a resurgence of "cyber attacks" against Japanese websites: embassy sites, national agencies, ministry of Defense, of Foreign affairs, universities and corporations.

Who are these patriot hackers whose actions are simultaneously the illustration of the "people's war" concept and a method of "active defense"? Are they a reply to external attacks, threats to enemy systems, or protection of the country's own systems? The increasing number of attacks since the end of the 1990s due to the exponential increase of Chinese Internet users is not only defensive. They target research centers, corporations and government departments of all the industrialized countries. The attacks have many goals including information theft, espionage, ideological demands and destabilization. It is very difficult to demonstrate the involvement of authorities in these actions that we credit to cyber criminality, or organized groups of hackers, especially when we can demonstrate with certainty that they come from China and that the parties responsible are actually Chinese!

2.2.3.8. *Nationalist hacking or simply cyber criminality?*

As in the rest of the world, with the growth of networks, the exponential increase of the number of Internet users, criminality has quickly spread in the Chinese cyberspace. The first cyber criminality acts were recorded in China in the mid 1980s. The first victim was the banking system.

Until the middle of the 1990s, cyber criminality was simple in its form (mostly crimes against property). Public interest in this new phenomenon grew with the emergence of the virus. In 1989, political propaganda viruses started appearing, resulting in government reaction as the virus penetrated sensitive fields. The second cyber criminality period started in 1996 with the massive expansion and exponential growth of networks and numbers of users, even though the Internet was relatively late in arriving in China.

System hacking is severely punished (with up to a death sentence). But when hackers target foreign systems, the government, because of its silence and the lack of reaction of law enforcement authorities, seems to support these actions.

Trojan horse attacks targeting Western corporations were recently recorded all over the world. In 2004, reverse engineering of the Myfip Trojan horse revealed that it sends data stolen from its victims to an Internet user located in Tianjin, the third biggest city in China and second hub of the electronics industry. The source of the Netthief Trojan horse that attacked companies in the United Kingdom was also located in China. Trojan horses go after sensitive data; IP and commercial secrets. The finger is pointed at continental China. Taiwan is not to be out done: according to a report from the American Department of Defense "Taiwan Strait Posture Status", Taiwan is the global leader in the development of anti-virus techniques, but also home to a large number of recent viruses (among the most well-known are Bloody of 6/4 in 1990, Michelangelo in 1992 and Chernobyl in 1998).

There is nothing that proves that the Chinese authorities directly support or sponsor these activities. But by not punishing them, in the eyes of the victims, they support them. Beijing of course denies the involvement of the State in hacker acts targeting foreign interests, despite numerous international allegations.

2.2.3.9. Can the United States remain a victim without reacting?

The potential Chinese threat raises awareness. In its annual report of 2005, the US–China Economic and Security Review Commission recommends that Congress mandate an investigation conducted by the appropriate agencies, involving cyber attacks against American networks from China.

If proof could be made that China is responsible for these attacks, that it is an accomplice or that, because of negligence, it lets its citizens attack networks then, insofar as these threats constitute hostile acts against the United States, Congress could ask the President to advise on the measures to take against China, in accordance with current laws, or ask that measures be taken to discourage attacks against American networks.

2.2.3.10. *The development of the Chinese Internet*

Regardless of controls and legal or political measures, it is clear that the number of attacks and their power will only grow in proportion to the increase in the number of Internet users in China. In 2005, Asia, representing 60% of the Earth's population, had over 240 million Internet users[20]. China represented over half of this potential, thus becoming the second largest personal computer market in the world.

In 2009, Asia represented 42% of world internet users; in 2009 Q1, China had 298 millions internet users.[21] The statistics are impressive. The arrival of China in the Internet world is an opportunity for accelerated development of its economy and a new economic openness for the most remote regions. For the rest of the world, this arrival is at least as important as the accession of China among the first worldwide economic powers. As the Internet is more prevalent in all the country's provinces and cities, it must become the backbone of the communication system and one of the driving forces of economic development for the 21st Century. In 1993, China initiated the large "Golden Projects" program, still in progress, aimed at providing the country with Chinese telecommunications and information infrastructures necessary for economic development, as well as the development of economic information networks, a customs information network, connecting financial centers and networks linking 12,000 small- to medium-sized companies and large corporations. The country's infrastructures have quickly modernized. At the end of 2004, China connected 25 universities together through a new generation backbone Cernet2 (China Education and Research Network 2), a first IPv6 protocol network with record throughputs of 40 Gb/s. China thus offers the image of a country with state-of-the-art innovation, with its own Silicon Valley (Zhongguancun), or strategic "corridor", concentrating 75% of the Chinese market in the field of telecommunications (Beijing – Shanghai – Guangzhou). The Internet has rapidly become one of the most sensitive infrastructures in the country by its importance and penetration. China, just like all modern countries, is more and more dependent on its information systems.

2.2.4. *Why is China intensifying the modernization of its armies?*

China has long been a weak country in terms of its military. But its economic growth since the 1990s has provided the means to invest in its defense. China's

---

20. *The approaching Chinese Cyber Storm*, July 21, 2005. http://www.netcost-security.fr.
21. Statistics provided by http://www.internetworldstats.com/stats3.htm.

defense budget is now the second largest in the world after the United States, albeit far behind in absolute value[22].

This budget continues to grow every year in an impressive way. What is China looking for with this military growth? Does it simply want to be able to promote an image as a credible military force to the world?

Reinforcement of the technological military capabilities serves the strategic interests and political intentions of the country well in the Asia-Pacific zone, notably preparing the country to fight and win a short-term and high intensity conflict against Taiwan, with the United States or any other country that would come to the rescue of the island.

To the Americans, China cultivates ambiguity while modernizing its armed forces. When it conducts ballistic missile tests over the Taiwan Strait, it maintains that it has no aggressive designs against Taipei and calls for a peaceful reunification.

2.2.4.1. *Preparing for new wars?*

The Desert Storm operation resulted in the modernization of C4ISR systems and the development of information warfare, precision weapons and logistic capabilities.

The Allied Forces operation (1999) had a similar impact on the Chinese army thought process, confirming the first conclusions of the necessity of preparing for new wars, notably by observing how the Serbs could resist with technically inferior methods against the American attacker. The "three attacks, three defenses" principle is the direct result of these observations and conclusions of the Allied Forces operation; attack by aviation, cruise missiles, helicopters; defense against precision fire, electronic warfare and enemy reconnaissance.

2.2.4.2. *Arriving in the information age*

Military modernization is, then, based on a finite analysis of American military operations since the 1990s (American operations in Iraq in 1991 and 2003 and in Kosovo in 1999). The Gulf War of 1991 showed that an army built around technologies and methods inherited from the Soviet army was doomed to fail against the power of a modern military such as the United States, made possible because of its RMA based on technological progress.

Chinese priorities include getting to the information age, introducing and adopting technologies and information tools, solutions for increased mobility and

---

22. For more information of the strategic power of China, refer to [LIM 02].

precision strikes. Marine, ground and air forces are all benefiting from the major investments granted by the government.

The Chinese army's transformation is guided by the objectives of being able to fight and win a "limited local war under conditions of informatization" and modernizing an army that has long been guided by the "people's war" principle dear to Mao Zedong. What does this new doctrine mean? Engaging in short and high intensity conflicts, characterized by mobility, speed, long distance attacks occupying all spaces simultaneously; ground, air, sea, space, electromagnetic field and field of information relying on very deadly high-tech weapons (unconcerned about reducing human losses, or at least not focusing on the question like the United States does with its obsession with zero death).

2.2.4.3. Ambitions beyond Asia-Pacific?

The annual report to Congress "The Military Power of the People's Republic of China 2007"[23] states the concern of the United States with the increase in power of the Chinese army whose technological developments and profound transformation cannot be justified only by a possible conflict in the Strait of Taiwan.

The Chinese army now has great potential to confront the United States and engage in regional conflicts for resources or territory. The growth of China's military capabilities clearly has implications that go beyond the Asia-Pacific region. The strategy of banning access and the protection of air, sea and ground territories clearly expands to space and cyberspace. The report again uses the notion of China's "lack of transparency" involving its objectives and the very limited knowledge of the West about these objectives and China's motivations.

2.2.5. Technologies for army modernization

2.2.5.1. What technologies?

The military budget keeps increasing; over 14.7% in 2006. The effort will continue. In May 2006, China approved a new research and development plan for defense sciences and technologies focusing on solutions involving information technologies. These investments are used for acquisition and development:

– of anti-satellite weapons; nuclear warheads and lasers. In 2007, an American spy satellite was blinded by a Chinese laser as it passed over its territory[24]. The

23. http://www.defenselink.mil/pubs/pdfs/070523-China-Military-Power-final.pdf.
24. United States Space. CNES bureau of the French Embassy in the United States. Information accessed 24 April 2007 at www.techno-science.net.

satellites have high resolution sensors that lasers target to distort their capacities. The Americans conduct similar tests on their own satellites. Satellites are relatively easy targets because of their regular rotation around the globe. Their position is known at each moment. Furthermore, faced with a weapon intent on destroying them, satellites have no protection. A satellite can also be destroyed by ballistic missiles. In January 2007, China destroyed one of its meteorology satellites while testing the feasibility of this type of attack. The low orbit (865 km altitude) made the operation possible. China was strongly criticized for this test, which created a precedent. Should we have the right to destroy satellites in orbit, leading to the "pollution" of space with debris, a threat to surrounding satellites in orbit? China was criticized but the United States and Russia had already proceeded with such tests;

– of parasite microsatellites that could hang on to enemy satellites, paralyze them, destroy them or divert the information that they gather;

– of information technologies. The Chinese army is involved in a double construction: mechanization and informatization. It wants to "digitize" its equipment and weapons with communications systems and sensors that are more precise and puts all its efforts in C4ISR infrastructures, networking and information warfare.

2.2.5.2. *Acquisition methods*

In order to develop its information warfare capacities, China needs leading edge technologies that it would like to acquire in different ways.

In 1998, China initiated a wave of reforms of military acquisitions. Acquisitions and development are done in the context of large pluriannual projects, resulting, for example, in the "998 State Security Project"[25]. One of its main objectives is the development of concepts and weapons (missiles, power weapons, nuclear weapons) to counter supremacy by any other power. The project was adopted by the central committee of the Chinese communist party in August 1999 [WEN 00]. In 2000, the objectives of Project 122 were the reinforcement of the Chinese army, its counter-attack capacities and the development of a new generation of high-tech and nuclear weapons. Project 126 covers the development of spatial/aeronautical technologies, electronic/information technology systems, strategic defense systems, counter-attack, optical lasers and a development program for new material. The research and development program 863 implemented in 1986 (extended by program 973) covers military and civilian projects and puts a priority on dual technology projects.

---

25. Hearing on Military Modernization and Cross-Strait Balance, 6 February 2004. http://www.uscc.gov/hearings/2004hearings/transcripts/04_02_06.pdf.

Research and development is carried out jointly between civilian and military centers. Since China allocates a large budget to defense (approximately 9% of its GDP)[26], it can afford to invest in the development of information warfare.

In this frantic race for modernization, China uses any means, including illegal means, to acquire what it needs. The United States condemns aggressive Chinese espionage. Since 2000, almost 400 investigations have been conducted in the United States involving illicit weapon and technology exports to China.

2.2.5.3. Dependence on foreign countries

China is still not able to produce its own leading edge technologies and thus greatly depends on imports. Russia (at 80%) and Israel have been China's major suppliers of weapons and military technologies over the last ten years.

The Chinese army still depends greatly on foreign military technologies. Some of the "historical" suppliers are Russia (destroyers, submarines and aircraft) and the United States. The European Union confirmed an embargo on sales of weapons to China in April 2004 because of pressure from the United States, in particular, and from human rights groups. But China sees in this embargo a remnant of the Cold War. Besides, can the EU resist the lure of this huge market?

Parallel to the development of solutions within its own industries, China is a powerful importer of technologies for building an information warfare infrastructure. Under the Clinton administration, China imported supercomputers directly from the United States. How many may have landed in military laboratories for purposes other than what was initially expected? EU exports to China are under an embargo since the events of Tiananmen Square in 1989. Lifting that embargo would profit China and enable it to access dual use technologies. Cryptography technologies are under the control of member countries of the Wassenaar arrangements[27]. China is not a member, making industrial agreements in this area and acquisition of Western technologies difficult.

2.2.5.4. Transformation characteristics

Chinese military development raises concerns but the United States estimates that China will not catch up with them any time soon. In the long term, the capacity of China to produce its technologies itself will become urgent.

---

26. General Abe C. Lin, Comparison of the Information Warfare Capabilities of the ROC and PRC, December 27, 2000. http://cryptome.org/cn2-infowar.htm.
27. The arrangements (13 July 1996) are intended to limit the export of dual use weapons, items and technologies.

The Chinese army's transformation is interesting on several levels:

– by the creation of an army within the army. Approximately 15% of ground forces are specifically trained to engage in quick attacks supported by missile strikes and precision fire from the air and by sea, and equipped with "high-tech" equipment (C4ISR systems, capacity of offensive information warfare)[28]. This type of strategy is intended to prepare an elite army that is modern and can quickly intervene in conflicts limited in time and space. An intervention against Taiwan obviously comes to mind, but it could be local conflicts of a different nature, for example, conflicts over natural resources;

– the informatization implies a fundamental change from a war centered on platforms to Network Centric Warfare;

– more than in any other country in the Asia-Pacific region, the transformation of the Chinese army occurred by using the United States as a model. Is the objective then to one day be able to resemble the enemy and beat him with the same weapons?

The development of China is presented as being particularly aggressive. Any means seem acceptable to reinforce its civilian and military industry, and the boundary between the two is very small since civilian industry is at the service of national security. China must grow technologically and acquire as many technologies and as much know-how as possible, and very quickly, to feed its economy, progress and modernization (especially of its armies). The Americans see the practice of economic intelligence in the Western and Japanese model (officially encouraged by the Chinese government) as illicit practices, bordering on espionage. This battle for the acquisition of strategic and technological information also involves infringing on intellectual property rights (copying of patents, breach of industrial secrets, reverse engineering). The programs for science and technology are based on the assimilation of foreign sciences and technologies, and the civilian–military relation is at the heart of these developments.

The role of China in the proliferation of weapons of mass destruction and other weapons, including dual use technologies, is another subject of concern for the Americans. However, there is only one American officer based in continental China responsible for controlling American exports, and notably to ensure that dual use technologies and items licensed in the US are really used where and how they are supposed to be according to the license. Similarly, there is only one officer in Hong Kong responsible for verifying that dual use items licensed for limited use in Hong Kong remain in Hong Kong and are not transferred to the Chinese continent. The

---

28. Richard A. Bitzinger, *China adapts to US defense transformation*, 11 October 2006. http://www.isn.ethz.ch/news/sw/details.cfm?ID=16778.

weakness of human resources available makes any real control of the use of these items once they are acquired impossible, even under license.

In the three-way USA–Taiwan–China relationship, the balance of power is now unfavorable to Taiwan which would be unable alone to resist an attack launched by China. And yet, China is still lacking in a real integrated C4ISR architecture, which prevents it from launching efficient joint operations. Additionally, experts estimate that the United States will find itself in a "window of vulnerability" period between 2008 and 2015, the time needed for the USA to develop ballistic anti-missile defense systems.

2.2.6. In search of interpretations: the concept of "shashoujian"

"Shashoujian", which can be translated as "assassin's mace", is a relatively common expression in China, expressing the means and methods by which it is possible to overcome a seemingly insurmountable obstacle. This involves an action or a quality, offering a strategic advantage, when it is used for a specific purpose, in a particular manner and at a specific time[29].

The term appeared in the annual "US–China Security Review Commission Report 2002", then used again in the annual reports to Congress "Military Power of the People's Republic of China" of 2004 and 2005. It certainly intrigued American observers, who immediately saw a new mystery in contemporary Chinese strategic thinking and it therefore had to be decoded as soon as possible. The American Department of Defense claimed that China intensively pursued the development and acquisition of asymmetric "assassin's mace" type solutions, recognizing at the same time its inability to say with precision if this term indicated specific technologies, concepts or a strategy.

The term is not recent (it is thought to date back to the Tang period) but it has reemerged recently in the context of the debates involving the modernization of Chinese armies in the middle of the 1990s, after China became really aware of its backwardness compared to the undeniable technological superiority of the Americans. The term is used to describe a secret weapon, a platform, a dissuasive system or a tool helping to reach a political/psychological/military victory with a single decisive, fatal battle. The military concept of "shashoujian" cannot be reduced to the idea of a "magic" weapon, to the concept of *Blitzkrieg* or to the idea of launching an abrupt and total attack (an electronic Pearl Harbor, for instance) that would make it possible to paralyze an enemy before even starting a war. The concept of "shashoujian" focuses more on the capabilities of the "inferior" enemy in

---

29. Also read [JOH 02].

an asymmetric conflict, the possibility for that enemy to win the war despite its inferiority.

Why has the term come back in the military world? When the Taiwanese President Lee Teng-Hui wanted to confirm the position of Taiwan in relation to Beijing, China replied with a demonstration of force by firing ballistic missiles off the Taiwanese coast. The United States reacted immediately by sending a fleet in a show of support for Taiwan. President Jiang Zemin then asked his army what possibilities there were. The response was: "Nothing!" Politically powerless against the United States, the Chinese government has since strived to develop new capabilities enabling it to one day force its will. Chinese capabilities are and will remain for a long time inferior to the United States, but they need to find a way to take advantage of such a situation that is *a priori* unfavorable, which would be possible with an "assassin's mace", enabling it to win in the Taiwan Strait in an asymmetric situation. This "shashoujian" is therefore mainly a general principle, an idea, a concept, more than a specific technology. That is what will make China able to impose itself on a more powerful enemy, for example by making an American intervention useless, too costly and/or too risky. "Shashoujian" could consist of a diplomatic opportunity, a strategic manoeuver, the use of speed (a long-range missile strike that American ships would not have time to detect), or the use of submarines, computer network attacks, communications satellite attacks and information warfare to deteriorate American C4ISR systems, the effect of surprise in taking a military advantage and pursuing through diplomacy, running the risk of a generalized conflict which the United States would not want to engage in. We can imagine solutions and different configurations. The only option available to China at present is to prepare for asymmetric conflicts if it finds itself at war with the great powers.

What are the expected effects of "shashoujian" type strikes?

– dissuasion. This is the equivalent of the Sun Tzu formula: "Winning without fighting". Today, ballistic missiles and submarines are considered shashoujian type forces used as the basis of psychological warfare;

– decapitation. i.e. killing the enemy in one clear and fatal shot. That is the ideal goal;

– blinding, paralyzing, disintegrating. It is the acupuncture war (*dianxue zhan*) that must have systemic effects on enemy structure and military organization. Chinese strategists discuss the importance of shashoujian strikes on critical infrastructures: C2 centers, networks, intelligence systems, sensor platforms and military logistic systems. Such systems are taken as a source of weakness of the superior enemy, more vulnerable to attacks. Attacking weak points, and especially vital points, paralyzes the adversary and then initiates the disintegration of a superior force.

2.2.7. *2008 DoD report concerning Chinese military power*

In March 2008, the United States Department of Defense published its annual report on the military power of the People's Republic of China[30]. The report insists once more on the concerning development of seemingly aggressive military capacities and doctrines and strategies in China. China, which has become a vital partner internationally, still represents a serious threat to peace in the world. The report questions once more the place that information warfare has in the constitution of this "Chinese threat". But could the report be revealing American perceptions, psychology or strategy instead of being a strictly objective description of the Chinese reality that it wants to conquer?

The 2008 report has seven chapters, with a summary, a glossary of acronyms and appendices:

– Chapter 1: Key developments.

– Chapter 2: Understanding China's strategy.

– Chapter 3: China's military strategy and doctrine.

– Chapter 4: Force modernization goals and trends.

– Chapter 5: Resources for force modernization.

– Chapter 6: Force modernization and security in the Taiwan Strait.

– A chapter dedicated to human capital in the PLA modernization.

– Appendices proposing a series of quantitative data on the military forces of China and Taiwan.

As an introduction, the report highlights the major role that China now plays on the international scene, achieved through the unconditional support of the United States: "No country has done more [than the United States] to assist, facilitate and encourage China's national development and its integration in the international system"[31]. Uncertainties surround the course chosen by China however: what is the purpose of the expansion of the Chinese military power, how will this power be used?

The new China–United States, China–Asia, China–rest of the world balances of power quickly become the major subject. On one side, there is the United States with peaceful intentions, and on the other, China, seemingly peaceful but suspected

---

30. The report can be downloaded in full at the address http://www.defenselink.mil/pubs/pdfs/China_Military_Report_08.pdf.
31. Page 1 of the 2008 report.

of not remaining that way, of wanting to switch from simply ensuring its defense to an aggressive player, preparing local wars[32] with the help of high-tech resources ("local wars under conditions of informatization")[33] and able to confront the United States in a military context (this idea taken from the 2006 Quadrennial Defense Review Report[34]). According to the United States, China is preparing for the possibility of a conflict in the Taiwan Strait, including in case of American intervention. In order to quickly modernize its armies and achieve its RMA[35], China has agreed to significant efforts and investments: acquisition of state-of-the-art weapons, notably from foreign countries, modernization of its nuclear arsenal, development of a strong technological and scientific industry, and reformulation of its doctrines, thus affecting the army organization to its core.

Chinese doctrine is perceived as a free mix of ancient and modern sources, including strategists of the era of Imperial China and Chinese Communist Party icons. This multitude of sources is the reason why Westerners do not understand China, and because of this, study of Chinese military strategy remains a fundamentally inaccurate science. This comment is surprising: is there an army with a history that is not today built on both the past and the present? The report identifies a few "concepts" deemed vital to the understanding of Chinese action today and in the future.

2.2.7.1. *The 24 character strategy*

"Calmly observe, secure the position, face the events with calm, hide our capacities and wait for the right moment, try to maintain a low profile, and never claim leadership". This sentence, written in 24 Chinese characters and attributed to Deng Xiaoping was used as a guide for the Chinese system of foreign affairs and security policy early in the 1990s. Some elements of this strategy continue to be used by the heads of Chinese security in the context of diplomatic and military affairs. This strategy is instructive in that it suggests maximizing the options to

---

32. To defend territories where China claims sovereignty, and for the "One China" principle to be respected: territories include Taiwan, the Paracel and Spratly islands, islands in the South China seas, etc. These territories are claimed by many countries in the region: Brunei, The Philippines, Malaysia, Vietnam, Russia, Japan, India, etc. For a map of territorial conflicts, see page 11 of the 2008 report.
33. "Informatization" here means operation environments characterized by the jamming of communications, electronic surveillance, and precision weapons.
34. 2006 Quadrennial Defense Review Report: "China has the greatest potential to compete militarily with the United States...". Downloadable report at http://www.comw.org/qdr/qdr2006.pdf.
35. Revolution in Military Affairs. The expression represents the process of modernization of armies in the context of a technological revolution.

come without useless provocations. The Americans see in this concept one of the keys for interpreting Chinese attitudes internationally [MED 07].

2.2.7.2. *The Chinese opportunism*

Chinese leaders have described the first 20 years of the 21st Century as a period of opportunity[36], providing peaceful regional and international conditions, and conducive for China to dominate regionally and have a global influence. This means that during this period of opportunities, the country must be able to seize its chances; every occasion should be used for its benefit. Opportunism does not mean playing wait-and-see, however. It can also involve frequent changes of policy, tactics and economics, according to the context. Opportunism involves a strong capacity to react and to adapt. Opportunism is often considered as an attitude that ignores moral principles. Should we increase political and economic influence at any cost? Should we be able to abandon political or ideological principles considered as fundamental to expand our political influence? How can these opportunities materialize: through alliances, collaboration agreements, by exploiting the weaknesses of other nations, by organizing the exploitation of all the flaws of the international system and, if so, then why not include the information systems that we know are so fragile? But opportunism is not an option without risk. As early as 1928, Leon Trotsky, writing about the Chinese revolution involving the "classic mistakes of opportunism", mentioned these risks that ideological movements take when they sink into opportunism[37].

2.2.7.3. *Asymmetric war and the concept of "shashoujian"*

The report uses the famous concept of the "assassin's mace" ("shashoujian" in Chinese)[38]. It appeared in the annual report "US–China Security Review Commission Report 2002", and was then used again in the 2004 and 2005 annual reports to Congress "Military Power of the People's Republic of China", the term certainly intriguing American observers who immediately saw a new mystery in contemporary Chinese strategic thinking. The 2008 report goes back once more to this concept, defining "shashoujian" programs as an integral part of the Chinese asymmetric war strategy, giving a technologically inferior party military advantages over technologically superior adversaries, in order to change the direction of the war. The descriptions of the use and effects of "shashoujian" type platforms are compliant with the Chinese asymmetric war strategy and mainly consist in the integration of modern and older technologies used in an innovative way. Would cyber aggressions carried out in peacetime come from the preparation of these

---

36. Chapter 2, page 9 of the 2008 report.
37. http://www.zhongguo.org/trotsky/revbetrayed/images/China/27.htm "Leon Trotsky on China. The classic mistakes of opportunism." January 1928.
38. See page 20 from the 2008 report.

solutions, by providing a player with the flaws of potential adversaries? Regardless of the solutions being developed, American intelligence estimates that China will have to wait at least 10 years before having a modern army able to beat a medium-sized adversary[39].

2.2.7.4. *Place of the "information warfare" concept in the report*

The concept of "information warfare" is addressed in its own section within the 4th chapter on the objectives of army modernization. The terms of the report remain vague, simply indicating that military strategists have a deep understanding of the concept, its methods and uses. Text from a Chinese report published in the "Liberation Army Daily" review[40] in November 2006 defines the concept of information warfare. This quotation, already present in the 2007 DoD Report, does not bring any new information for identifying a specifically Chinese approach to the concept. Information warfare is "the mechanism to take control of the enemy in a war under informatization conditions, finds its strongest expression in our capacity or not to use several methods to obtain and ensure efficient circulation of information, our capacity or not to fully use permeability, sharing property and connection of information to achieve organic fusion of materials, energy and information, in order to create a combined combat force, and in our capacity or not to use efficient methods to weaken superiority of information of the enemy and the operations efficiency of the enemy computer equipment".

Data relative to investments is then provided, but without a statistical approach. It simply states, as in previous reports, that the Chinese army invests (in acquisition or development?) in methods of electronic counter-measures, defense against electronic attacks (angle type reflectors, false target generators) and CNO (Computer Network Operations)[41] to dominate the electromagnetic spectrum early in the conflict.

The report mentions the creation of special units of information warfare in China. According to the Department of Defense, China has integrated specialized units of information warfare and developed viruses to paralyze enemy systems. But again, this is information already published in previous Department of Defense reports.

No information relative to information warfare in the 2008 report is any different from the contents of the previous reports. Does this mean that intelligence departments have nothing new to add to the report about this subject? Or would it

---

39. See Chapter 4, page 22, of the 2008 report.
40. http://www.pladaily.com.cn/.
41. CNO: Computer Network Operations. This military concept from American doctrine groups CNA, CND and CNE.

mean that the subject may have been put somewhat aside to concentrate on other objects of concern like the tension in the Taiwan Strait, the development of human potential or the arsenal of ballistic missiles? Would information on information warfare not offer sufficiently interesting arguments to feed the image of the "Chinese threat"? Even though several countries brought accusations against the Chinese army in 2007 involving aggressions against government information systems, nothing in this chapter establishes any link between the events and the PLA; there is no constructive comment to agree with the accusations or to contradict them. The report is of no help in better understanding the Chinese doctrine and strategy in terms of information warfare, which appears not to have changed in the last few years.

2.2.7.5. Cyberwar methods

By "cyberwar" the Americans mean confrontations in networks, hacker wars conducted by the military. Non military hacker warfare, confrontations between hacktivists and aggressive maneuvers in cyberspace by non military is covered in the concept of "netwar", not discussed in this report. In Chapter I "Key developments"[42], there is a section dedicated to cyberwar methods. During 2007, several attacks against computer networks occurred around the world, including the information systems of the United States government, victims of intrusions that seem to come from continental China. These intrusions would require significant skills and means. The report recognizes that there is no certainty that these intrusions were led by, or with the support of, the Chinese army or other Chinese government elements. It does maintain, however, that the development of cyberwar capacities is compliant with the doctrines published by the Chinese army on this subject. Some of the now famous incidents of 2007 include:

– The Department of Defense and other agencies or departments of the United States government, as well as contractors or think tanks linked to defense, were the targets of several intrusions in their systems, and many of them seemed to come from continental China.

– The Vice-president of the German Intelligence Department, Hans Elmar Remberg, publicly accused China of supporting daily intrusions in information systems. These intrusions were suspected to be for the purpose of stealing information so that China can catch up technologically as soon as possible.

– In September 2007, the French Secretary General for national defense confirmed that the government's information systems were the target of attacks from China.

---

42. Pages 3 and 4 of the 2008 report.

– Aggressions seeming to come from China affected British companies, and the CEO of MI5 alerted 300 financial institutions in the country of risks of aggression from China.

2.2.7.6. *From cyberwar to espionage*

No revelations or any new information can be found from reading the press or from the numerous articles on the Internet, and the American intelligence services did not add to the 2008 report with respect to Chinese involvement.

On the other hand, even though mention of the facts is preceded by a short sentence giving China the benefit of the doubt (because it is technically impossible to identify with certainty the authors of these acts, and it is unclear if these intrusions were conducted by, or with the endorsement of, the PLA or other elements of the PRC government), the whole section can be understood as a clear denunciation of China.

The actions are attributed to China, guilty or innocent. The motives of these attacks do not seem to have been the subject of a deeper analysis, as they are presented as obvious. Economic espionage is the only argument that can be proposed, because of the nature of targets affected or attempted. China wants to quickly access high technologies. The Federal Bureau of Investigation (FBI)[43] and the Immigration and Customs Enforcement (ICE)[44] have named China as the major threat in terms of espionage against the United States. In the last few years, we have seen an increase in investigations involving illicit weapon and technology exports to China. As with the cyber aggressions of 2007, the report provides examples:

– In December 2007 a resident of California was sentenced to two years in prison for his involvement in illegal export activities of night vision technologies to China.

– The ex-director of a research institute linked to the Russian space agency was sentenced to 11 years in prison for having transmitted classified technologies to China.

This economic espionage seems to be caused by the Chinese army and government because accusing fingers have declared them as being at the origin of the 2007 attacks. The report is not meant to propose interpretations. Some questions should be raised, however. Is espionage the only reason for the attacks against information systems? Is China the only possible source? Can other motives explain acts of aggression, such as target observation, implementation of tactics and aggressive operation methods, with the purpose of more ambitious actions in the future or to demonstrate power? Different hypotheses are completely ignored in this report.

---

43. http://www.fbi.gov/.
44. http://www.ice.gov/.

2.2.7.7. *The military doctrine: the duality of the Chinese strategy*

The few lines dedicated to the recent developments of the Chinese military doctrine do not identify any major evolution of the information warfare concept. Only the firm directives instructing the armies to train in computerized environments and integrate leading edge technologies in their structures are mentioned. The fundamental texts have remained essentially the same since 1993, reflecting the impact that the 1991 Gulf War had on military doctrines. However, it seems that today China is shifting from "developing" its forces consisting in preparing them for modern wars, to wars in the information age, to training for "winning" these wars[45]. The strategy remains active defense, consisting in not engaging in a war of aggression, but only engaging in defense wars for national sovereignty and territory integrity. Once hostilities have started, the essence of active defense is to take initiative and annihilate the enemy. But the definition of the attack against the sovereignty of China remains vague. Preemptive actions have been conducted in the name of the defense strategy; for example, China's interventions during the Korean war (1950-1953) to help Korea resist against the United States. The actions carried out during border conflicts are presented as self-defense counter-attacks. The idea is to protect interests perceived as central by China through actions that may be preemptive, preventive, coercive, etc. Striking after the enemy strikes does not mean passively waiting for the enemy to use force. This Chinese strategy thus justifies offensive military actions (said to be preemptive) at operational and tactical levels, under the pretense of a strategic defensive posture. Finally, the Chinese military doctrine clarifies that an enemy strike is not limited to conventional kinetic military operations. An enemy strike can also be defined in political terms. Could the reasoning be taken further? By supposing that the cyber-aggressions encountered by a large number of countries in 2007 were in fact Chinese, would they be part of these operational and tactical offensive actions justified by a defense strategy? Could the 2007 aggressions be a form of defensive reaction? Is China's informational space a domain of sovereignty that the government is ready to defend based on the same arguments and strategies that it uses for its territorial conflicts with neighboring countries? Why then, if that is the case, would China not have claimed responsibility for these actions?

2.2.7.8. *The capacities of anti-access/area denial capabilities*

This concept[46] captures the attention of the report's writers. The strategy consists of creating an insurmountable zone for anyone who would want to penetrate it in the context of the preparation of a confrontation with Taiwan, and is mainly based on the deployment of a nuclear arsenal, ballistic missiles, or even anti-satellite weapons. It involves ground, sea and air dimensions. This strategy would

---

45. Chapter 3, page 16 of the 2008 report.
46. See also [CLI 07].

now extend to cyberspace[47] and consist of information control (dominance of information). China is developing operations security, electronic warfare, information warfare and deception solutions. Information dominance involves using civilian and military power instruments in all dimensions of the modern combat space[48].

2.2.7.9. *Cartographic absence of information warfare resources*

The report proposes 17 illustrations (diagrams, figures) relative to:

– the space of Chinese military influence (territories that are subject to dispute, the extent of maritime power and the range of ballistic missiles)[49];

– army potential in terms of equipment (conventional and ballistic missiles)[50], investments (defense budget)[51], and efforts in the development of a modern system by force (ground, air, sea, space)[52];

– the balance of power in the Taiwan Strait, in ground, air and naval forces[53].

Several sections in the report are dedicated to the doctrines and methods underlying Chinese information operations. However, capacities in terms of information and communication technologies for military use, and in terms of resources allocated to information warfare, are not listed. No table or diagram presents the respective potentials of continental China and Taiwan in terms of information warfare resources (location or number of cyber units integrated to armies, scope of deployed C4ISR systems, inventory of informational weapons, etc.). And yet, the information space is now perceived by the United States as a field in itself, in the same way as the more traditional arenas (ground, air, sea, space). Maps of that space would be interesting but, in the absence of maps showing Chinese information warfare resources, we can attempt to advance some explanation:

– either these resources do not exist (highly unlikely);

– or they do exist but are not significant and do not deserve to be represented. This second option would put into question all the theories put forward by the series of reports on the Chinese military power published by the DoD since 2002;

---

47. Chapter 4, page 22 of the 2008 report.
48. Chapter 4, page 24 of the 2008 report.
49. Figures 1, 2 and 3 of the 2008 report.
50. Figures 4 and 5 of the 2008 report.
51. Figures 6 and 7 of the 2008 report.
52. Page 8 of the 2008 report.
53. Figures 9 to 17 of the 2008 report.

– or the resources exist but their location, measurement and identification are impossible. By their nature, they do not lend themselves to statistics. It is easier to count the number of nuclear warheads than informational weapons. We must find other units of measurement;

– or again, these resources are identified but the Americans do not wish to show them, either because they want to keep their knowledge confidential, or because they prefer to focus the report on other themes.

2.2.7.10. *Objective portrait of China or reflection of American opinion?*

One of the characteristics of this report, which is an attempt at painting a picture, remains the admission of being unable to complete it. "The international community has limited knowledge of the motivations, decision-making, and key capabilities supporting China's military modernization"[54]. Doubts, unknowns, uncertainties are the important variables of this report. Several times, the text emphasizes the absence of knowledge, lack of vision, the difficulty in understanding Chinese thinking, its objectives and its strategies. This is obviously not presented as a lack of information based on American flaws, but as the problem with China's communication of information, explanations, openness and clarification. "China continues to promulgate incomplete defense expenditure figures…". The report again denounces the "lack of transparency" of Chinese affairs, a source of risk for stability and presents China as a player who conceals, who lacks sincerity. China continues to "engage in actions that appear inconsistent with its declaratory policies"[55], "less clear are the specific strategies and plans Beijing has developed to achieve these objectives"[56], etc. There are many unknowns in the eyes of the Americans.

In Chapter 2, the authors write "China's leaders have not publicly articulated an explicit, overarching 'grand strategy' that outlines national strategic objectives and the means to achieve them […]. Although such vagueness may reflect a deliberate effort to conceal intentions and capabilities, as implied in Deng Xiaoping's '24-character strategy'… it may reflect […] disagreements and debates among China's leaders"[57].

It appears impossible to trust this speaker who is not really a speaker because he would lie, conceal, hide his truth. China is portrayed as an underhanded menace threatening the rest of the world. The United States appears as a legitimate informer, justice of the peace, guarantor of balances. The vision of the world remains divided; what is not understood, seen, heard, shown or said is obviously suspect. On one side there is truth. On the other side, there is lying, a "lack of transparency", the

---

54. Page 1 of the 2008 report.
55. Ibid.
56. Chapter 2, page 9 of the 2008 report.
57. Chapter 2, page 8 of the 2008 report.

adversary that we make up. Denouncing ambiguity, duality and opacity is confirmation that China has secrets to hide: we remember the inventory of chemical weapons hidden in Iraq which was the argument that served in part to justify the military intervention in that country. Accusing a party of lying and concealing in a security context makes the adversary a threat and demonizes it.

Is the "Chinese threat" a real threat or is it mainly an intellectual construction? Where is the reality in the description made by the report? And is not the description of this reality written under the influence of what we might call an American feeling of insecurity? China has for centuries been the subject of great fascination. It is today presented as both:

– attractive:

   - mainly commercial interests,

   - cultural attractions;

– source of risk and threats:

   - because of its political regime, survivor of the communist era and awakening cold war fears (of a nuclear threat),

   - because of its growing power that no one knows the limits of (competitive supremacy with the United States?),

   - challenging the world balance centered until now, in financial, political, military and cultural terms, on the role of the United States,

   - challenging the future of the planet: a nuclear power, a polluting power, etc.

Is China first and foremost a strategic threat to the United States or a commercial godsend? In dealing with China, should we collaborate or confront? In fact, which conjunction is more relevant here: "or" or "and"? Shouldn't the questions be reformulated as "Is China a strategic threat and a commercial godsend for the United States?" "Must we collaborate and confront?"[58].

The report on Chinese military power is an attempt at defining what China is, what it represents, the course it is taking and the consequences of its choices for the rest of the world.

But is the subject of study seen by the Americans with the objectivity and impartiality required of its analysis? Are there not too many traditions, biases, ulterior motives and predefined objectives in the methodology? The report on Chinese military power could be called "Report on the Chinese threat". The same

---

58. See for example HYPERLINK "http://www.cato.org/pubs/pas/pa465.pdf" "Is Chinese Military Modernization a Threat to the United States?" Even Eland. January 23, 2003.

elements being used from year to year, the lack of updates on the words or data just contribute in rehashing the same simple ideas that will be used in the media all over the world as a source of reference. The views promoted by official reports and the media coverage transform the "Chinese threat" into social reality[59]. The report does not identify a Chinese threat; it is a fabrication of the threat. This Chinese threat connects with the image of a more conventional enemy. Whereas the last decade completely focused on terrorism, an elusive threat, the Chinese threat offers an identified enemy that could be fought with controlled weapons. With the Chinese threat, we also connect with the figure of the spying enemy, whereas terrorism offered only a killer enemy. But the Chinese threat is no longer the same as the old Soviet threat, because between the two there has been the fight against terrorism and the revolution of information technologies. Terrorism changed the feeling of invincibility that was at the core of American society. US–Chinese relations are brought up in this new context of vulnerability. We all know that threats are no longer only nuclear and that a country can be affected remotely, notably through cyber attacks. A "threat" exploits a "vulnerability". If there is a feeling of threat, it is because there is a feeling of vulnerability, of weakness. Doesn't the "Chinese threat" feed a new form of paranoia in American society?

2.2.7.11. *What do the Chinese think of the report?*

The Chinese reacted to the publication of the report quickly. As soon as it was published, comments have been feeding China's Internet sites and traditional media. Here are the most frequently written comments in media articles[60] and from Chinese officials on 4 March 2008[61]:

– The sources of information for this report are questionable. It would seem that complete sections were developed from information taken from the Internet, with no validation of sources and accuracy of content. The information proposed by the report is therefore not reliable.

– The report perpetuates the cold war mentality. This report is the only one published by the Department of Defense involving a particular country, China. During the cold war, the United States published an annual report on the Soviet

---

59. "The "China Threat' in American Self-Imagination:The Discursive Construction of Other as Power Politics". Chengxin Pan. http://www.accessmylibrary.com/coms2/summary_0286-14132948_ITM.
60. Google search from the following keywords 由国防部中国军力报告 2008年.
61. http://news.xinhuanet.com/mil/2008-03/07/content_7736310.htm "The Pentagon report perpetuates the cold war mentality". 7 March 2008.
http://209.85.135.104/translate_c?hl=fr&langpair=zh%7Cen&u=http://news.xinhuanet.com/n ewscenter/2008-03/04/content_7716738.htm: the spokesman for the Chinese Defense minister categorically opposes the contents of the American report.
http://www.pladaily.com.cn/site1/xwpdxw/2008-03/14/content_1163772.htm 14 March 2008.

Union. When the cold war situation relaxed in 1991, the Americans stopped their annual publication. Less than ten years later in 2000, their attention switched to China. For the Chinese, this focus is unacceptable and is revealing of the American mentality of naming an enemy to justify its military budget, its presence and actions all over the world. The attitude of the United States represents a serious violation of international relations standards.

– The partisan presentation of the China–Taiwan relationship, pro-Taiwanese, making the island a weaker player, is in fact an excuse to reinforce American presence in the Pacific and intensify weapon sales to Taiwan.

– The report distorts truths, false ideas are in abundance because of the very strong subjectivity of the authors of the report, because of bias, preconceived ideas and the ideology that the methodology implies.

– The Chinese are shocked by the accusations made against them in the report: accusations against the Chinese government which allegedly manipulates public opinion, attempting to deteriorate relations between China and foreign countries, an attitude that would be at the source of tensions in the region, etc.

– Chinese culture is peaceful. Historically the country has always been peaceful and will continue to be that way. In 1974, Deng Xiaoping claimed that China would never strive to become a predominant power; the American report prefers to only retain his "24-character strategy", more useful to demonstrate the hidden character of the Chinese threat ("hide our capacities and wait for the right moment"). In fact, aren't the vision and American analysis warped because the writers cannot discern or find the arguments, able to demonstrate that China is a potential threat, that they are looking for?

– The report continues to spread a false and ridiculous "theory of the Chinese threat" and the tone of the report has not changed since the first document was published in 2002. It spreads a false truth on the state of Chinese military power. On the other hand, the development of appropriate military capabilities is a legitimate right for any sovereign government. It is also legitimate that China has an army in relation to the status that its new economic power gives it; both forms of power mutually support each other. Finally, because of its military capacities, China participates in maintaining peace in the world. Since 1990, it has participated in United Nations peace operations in Cambodia, Congo, Liberia, Sudan and Lebanon.

– "China's opacity" is "nonsense", is another comment. How can we speak of opacity with military choices when we know that the country has carried out 18 joint military drills with international forces since 2002? On the contrary, transparency has increased and this should be written in the report because China now submits to the system of military transparency of the United Nations.

2.2.7.12. *Annual reports from the American Department of Defense on the Soviet Union: From the Soviet Union to China*

The series of reports on Chinese military power is the equivalent of the long series of reports on "The Soviet military power" published from 1981 to 1991[62]. The first publication of this report on the Soviet Union was a secret modified version, initially addressed to NATO authorities and written by the intelligence agency of the American Defense Department. The report addressed the inventory of Soviet military capacities, "the devil's empire" whose intentions represented a threat to the world. The content of the report justified the fact that NATO countries invested in their military. But, subsequently, reports made public could only demonstrate the problems that American intelligence departments had in understanding the actual situation in the Soviet empire, and did not lead to any really new information on the position and role of the Soviet Union. The United States stopped publishing reports on Russia. A few years later, in 2000, it started looking at China, the idea being probably that one day, the United States would once again confront an enemy and that this role would be played by China and not India, Russia or Europe. Multiple observers in the world denounced the content of this report which at most draws, and at worst manufactures, the image of the next biggest enemy to the United States, and thus to the world. The accusations made against China are often identical to the ones that were made in the publications on the Soviet Union: lack of transparency, army modernization, race to weaponry, massive investments in defense, etc. And, as with the Soviet Union, the report on China is the only report from the DoD that has been made public.

2.2.7.13. *Identification of similarities between Russian and Chinese strategies?*

Is it possible to identify similarities between Russian and Chinese strategies? The report on the Soviet Union from 1981 described the Soviet concept "as an infrastructure of influence", that would consist in the mix and intervention of war forces including unconventional, diplomatic, traditional intergovernmental, military council, treatises, agreements and support for terrorist organizations and pro-Soviet guerrilla groups, economic support, cultural support, media, and the use of active measures such as propaganda. This "infrastructure of influence" thus grouped the series of methods of space penetration that remained inaccessible to Soviet military forces[63]. The report on Chinese military power again uses this approach to an extent by recalling the existence of the Chinese concept of the "three wars", approved by the Central Committee of the Communist Party in 2003, that would define the non kinetic way to conduct modern warfare: psychological warfare (use of propaganda,

---

62. http://www.fas.org/irp/dia/product/smp_index.htm.
63. Soviet Military Power. By Edgar Ulsamer, Senior Editor (Policy & Technology) December 1981, Vol. 64, No. 12 http://www.afa.org/magazine/dec1981/1281 sovietpower.asp.

deception, threat and pressure to affect the capacity of understanding and decision of the enemy), media war (dissemination of information to influence public opinion and obtain the support of national and international opinion for Chinese military interventions), legal war (using national and international laws to ensure the support of the international community and manage the possible repercussions of Chinese military actions)[64].

The object of this 2008 report from the American Department of Defense is to attempt to respond to the question "must we fear China?", or more precisely perhaps, "must the United States fear China?" There are still many uncertainties, grey areas and misunderstandings. Because China does not communicate information in the standard format desired by American observers, because Westerners may not always understand all the intricacies of the language... Whatever the reasons, the United States interpret these grey areas and zones of silence as deliberate, so that China can hide its cards. Even while the United States congratulates itself on China's accession to the role of new peaceful economic player, it does not miss an opportunity to depict China as "the" threat, wrapped up once more in its role as "hero" ready to defend humanity against the "big bad wolf".

The series of attacks against Western information systems in 2007 have led to accusations against China. Are the reactions justified, and is there proof? Or are these reactions the result of the power of influence that the repeated views (including those found in official reports) describing a dominating power have on our minds?

While Western countries denounce China's actions in cyberspace, potentially providing arguments in favor of the American position, agreeing with its predictions and observations, paradoxically the 2008 Department of Defense report only gives the "information warfare" chapter a relative, perhaps even minimal, significance. In this period of so-called major risks of attacks against sensitive State information systems and attacks in the information field, very little is written in the report about information warfare, especially nothing new or very concrete. This may mean that the United States does not think the cyberspace threat is major, but simply an element among others constituting the Chinese threat.

2.3. Relations between Beijing and Taipei

The Pacific is the theater of conflict. China wants to keep Taiwan, and the military could intervene if Taiwan proclaimed its independence. In that case, the United States and Japan would very probably be involved.

---

64. Page 19 of the 2008 report.

On 14 March 2005, Beijing proclaimed an anti-secession law to reaffirm China's unity and prepare for the possibility of the proclamation of secession by Taiwan. The law is based on the principle of Chinese unity (Article 1) and Taiwan is only a part of it. Beijing will never accept independence. The question of Taiwan is an internal affair that accepts no interference from foreign forces (Articles 2 and 3). Article 6 lists the methods that Beijing plans to use for the achievement and maintenance of unification: peaceful methods (cultural, economic and scientific exchanges) as well as "other methods" that are not specified. Information warfare maneuvers in this case could be entirely possible. Taiwan is under permanent pressure fearing that China may attempt a computer attack instead of a conventional invasion.

But China is not alone with regard to Taiwan and is not free to act. Threats from China against Taiwan represent an indirect threat against the United States because of the formal relationship connecting the government of Taipei to the Americans. The "Taiwan Relations Act" of 1979 in fact indicates that the Americans will provide Taiwan with defensive weapons and will maintain capabilities to resist any use of force or any other form of coercion that would threaten the security of Taiwan. The United States insists that Beijing and Taipei take measures to avoid the increase in tensions existing between the two shores of the Strait. But events have gone against that wish.

Adhering to the principle that demonstrating our forces to intimidate or dissuade an adversary can be useful, Beijing concentrates its troops in regions facing Taiwan, displaying its new military methods: missiles, precision weapons and submarines.

Beijing could still use CNA attacks against the political, military and economic infrastructure of Taiwan to undermine the confidence of the population toward its leaders, and information operations at different levels to convince the population of the legitimacy of its action, and demonstrating that military operations are only targeting military infrastructures and not the population.

To this day, China has not intervened in Taiwan for two major reasons:

– because of the presence of the United States and the prospect of a confrontation for which it may not be prepared;

– because of the economic and political impact that this conflict would have. China is in full economic growth; starting a war would jeopardize that momentum.

2.3.1. *The assassin's mace against the strategy of the scorpion*

In the conflict opposing Beijing to Taipei, China will have to take the initiative of an attack if it wants to one day reach its goals. It must cross the Taiwan Strait to attack or finalize its offensive. But Chen Shui-Bian, who became President of Taiwan in 2000, announced a new policy to win a conflict against China outside of Taiwan, directly on the Chinese continent.

This strategy, known as the "strategy of the scorpion", consists of acquiring capabilities to strike vital targets and sensitive infrastructures on Chinese soil; attacking a few, but identified and selected, targets such as electric dams. Is this an economy of method for Taiwan? The objective is to make the invasion of the island too expensive for Beijing. But even if Taiwan reached these targets, would the effect really be dissuasive? Taiwan's position, its strategy of the scorpion, is supported by the United States who continues to provide the island with weapons, and by the government which maintains the allocation of substantial weaponry budgets.

2.3.2. *Cyber-attacks against Taiwan: psychological effects*

In July 2006, the Taipei Times site published an article titled "Legislature rattled by PLA hacker attack" (17 July 2006)[65]. The press echoed computer security incidents affecting Taiwanese political parties (KMT, Chinese nationalist party, DPP, Democratic Progressive Party and the Taiwanese Solidarity Union, TSU).

Intrusions, Trojan horses, attack against data confidentiality, the attacks seemed to come from Chinese hackers based in Fujian. This name has become synonymous with "hackers organized in special units of the Chinese army". The information is not confirmed by official Taiwanese sources. In the permanent psychological war taking place between Beijing and Taipei, the use of attacks and announcements of attacks on networks against sensitive infrastructures is frequent and is intended to influence opinions and behavior. This article is interesting because it shows how it is possible to feed public opinion with emotions toward a potential enemy, while remaining short, vague and using unconfirmed information. We have:

– rumors. Nobody knows anything officially. Sources are unofficial. Did the attackers have Taiwanese help? Nobody really knows who found the virus: the Justice department? The security center of the technology department?

– the presumed guilty (PLA hackers), all the easier to target as the feeling of threat seems to be heightened;

---

65. http://www.taipeitimes.com/News/taiwan/archives/2006/07/17/2003319181.

– denial from an official government organ (the Information and Technology Department);

– confusion. Viruses? Worms? Which type of attack was used? What was stolen? Has sensitive data really been stolen? There are actually very few concrete elements. The only information that seems certain is technical (the offensive virus is BKDR_BIFROSE_JH);

– the expression of fear: involving a guilty party without firm proof (but is it possible to make up that proof?), maintaining again that the level of security of information systems in Taiwan is now such (with firewalls and antivirus software) that it is hard for a single hacker, not having the benefit of accomplices, to penetrate its networks. Reasserting that there is a threat emanating from PLA hackers who would be able to attack Taiwanese information systems. The fear is not only fueled by confusion, the vague feeling of a possible threat, but also by the publication of this article and all the ones written in the same vein (nothing is clearly stated, there are questionable sources, everything is contradictory).

A few months earlier, on 16 June 2004, the site published an article involving Fujian hackers: "Beijing wages cyberwar against DPP Headquarters"[66] in which the same ingredients from the 2006 articles were involved:

– involvement of continental China, damages and a guilty party was designated: "an army of hackers based in China has broken into Democratic Progressive Party (DPP) databases, stealing classified information such as President Chen Shi-Bian's personal itinerary [...] the Ministry of National Defense [...] deems a systematic information attack launched by China as military warfare";

– reminder of the permanence of threat and actions from China, presented as an aggressive neighbor: "this is not the first time that China has conducted information warfare against Taiwan. The cabinet discovered that hackers in Hubei and Fujian provinces had spread 23 different Trojan horse programs to the networks of ten private high-tech companies in Taiwan and used them as a springboard to break into at least 30 different government agencies and 50 private companies";

– the attacks target national security and its main backers; National Police Administration, Defense Ministry, Central Bank and the Central Election Commission;

– the attacks are intended to profoundly damage the country's infrastructures: "the Cabinet suspected that the program was likely aimed at paralyzing the nation's computer systems, stealing sensitive government information or preparing computers for future information warfare";

66. http://www.taipeitimes.com/News/taiwan/archives/2006/07/17/2003175231.

– sources remain undetermined: "according to a Cabinet official who asked not to be named";

– the incident is happening on the field of diplomacy. The information that was stolen was classified and involved high level encounters, notably with the United States.

On 23 June 2004, a new article[67] had similar elements:

– a victim was presented, the DPP site was a victim of defacing. Two Taiwanese political leaders were represented naked, wearing two Japanese kimonos on their shoulders. Slogans accompanied the images: "Opposition to Taiwan's independence". Another image represented a Chinese soldier ready to fire and declaring himself proud of being a Chinese soldier. Attacks against the DPP party are increasing;

– a presumed guilty person is identified, the attack allegedly comes from continental China: "we think that the PLA takes cyber attacks very seriously as they tend to paralyze information operations of strategic targets. These attacks are part of an effort to remove the leaders of Taiwan in a surprise attack";

– reminder (hammering) of the Chinese threat. To make the threat ever stronger in people's minds, previous political tensions resulting in intensive hacking campaigns against Taiwan were recalled. This threat was once again demonstrated by the drills that China was preparing to carry out on the island of Dongshan in June and July of 2004, a few miles from Taiwan. "We think that cyber warfare will be part of these drills";

– for the enemy, there is a reminder of Taiwanese technical capabilities in terms of defense as well as alliances with the United States and Japan: "Taiwan recently carried out war simulations on computers, these drills can be coordinated with the United States and Japan".

2.3.3. *Taiwan and information warfare*

Taiwan is one of the most popular targets in the world. According to the central information agency of Taiwan, the country has the highest number of attacks by hackers. An identical report indicates that Taiwan experienced 250,000 attacks between 1996 and 2000. The PLA is highly suspected of having special information warfare units and of being the instigator of numerous network attacks against Taiwan[68].

---

67. Published at http://www.etaiwannews.com/Taiwan/2004/06/23/1087958173.htm.
68. Suspected Chinese Hacker Attacks Target AIT, Taipei Times, 19 June 2006.

Taiwan developed its information warfare capabilities (defensive and offensive) and acquired alert systems (attack detection) in an attempt to turn around its purely defensive situation. The Taiwanese army thinks that superiority of electronic warfare is one of the most economic and efficient strategies.

In 2003, Taiwan estimated that Beijing was abandoning its strategy of dissuasion for a new "paralysis warfare" strategy which would consist of information warfare, ballistic missile attacks, precision strikes and capturing assets with special units[69]. Based on these conclusions and to counter new threats, Taiwan built its defense policy on new high-tech weapons.

The methods deployed are intended to stay on top in the information field:

– according to Chinese media, the Taiwanese army is developing viruses to be used in times of war[70], relying on the diffusion of the CIH virus first appearing in Taiwan in 1998 and affecting the computers of the Tatung Institute of Technology (TIT). The virus is also known as Chernobyl, PE_CIH, WIN95, CIH 1.x, Win95.CIH, Win32/CIH, W95/CIH.1003. It was called Chernobyl because it was activated on April 26. The CIH virus caused serious damage everywhere in the world. South Korea reported financial losses of about 250 million US dollars one year after the virus was spread. Its presumed creator is Chen Ing Hau (Chén Yínghảo)[71], who was arrested in September 2000 by Taiwanese law enforcement authorities. He developed this virus while a student but when the application spread and its significance increased, he was doing his military service. This explains the interpretation of a link between the army and virus developers. Continental China is not to be undone, however, since several viruses were also attributed to it (Lion, Adore, Code Red worms);

– reinforcement of the security of information systems, to protect against network attacks from continental China, or to protect against the effects of electromagnetic pulse weapons;

– development of software and hardware for electronic warfare (surveillance, electronic attacks, electronic protection);

– a long-term project to create a computerized army. The first information warfare units should have been created in 2005 and be operational by 2008. In 2000, the annual joint drill of armies ("hankuang" in Chinese), introduced EMP attack simulations. The science and technology institute of Chungshan began to develop a war simulation system in 1997 that was tested for the first time during Hankuang

69. China Developing Paralysis Warfare, Taipei Times October 8, 2003. http://www.taipeitimes.com/News/front/archives/2003/10/08/2003070830.
70. http://mil.fjii.fj.vnet.cn article from July 30, 2002.
71. http://www.sophos.com/pressoffice/news/articles/2000/09/va_cihauthor.html.

No. 15 in 1999. In 2002 during military exercises ("hankuang" No. 18), the efforts focused on reinforcing electronic counter measures (antivirus systems), and included computer simulations of an invasion of Taiwan by Chinese military troops. This exercise (code name Lushen No. 2) was the first completed by the information warfare unit created within the Taiwanese army in 2001, the "Task Force Tiger" group. The drills simulated information warfare, electronic warfare, air space control, navy space control and counter attack on the Chinese continent. Taiwanese national defense university professors played the role of the Chinese army in this information warfare battle simulation. Their action consisted of using the Internet to broadcast false information, conceal the movements of troops to spread confusion within the Taiwanese army, carry out intelligence warfare and psychological operations, then launch attacks against networks (viruses, logic bombs). The Taiwanese special unit countered this assault by protecting their systems from hacking type attacks, and shot back viruses to the attacker's networks. In the simulation, the Taiwanese camp was victorious since it succeeded in penetrating the enemy's information systems. American observers were impressed by the capacity of the Taiwanese to fight in the field of information, which they judged as superior to those of the Chinese[72]. Since then, all annual drills have information warfare simulation phases. But we must not forget that these are just simulations. Even though they are extremely useful for training purposes, we must be careful in making definite conclusions on the real capabilities of an army until the tools and methods proposed in simulation are used in real live, real war, situations;

– development of military alert (detection) and reconnaissance systems, development and acquisition of long range radars (from 1,000 to 6,000 km. Even though costs may limit ambitions, with such radars, reaction time would be of 15 to 20 minutes), command systems, reconnaissance satellites in cooperation with foreign countries. In 1998, Taiwan developed a satellite in cooperation with Singapore that was later launched by France. Taiwan also developed its own satellites, ROCSat-1 (renamed FormoSat-1 in 2004)[73], a low orbit observation satellite launched by the Americans (FormotSat-2) and FormoSat-3. With these satellites, Taiwan can observe Southeastern Asia and the continent;

– development of anti-missile systems;

– development of SIGINT capabilities;

– the Taiwanese army is presumed to have developed thousands of viruses that could be used to counter an attack from Chinese forces[74]. Can the information transmitted by the Taiwanese press be verified?

---

72. Taipei Times, 27 April 2002.

73. http://directory.eoportal.org/info_FormoSat1ROCSat1RepublicofChinaSatellite1.html.

74. Computer Virus Warfare developed by the Military, Taipei Times, 10 January 2000.

Chapter 3

India

Today, with a population of 1.095 billion people, India is one of the most populated countries in the world. It is also a country in development that the West is watching (albeit not as closely as it watches China), and a country that wants to become one of the great powers of the world. However, the weight of its historical past is strong and its social structure does not make India the power that China is in terms of culture, politics and economy. Its rural population, which is its most significant part (containing 70% of the total population), is also the poorest (a mere 20% of GDP). This significant imbalance hampers the entry of India into cyberspace, and in the development of an information society culture. India is facing a great number of social, ethnic and religious problems which are sources of internal and external conflict, an additional barrier to the smooth development of a modern industrial society, including religious conflicts between Hindu (India is 80% Hindu) and Muslim communities, terrorism, uprisings, border conflicts with neighboring countries (Pakistan, China) and nuclear threat.

3.1. Entry into information society

Only nations already ensconced in the information age can aspire to use information warfare (or be its victims) because they are equipped with highly developed communication systems to which they have become almost completely dependent. Is India in this situation?

Its Internet network is certainly developing and its intellectual elite is able to create the best companies in the world in the field of information and communication technologies. Relying on high-level and extremely selective universities, the country trains an elite who then supports the creation and development of high-tech research and industry: Sabeer Bhatia (co-founder of Hotmail), S. Gopalkrishnan (co-founder of Infosys), Rajat Gupta (who managed McKinsey & Co for a few years) and Vinod Khosla (co-founder of Sun Microsystems Inc.) all come from the famous Indian Institutes of Technologies (IIT). Indian "Silicon Valleys" (the famous "Silicon Triangle" made up of Bangalore, Chennai and Hyderabad) are thriving, the ICT industry is highly dynamic, and the software industry in India is among the most powerful in the world. India attracts companies worldwide, but is that enough to provide the country with the means to actively carry out information warfare? The image of India is that of a country anchored in its past, a society that is profoundly unequal with its extremes of poverty and colossal wealth. These images represent ancient times for the Western world but all the splendors of Hollywood's artificial gildings cannot change a thing, nor can some of the legendary fortunes built in a short time with the help of information technologies. It is not the image of a nation invested in cyberspace that is projected by India. Is India able to control the complex machinery of information warfare?

3.1.1. *Has India entered the age of information?*

Despite the efforts of the government to expand the Internet network beyond academia, it remains underdeveloped. The number of Internet users only reached 50 million people in 2005. Communications are still slow and expensive.

Internet penetration is estimated at approximately 10% of the urban population in India, whereas total penetration is 2.25%. The country's ten major cities[1], which also encompass the high-tech industries, account for over 50% of all Internet users in the country. The Internet is obviously an urban phenomenon; it does not play any role in opening up the provinces and countryside. It is for city-dwellers, mostly men (75% of Internet users), even though city-dwellers only represent 25% of the Indian population; in cities it is also for the young: 70% are less than 30 years old. The Internet was used by a digital minority in India in 2006. Internet population trends follow world trends: in 2006 it was affected by the blog phenomenon with 85% of Internet users saying they read or participated in blogs[2].

In 2009, although the percentage of Internet users remains low compared to the country's population, India is the third country in Asia, in absolute numbers of Internet users, with 81 million users, following China (298 millions users) and Japan

---

1. Delhi, Mumbai, Bangalore, Hyderabad, Chennai, Kolkata, Pune, Ahmedabad, Kochi, Lucknow.
2. India Online 2006 annual report, written by JuxtConsult. http://www.juxtconsult.com.

(94 millions users). The population of Internet users increased 1,520% over the period 2000–2008.[3]

Internet development in India has experienced chaotic moments with no connection to technological or economic and industrial issues. Cellular telephony and Internet services were banned in Jamu, Kashmir, and in the northeast until 2002 for reasons of security because of political tensions and insurrection; the government decided only as recently as August 2002 to give access to vital communication methods in these regions, so the local population can at last benefit from technological progress.

3.1.2. Security of information systems

As well as the Internet's slow development, India appears to be vulnerable to attacks against its information systems. Victims of recent attacks include the army, the research sector (defacement of the Indian Science Congress Association site in 1999 is one of the incidents that attracted the most attention), the Indian Science Congress (ISC) 2000, the National Informatics Center (NIC) and the Videsh Sanchar Nigam Limited (VSNL) sites, as well as the Indian ministry of foreign affairs, the ministry of Information Technologies site, and private sites such as Sony, Mercedes and other foreign and Indian interests.

According to Ernst & Young, India is the most vulnerable country for cyber attacks[4]. India's vital information systems (its banking sector, stock exchange, telecommunications networks and Internet) seem to be very vulnerable to attacks, lacking in efficient intrusion detection systems[5]: 30% of Supervisory Control & Data Systems (SCADA) networks controlling energy, water and dam distribution systems can be accessed by modem.

CERT-In (a center based in Delhi and another one at the Indian Institute of Science in Bangalore), created in January 2004, watches for attacks and provides reactive services to increase Internet security in India.

But technology is not the only solution to India's security problems. Political stabilization of international relations with neighboring countries could be one of the conditions of appeasement of cyber conflicts. In fact, many attacks seem politically motivated.

---

3. Statistics from: http://www.internetworldstats.com/stats3.htm.
4. http://lists.jammed.com/ISN/2003/04/0104.html.
5. Ravi Visvesvaraya Prasad, *Cyber Menace: Integrated Defensive Policy Needed*, Times of India, www.securityfocus.com, 20 May 2003.

Regardless of the reasons, public opinion only remember the attacks, and experts can see the flaws in the security of Indian systems. Does this mean that the government is unable to contain an attack against its networks? If that is not the case, was it as a result of the Indian government's negligence when, two months after the attack, the Foreign Affairs Department site was still not up?

3.2. Information warfare: development and adoption of the doctrine

3.2.1. *The military doctrine*

The military doctrine[6] of information warfare is globally designed according to Western conceptual models: C2 warfare, intelligence warfare, military deception, electronic warfare, cyber warfare, psychological warfare, network centric warfare and the role of the media are the main components of the Indian doctrine.

In 2001, the Indian government published "Challenges for managing national security" in which it recognized that the Indian battlefield will have to be digital and transparent, and will experience exponential growth in the deployment of electronic equipment, indicating the predominance of the electromagnetic spectrum. India must maintain modernized conventional armed forces.

In 1998, the Indian army announced a turning point in its doctrine embracing the new constraints of electronic warfare and capacities of information operations. This new doctrine, also called the IT-Roadmap, proposed ambitious plans to be in place by 2008. General Ved Prakash Malik, who was commanding the army during the Kargil conflict, was also one of the major architects of this new doctrine. The logbook is intended to develop a solid information technology infrastructure to act as a power intensifier. Software becomes more important than hardware. Industry standards are increasingly open and homogenous, making access easier. General Malik supported the use of off-the-shelf technologies.

To prepare for 21st Century wars, India entered into the information age. Information warfare was one of the major components of the new army doctrine[7] at that time. The evolution of the doctrine, which encourages a profound transformation of the armies themselves, makes India one of the most powerful nations. It is also intended to support the country's economic and social

---

6. Also read [ASH 02].
7. The complete text is available at http://indianarmy.nic.in/indianarmydoctrine.htm.

development, by ensuring its security and peace: "The defense of India calls for the defense of its physical, economic and cultural identity"[8].

3.2.1.1. *The new army doctrine of 2004*

The threats of armed conflicts with neighboring countries, and the entry in the information age along with new national security challenges, have forced the army to begin a transformation, the outline of which is traced to the warfare doctrine published in 2004 and which is already a large part of India's information warfare.

Military operations must be organized and the security of strategic (economic and political) information must be ensured. At the juncture between the 20th and 21st Centuries, India questioned the importance of major evolutions in the field of information technologies for its national security. It observed transformations in Western military, the American model, as well as the evolutions (some would call them revolutions) emerging from the introduction of ICTs in the military environment, their impact on the way to fight a war, and it also observed how control of information makes it possible to dominate the battlefield even though it does not ensure all victories. India acquired nuclear weapons, but these weapons are no longer a solution for the balance of peace, as proved by the crises and conflicts multiplying within and around its territory. The new nature of asymmetric conflicts must bring about new solutions.

The working paper published in 1998, covering the next ten years, announced the necessity for the army to engage in a path to ideological renewal to take into consideration new forms of war, including information warfare. This path also included the establishment of new partnerships between the civil sector and military industries: "The defense forces adopted information warfare doctrines [...]. There is an increasing partnership between defense and private industry for the evolution of computer security and in the telecommunications of defense information infrastructures [...]" [BAK 01].

The doctrine published in October 2004, organized in two main parts (the first part is the only one made public), must be reviewed every five years and published every ten years. This first version is in force until October 2009.

Much space is given to information warfare in this document:

– the theme is addressed in the introduction;

– it is widely discussed in Chapter 2 of the doctrine, "Understanding war", Section 5 "Different types of war";

---

8. Quote from Section 1.5 of the new war doctrine of the Indian army.

– the theme is also discussed in Chapter 3, "Operations perspectives", Section 7 "Elements of operational success", and Section 10 "Impact of technologies on operations and revolution in military affairs".

While attempting to introduce 21st Century modernity into the armed forces, the doctrine still recalls past history and military tradition with numerous quotations from statesmen, servicemen and strategists.

The quotes anchor the military tradition in its past, and ancient principles are not lacking in relevance to the modern environment: fundamentals of war cannot be forgotten with modernism: "There are a small number of fundamental war principles that we cannot ignore without risk, and where, on the contrary, the application has always been successful" (Jomini, *Précis de l'art de la guerre*, 1838). Modernism must not make us forget that war is an art, and as any art, cannot be reduced to instructions but must rely on human genius: "War… should be conducted according to the principles and rules of art" (Napoleon, *War maxims*, 1831), "War is a science included in art for its application" (Sir Basil Liddell Hart, 1929). Modernization of armies by the introduction of new technologies is not sufficient in itself: "The instruments of battle only have value if we know how to use them" (Ardant du Picq, 1870).

Some quotations draw on tradition: Confucius (500 BC), *Bhagawad Gita* (sacred Hindu text), Sun Tzu (400-320 BC).

General NC Vij recalls in the introduction to the doctrine that progress brought about by new technologies mandates new strategic thinking. Technology alone does not transform a doctrine, but leads to a new approach of the conduct and organization of operations. The challenge is complex because the shadow of possible conflicts is wide and theatres of operations are numerous. The adaptability capabilities of the Indian army must be strong. To build a doctrine over time, it is first necessary to try to imagine how future wars will be fought. The wars of today, liable to be longer, provide a precise clue.

Two types of conflict must, then, be considered: conventional wars and unconventional wars, including asymmetric wars which are the most remarkable type of this period of history. They will not replace conventional wars (Chapter 1.11 of the doctrine) but they take up so much space in the environment of modern conflicts that the army had to propose a new doctrine in 2007 (see section 3.2.1.2 below) specifically dedicated to it. Modern wars will be characterized (Chapter 1.12 of the doctrine) by their suddenness, brevity, intensity, the non-linearity of the conduct of their operations, intensity, depth, the concentration of the fire power and resources, by the necessary integration of armies jointly involved and in a coordinated way in operations, by the major role of information, surveillance, control of information for a perfect vision of the theatre of operations which can decide the outcome of the battles, maybe more so than the forces engaged. The transformation of armies must prepare them to carry out information warfare and network centric wars. These wars are characterized by their new forms, which are low intensity conflicts (LIC), terrorism, insurrection and "proxy wars" (wars conducted between countries using non-military players to fight in their name, in the form of cyberwars through hackers. In these "proxy wars", at least one of the countries uses a third party to fight in its place. The governments provide financial and logistical support to these fighters). In this context, information warfare is an essential "power intensifier" and its control is mandatory to aspire to victory. The introduction of these technological, ideological and organizational evolutions involves a deep evolution in styles of command that must consider decentralization of processes.

The definition of information warfare (Chapter 1) presents superiority of information as the absolute objective. In order to reach this goal, we must carry out a series of actions affecting information, processes based on information, and the enemy's information systems and networks, while protecting the information, processes, information systems and networks of our own camp. This approach is not very original if we compare it to the United States.

Information provided to C2s must be accurate and timely. This information must shorten the OODA loop. Information warfare has an impact on the "Observation – Orientation – Decision" of the enemy phases: it makes it possible to disrupt the cycle (disrupt its observation, corrupt its orientation and distort its decision).

The doctrine has six major goals:

– develop and maintain detailed basic information on enemy capabilities and predict their possible actions;

– deprive the adversary of information on us and our allies;

– influence perception, plans, actions and will of the enemy in order to send in our own forces with the offensive use of IW techniques;

– influence non-combatants and neutral organizations to encourage them to support the missions of our camp;

– protect our own decision processes, our information and information systems;

– deteriorate enemy information systems.

3.2.1.1.1. Seven components of information warfare identified by the Indian military

Command and control warfare (C2W). The goal is to influence, block access to information, deteriorate or destroy enemy C2 capabilities, while protecting our own C2 systems against such actions. C2W operations integrate and synchronize the 5 components found in American doctrines: electronic warfare (EW) capabilities, military deception, physical destruction, psychological operations (Psyops) and operations security.

Intelligence-based warfare (IBW) is a traditional component of information warfare. Intelligence is directly introduced in operations to give transparence to the battlefield. IBW is intended to create asymmetry in transparence or in situational conscience in relation to the enemy (i.e. seeing better and before the enemy). This capability of seeing also conditions the capability of striking the enemy, from farther and with more precision. The challenge is to see as best as possible, as quickly as possible without becoming a target ourselves. This capacity of vision supported by intelligence will make it possible to operate by surprise to destabilize the enemy, forcing him to fight in unfavorable conditions by reducing his reaction time. Speed is one of the key words of this doctrine. It is better to see but we must also reduce information and command circulation time: "Cyberwar will be to the 21st Century what blitzkrieg was to the 20th Century"[9].

Electronic warfare (EW) is aimed at the domination of the electromagnetic spectrum through a series of military actions. The techniques consist of blocking, deteriorating, delaying and paralyzing information in order to create a false image, to deceive the enemy and make him come to the wrong conclusions and make the wrong decisions. The introduction of integrated and automated electronic warfare systems were a significant development, providing a high level of information, for intercepting and jamming information. In 2004, the army acquired mobile cutting edge electronic warfare system with the *Samyukta* system, developed by the Indian civilian industry[10], ensuring electromagnetic spectrum domination.

Psychological warfare (PSYWAR) is implemented through mass media such as the written press, radio, television and distribution of tracts. The ICTs make it possible to carry out more subtle psychological actions. In order to be efficient, psychological operations (PSYOPS) must be carried out in conjunction with other operations. In times of peace, or in LIC type operations, psychological operations can be qualified as "psychological initiatives". This section of the doctrine clearly indicates that during peacetime, operations to manipulate public opinion are and

---

9. General Malik. Comments noted in [BIL 04].
10. http://www.deccanherald.com/deccanherald/jan202004/n11.asp

must be carried out (without clarifying if we are talking about the national population or the population of other countries).

Cyber warfare group techniques are used to destroy, deteriorate, exploit or compromise enemy computer systems. Cyber warfare includes hacking type attacks against enemy computers. Computer hacking can authorize the deterioration of the enemy C2 structure. The doctrine clearly distinguishes between cyber warfare and network centric warfare.

Network centric warfare (NCW) focuses on the combat force that can be generated by the efficient connection or networking of the war machine. The three major elements constituting this system are a surveillance grid (a sensor grid covering the complete battlefield), a communications grid (to increase the potential of the telecommunications infrastructure, all networks must be seen as virtual grids covering the tactical, operational and strategic fields) and finally, a tactical grid (an abstract grid lists available weapons, classified according to their availability and degree of usefulness in relation to an order of enemy battle).

Economic information warfare (EIW) uses information as a destabilizing power against the enemy's economy. It is important to point out that this economic warfare is presented as a subset of the military warfare doctrine! This means that operations conducted by India in the economic field are controlled by the military.

Finally, Chapter 3, Section 10 of the doctrine is dedicated to the impact of technology on operations, and the revolution in military affairs goes back to the capabilities offered by information systems in terms of collection, processing and control of information and coordination of data from the different agencies. These are all advantages to whoever can control information and information systems. The doctrine does, however, highlight a few flaws inherent to systems that can be challenging:

– "these systems are vulnerable to attacks from the enemy and the impact on the conduct of operations would be proportional to our state of dependence on these systems";

– the risk of information overload weighs heavy on the decision process. C4I2SR systems (Command, Control, Communication, Computers, Intelligence, Information, Surveillance and Reconnaissance) process and provide a significant volume of data; the risk would be saturating the decision-makers and systems;

– the effect of surprise is a theoretical ideal but increasingly difficult to attain in this complex information environment. It is increasingly difficult to implement military deception, to blind and deceive enemy surveillance.

This approach to information warfare does not rely on military tradition. The only reminder is the basic principles. It remains pragmatic and uninventive, mainly using the components as defined by the Americans. But is there a way to do it differently? The doctrine, then, may be the reflection of Western models. It is mostly an adaptation of the current context and the product of observation of events in the world, as well as understanding the lessons from 20 years of wars fought by the United States.

3.2.1.2. *The 2007 doctrine for sub-conventional operations*

The Indian army was the first to propose a doctrine for sub-conventional operations by proposing strategies for the conduct of counter insurrection operations in urban and rural zones. This doctrine is the result of experience gathered through 40 years of fighting against insurrection. The doctrine was made public and can be accessed on line at the army's website[11].

The object of the doctrine is the fight against terrorism, insurrection or any other form of asymmetric conflict where the *modus operandi* from the weakest side is the unpredictability of the action, irrationality, indiscrimination and forms of conflict found in both peacetime and wartime; peace is disrupted by a war that does not have a name. Information warfare and cyberwar have given a new dimension to these forms of conflict. Information warfare is part of the new threat, in the same way as weapons of mass destruction.

On Page 61 of the doctrinal text, there is a chapter called "Cyber-terrorism and information warfare":

– emerging asymmetric threats include the proliferation of technologies linked to the use of cyber techniques and information warfare techniques;

– these technologies can be used to destroy the targets' links to information or economies, regardless of borders;

– terrorists and civilian parties could target C4I2SR infrastructures (Command, Control, Communications, Computers, Intelligence, Interoperability, Surveillance and Reconnaissance), services, financial services and banking industries, the transport sector and energy distribution.

The text does not propose solutions for fighting against these information warfare threats. It is limited to listing the threats.

---

11. http://indianarmy.nic.in/indianarmydoctrine.htm.

3.2.1.3. *Weaknesses of the 2007 doctrine's application*

The weaknesses are at the operational level. The three services are not synchronized in their methods of information warfare, even though the Indian army has made great strides recently to acquire and develop C4ISR networks.

Civilian and military information systems are lacking in security. Progress made by India's national industry does not seem to be sufficiently used, for example in terms of radio and satellite systems. To reinforce the concept and its implementation, and to give a real dimension to information operations especially, analysts suggest thinking about the creation of net-forces based on the Chinese model, i.e. on the principle of a militia with specific skills. Can the model be applied to the army's territorial units? Even though CERTs[12] make it possible to respond to attacks against civilian infrastructures, they are only a reactive, defensive response. A proactive concept would be more appropriate[13].

3.2.2. *Official parties*

Information warfare is a responsibility of national security organizations. The Research and Analysis Wing (RAW) is one of India's intelligence agencies with no supervision and no accountability for its activities except to the Prime Minister. This agency is responsible for organizing campaigns of misinformation as well as intelligence actions (espionage) against countries threatening India's security, such as Pakistan and China.

Because reaching superiority of information (equivalent to superiority in the air, at sea and in space) is one of the major objectives of war in the age of knowledge, because using information smartly can have results as lethal as other forms of power, because information operations are as important as other forms of military operations, because these operations are extremely diverse and must be coordinated in order to be efficient and, finally, because the doctrines supporting this coordination must be formalized, the government decided to create the Defense Information Warfare Agency (DIWA), under the responsibility of the Integrated Defense High command. The role will be to coordinate the efforts of three departments (Air, Ground, Sea) and other intelligence agencies to handle all aspects of information warfare. The three departments have their own constraints and different ways of implementing information warfare. The DIWA is not meant to

---

12. Computer Emergency Response Teams.
13. Vinod Anand, *China Concepts and Capabilities of Information Warfare*, Strategic Analysis, vol. 30, n° 4, pp. 781-797, Institute for Defense Studies and Analyses, October-December 2006.

unify the practices, but to find common and integrated solutions. It is also responsible for the progression of the Indian information warfare doctrine.

The 1998 plan considered information technology training in order to transform the Indian army into a modern force. In 1999, the Army Institute of Information Technology (AIIT) introduced its first classes at its Hyderabad campus (presented as the future Indian Silicon Valley) to teach the basics of information warfare[14]. The Army Institute of Technology (AIT) in Pune, created in 1994, should be mentioned along with its Department of Information Technologies which teaches 60 students (each year) on programming techniques, notably[15] its telecommunications engineering department,[16] and has a computer engineering department educating 12 students, with themes such as concealing information[17], research and analysis of images, remote transactions, network management systems, storage in distributed systems and back-up systems. The small number of students means that selection is strict and only the best are trained. The Institute relies on the University of Pune, one of the most highly rated in India.

In 2003, the government proposed the creation of the Indian National Defense University (INDU), similar to the American and Chinese defense universities. Its mission was to be to train the military, change their way of thinking and learning, teaching the principles of information warfare and organizing simulations for military forces and intelligence services, as well as researching strategies through the National Institute of Strategic Studies (NISS) research center.

After the military, the civilian sector can also be a player in information warfare by supplying armies with the necessary technologies. The army's highest commanders, in 1998, expressed their wish for a quick and durable collaboration between the military and civilian sectors. The technologies that modern armies need are developed and sold by civilian companies. This idea of collaboration is contained in the 1998 working paper. Before 2000, production and supply of military technologies was only done by state-owned companies for reasons of security and ideology. This collaboration requires financial resources to acquire technologies, as well as flexibility and changes in thinking in armies which, as everywhere else in the world, are not necessarily open to the civilian world. Partnership and networking between both sectors can lead to synergies. The military understands that technologies from the private sector can contribute to reinforcing security, and not weaken it, as previously thought. Efforts must involve software, developing and using industry standards and the capacity to follow quick

---

14. http://www.mod.nic.in/reports/report01/cap3.pdf.
15. http://aitpune.com/itinformation.asp.
16. http://aitpune.com/etcinformation.asp.
17. http://aitpune.com/etcinformation.asp.

developments and progress in the field of information and communication technologies. In 2000, the National Defense Committee decided to establish strong partnerships between defense and the industry through programs. In 2002, the President of the National Defense Committee listed three axes of modernization: information technologies and information warfare; electronic warfare and C4I2 infrastructures (Command, Control, Communications, Computer, Information, Interoperability); and mobility.

The Indian army developed its network centric warfare methods[18] through these alliances, based on its (Army Static Switched Communication Network) ASCON network. Phase 3, called Mercury Thunder, was inaugurated in September 2006.

Development and acquisitions are carried out with Indian companies, as well as through international agreements such as, for example, with the United States or Russia.

3.2.3. Adoption of the information warfare doctrine

What is the perception of India's military concerning information warfare? It occupied a significant place in the 2004 doctrine, but does the military, which is the first party involved with its implementation, give it the same significance?

As important as the place given to information warfare in the new doctrine is, "we have not reached the level where information warfare can be considered as a new form of war. The goals and objectives of most of the conflicts in the world are identical as they were in industrial or agricultural societies. Today [...] information systems [...] operate as power intensifiers" (General Nikhil Kumar)[19].

"The general trend establishes sections between the different subsystems of information warfare. It is, in fact, a continuous process with several subsystems applied at different levels of a conflict such as an integrated weapon system. But the goals and objectives of the war remain the same. In the traditional sense, the ultimate goal of war policies is to win without having to go into battle. The ways to fight information warfare facilitate this art of the war" (General Subbash Chander)[20].

A study published in 2005, "Management of Information Warfare: Emerging paradigm" [HUS 05], written by Zafar Husain from the University of United Arab

---

18. See http://www.ciol.com/content/news/2006/106091401.asp.
19. [HUS 05]: p. 59.
20. [HUS 05]: p. 59.

Emirates, A.K. Pathak from the Indian Army and Ramkrishna Vyas from the International Institute of Professional Studies (India), provides an interesting view on the way the Indian military understands the concept of information warfare. The analysis is based on a survey carried out among a panel of 78 officers in the Indian army, in service for 15 to 30 years, with operational experience in the field. The vision of the military is important, because it determines to a great extent the way in which the revolution in Indian military affairs can be carried out and the place that information warfare will play in this transformation. The gap perceived between the potential offered by information warfare and its implementation is revealing of the cultural characteristics inherent to each nation, each army corps and their structural organization. The main results of this survey were as follows:

 − information warfare is a relevant and necessary concept for 82.3% of respondents;

  − the most cited components of information warfare are:

   - command and control warfare (C2W);

   - ISR;

   - cyberwar;

   - information security (Infosec);

   - the media;

   - in a very marginal way, from the responses, we find the following: economic warfare, hacker warfare, network warfare, satellite warfare and special operations;

  − priorities must be:

   - intelligence and surveillance (27%). In the different Indian analyses on information warfare methods, we find, in a recurring theme, that there is a particular interest in methods for information and intelligence gathering (ISR, SIGINT, ELINT, COMMINT, imaging and navigation methods);

   - security of operations (OPSEC) (21%);

   - electronic warfare (21%). All the officers questioned seem to find electronic warfare particularly important in the conduct of information warfare operations;

   - information security (9%);

   - deception (8%);

   - psychological operations (8%);

   - the media (4%);

   - smart weapons (2%).

Cyberwar seems to be the last of the priorities. Why? Is India still not dependent on cyberspace in the minds of the military? Does India think it will not have to experience this type of attack? Are its direct enemies not dependent enough on cyberspace to give it too much thought? The very low interest from the military toward psychological and media aspects is also revealing. They don't seem to be contaminated by the American model which now places these questions at the heart of information warfare.

Further, according to this survey:

– the budget allocated to armies should focus on intelligence and surveillance (20%), communications (16%), electronic warfare (14%), computer networks (13%), software (13%) and smart weapons (10%). Cryptography and information security are last with 6 and 8% of respondents, respectively. These choices are revealing about the feeling of threat involving information systems: it is not seen as very pressing;

– when officers were asked what measures would be best adapted to improve the efficiency of electronic warfare in low intensity conflicts, the creation of WAN type networks[21] to share information between units comes in last position;

– as for the impression of the impact of information warfare on mortality rates: 38% think information warfare can decrease mortality, 23% think it will not, 18% that it will limit collateral damages, 21% that information warfare increases mortality, going against the generally accepted idea that the main virtue of information warfare is to lean toward zero deaths. The decrease in mortality is therefore not significant;

– 61% think that information warfare has a dissuasive value but only against developed nations, because it is not very effective against under-developed or developing countries;

– 62% of officers estimate that the capabilities of individuals in terms of information warfare must be a criterion of promotion within armies, which is revealing of the importance that military officers are ready to give to IW. 98% approve the introduction of training specifically for IW in military training;

– as for the connections between the civilian and military sectors, only 2% disapprove of the involvement of civilian institutions in the development of information warfare.

---

21. Wide Area Network.

3.3. Understanding attacks against Indian cyberspace

3.3.1. *Indian site defacements: statistics*

3.3.1.1. *Site defacement: form*

The type of preferred attack against information systems, and the most widely reported to CERT-In especially, seems to be site defacement, which is an attack against information systems in the form of vandalism. Site defacement is also called web-jacking and cyber graffiti. The hacker can replace content on the home page only, or on several pages or even the whole site, with specific political or social messages in the form of claims, insults, threats and warnings.

Defacement can represent an important threat for commercial sites by affecting their image, their reputation and their credibility to partners or clients. This type of hacking is instantly visible, as opposed to other types. This is exactly what hackers are after: to be seen, to be heard, be known and attract the public's attention to a message or an idea.

For institutional sites, it can be more of a political attack, showing the weaknesses of the security levels implemented. Defacement, aside from the message on the screen, means "your security is inadequate, you are not serious, believable; we, hackers can do what' we want". Demonstrating the weakness of existing measures of security demeans the credibility of hosts, website creators and owners. Attackers simply take advantage of all the weaknesses, which become opportunities, to promote their political and ideological message using the site's audience.

More insidiously, an attack against a site can modify content very discretely. Just one word added or taken out, or a misplaced punctuation mark, can change the meaning of a sentence and make text say something entirely different.

Site defacement can also be a mainstay of organized psychological operations, an instrument of information warfare.

3.3.1.2. *Indian site defacements: CERT-In statistics*

In March 2007, the CERT-In published a detailed study of Indian site defacements for 2006[22] from which we find some interesting information:

– CERT counted 5,211 defaced Indian sites in 2006. Defacements are by far the most reported incidents: there are only 552 reported incidents of phishing, network

---

22. S.S. SARMA, GARIMA NARAYAN, *Analysis of Defaced Indian Websites – Year 2006*, Department of Information Technology, Ministry of Communications and Information Technology, Government of India, Cert-In White Paper CIWP-2007-02, 31 March 2007.

scans, worms and viruses. Cases of phishing go from 3 reported in 2003, to 339 in 2006; network scans from 11 to 177. There were (only?) 5 reported cases of viruses and worms in 2004, 95 in 2005 and 19 in 2006;

– the number of site defacements continues to increase: 342 in August 2004, 261 in July 2005 and 796 attacks in August 2005. But these comparisons do not necessarily make sense. We must analyze data over longer periods to be able to see a pattern;

– for site defacements, Top Level Domains (TLD) distribution is as follows: 3,177 involving .com, 1226 for .in, 443 for .org, 249 for .net, 104 for .info. The rest are insignificant, for example only 3 cases affect .edu. Distribution in relation to ccTLD shows that only 0.08% involves .mil.in and 5.95% for .gov.in. Sites with the .in extension are not all hosted in India; they can also be registered by people living outside of India. 61% of Indian sites attacked in 2006 were, in fact, hosted outside of India;

– Figure 3.1 shows the evolution of site defacements during 2005 and 2006. Significant peaks are recorded in January and August of 2005, but especially in August 2006. The form of the curve is made up of a succession of peaks and valleys, and not a regular progression, whilst the monthly average over both years is 413 incidents.

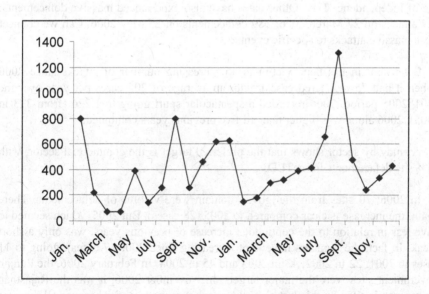

Figure 3.1. *Curve built from data published in the CERT-In report on site defacements in 2006, CIWP-2007-02. The diagram presents the number of Indian site defacements recorded monthly for 2005–2006*

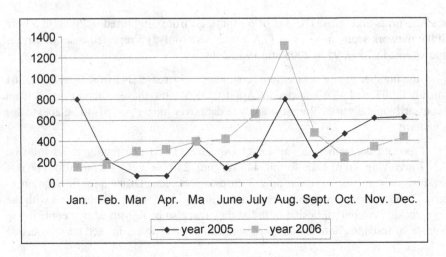

Figure 3.2. *Superimposed annual curves clearly show a renewal of energy in August. Taken from data published in the CERT-In report on site defacements in 2006, CIWP-2007-02*

The incident curves in Figure 3.2 present significant peaks in August 2005 and August 2006. The greatest number of defacements (320) occurred on August 14, the eve of Independence Day. Other dates have also experienced massive defacements: 227 attacks on 27 March 2006; 189 defacements on 25 May 2006. Can we connect these massive attacks to specific events?

Extension .in has been victim to an increasing number of attacks since 2000 (when it had 75 registered cases), with an average of 205 cases per year over the 2001–2005 period. 2006 recorded a spectacular spurt going to 1,226 (from 373 in 2005); 2006 alone was higher than all five previous years combined.

A study by sector shows that the preferred target is the commercial sector, with 85% site defacements for ccTLD.

In 2006, 70 sites from the .gov.in domain were victims of defacements. There again, the increase is clear compared to 2005 (28 cases). But 2005, which seemed to have less in relation to the continuous increase of previous years, was only a short break. In fact, the numbers have kept increasing since 2000 (7 cases), going to 11 cases in 2001, 22 in 2002, 43 in 2003 and 45 in 2004. In February 2006, the Punjab government sites were the major targets. In November 2006, it was the Rajasthan government's sites. In this last case, the attack was made easier because all the sites were on the same server in the United States and were defaced in two days.

3.3.1.3. *Indian site defacements: the authors*

Many authors of site defacements, in 2006 as in previous years, are identified by their signature, making statistical analysis easier. We can name a few:

– DeltahackingSecurityTEAM seems to be a specialist, among others, of massive defacements, and not only in India[23]. Its hunting ground is wide. The group leaves slogans on sites it attacks: "Nuclear Energy is our right! [...] No, Iran is not like others[...] Iran is Iran"[24] or "just for notice security"[25], "we love Iran[...] down with USA and Israel, stop war, you can't do anything with us, Iran is not a Terrorist, USA and Israel are Terrorists"[26];

– LORD, author of 434 Indian site defacements during 2006, mainly attacking Win 2003 servers. LORD is a group of Turkish hackers;

– CyberLord, author of 388 defacements, especially the author of all site attacks of August 14, 2006. CyberLord is a group of Turkish hackers;

– Yusufislam, 340 defacements; a group of Turkish hackers attacking forums;

– Devil-X, 194 defacements. This hacker group from Saudi Arabia is pro-Palestine, pro-Iraq, pro-Lebanon, anti-American, anti-Israel, calls for peace and sings the glory of Saddam Hussein. Like other hackers, it does not specifically attack India, but all sites where it can find an audience. Its attacks are sometimes co-signed (root-00);

– aLpTurkTegin, 183 defacements. A Turkish hacker group, launching messages against the PKK (a recognized terrorist organization), calling for respect for a Muslim Turkey, Kurdistan. May 21, 2007 the group counted 21,200 attacks in the world, including 15,210 mass defacements[27];

– other authors of site defacements include: kardeshackerlar; GOODY S3CURITY TEAM; b4d_m00d; crackers_child; ssh-2; crackers-child (103 ccTLD); EL_MuHaMMeD; and ihtilal.org.

This list is far from complete.

What could be the characteristics of these hackers attacking India?

---

23.   See   recent   attacks   in   Latvia   on   the   website   http://www.zone-h.lv/component/option,com_attacks/Itemid,16/filter_defacer,DeltahackingSecurityTEAM/.
24. http://www.savagekarma.com/ or those launched against Turkish sites http://tr.zone-h.org/component/option,com_attacks/Itemid,16/filter_defacer,DeltahackingSecurityTEAM/page,1.
25. On the Latvian website http://www.raznaslicis.lv/gallery/data/delta.html.
26. http://home.maskankerman.gov.ir/.
27. According to the site old.zone-h.org/defacements/filter/filter_defacer=aLpTurkTegin.

– hackers, fundamentally isolated, often network and form groups;

– the hackers attacking India also target other sites elsewhere in the world. Few groups specifically target India;

– do the signatures and pseudonyms used by hackers reflect reality? For example, is GForce Pakistan group, very active in 2004–2005 and motivated by defending their Muslim brothers, a group of Pakistani hackers? In this case, yes. Most of its members are Pakistani and work in the information technology industry. But the hackers could very well have been from another nationality and have the same name;

– it is very difficult to confirm the level of network warfare capabilities of the Pakistanis. There are not many publications to attest to the real nature of Pakistan's capabilities in terms of information warfare;

– hackers acting in the name of Pakistan can be Pakistanis living at home or abroad, as well as sympathizers;

– there are also pro-Pakistani hackers, anti-India hackers, anti-nuclear hackers, pro Muslim hackers;

– the attackers have the capacity of forming networks, groups cooperating together, able to combine their skills against targets anywhere in the world. The GForce Pakistan group does not only deface sites in India but has also defaced sites such as the National Oceanic and Atmospheric Administration, Defense Test and Evaluation Processional Institute, which depends on the American Department of Defense, and sites from Israel;

– hackers focus their defacing efforts on sites with a large audience: the Indian Science Congress, National Research Center, Indian National Information Technology Promotion, Indian Foreign Affairs Department, *Asian Age* newspaper, University of Bombay, Government of Gujarat;

– the groups do not seem to last very long: the Pakistani Hackers Club (Pakistan HC) was very active early in 2000. By 2006, it was no longer listed in the top 10 most toxic hackers against India (as was the same case for the above mentioned group, GForce Pakistan);

– individual hackers get together into small groups. These groups can then merge into more important organizations. Pro-Pakistani Anti-India Crew (AIC), PHC and GForce Pakistan groups have rallied to the Al Qaida Muslim Alliance;

– the groups denounce infringements of human rights by India, nuclear tests, crimes against Muslim communities, occupation by Indian troops, and alert the international community.

3.3.1.4. Indian site defacements: massive attacks and concentration

It is important to note that the majority of attacks originate from these few groups, which we can count on one hand. Even though the total number of defacements seems important, can the phenomenon be considered significant? We are far from describing the massive attacks involving large national and international Internet user communities, where thousands of sympathizers of a cause intervene.

Observations[28] from previous years show the same phenomenon of attack concentrated on only a few groups: in the 2000–2002 period, only five hacker groups were the authors of over 60% of recorded defacements. These groups are AIC (Anti India Crew), GForce Pakistan, Silver Lords, WFD and TheBuGz. The 135 remaining defacement authors in the list were only involved in less than 40%; .net, .org and .edu extensions are not very popular with these groups, unlike .com and .in extensions.

3.3.1.5. Indian site defacements: profile of attacks

These actions are sometimes massive because of the volume of attacks launched simultaneously, but isolated since they come from a few small number of groups.

The volume of forces focusing on these hostile actions is low. There are no confrontations involving hacker "armies" on both sides of a country.

Hackers defacing Indian sites also deface sites from other nations. Should we conclude that the attacks are not specifically aimed at India, but at what it actually represents? Or that these types of attacks are not aimed at a specific target but to defend a cause: to fight against nuclear proliferation, or fight against Islam?

3.3.2. Cyber crime or acts of aggression/acts of war?

Should the slogans signatures against a nation on defaced sites mean a hostile act or an act of war? Or are these CNA type operations carried out in the larger scope of information warfare initiated by an enemy? Are these CNAs intended as psychological or intelligence operations?

Even though statistics may not provide information on the nature of the attacks, they at least reveal the security flaws of the targeted sites and victimized institutions. Attacks by defacement do not always require cutting edge techniques, or taking

---

28. Refer to a study carried out on the 2000-2002 period available at http://www.firstmonday.org/issues/issue7_12/srijith/index.html.

advantage of published flaws. Rather, it is the victims who are not completely in control of the security of their information systems.

In order to interpret the information and statistics received, even though we do not really know which part of the iceberg they represent, it is important to place these numbers in their own political, social and economic context. The few violations disturbing cyberspace (albeit too numerous, disruptive and certainly reprehensible, and clearly grabbing media attention) have nothing to do with acts of "information warfare", or acts of war, in the strict sense of the term. The problem lies in our capacity to make this distinction.

There are numerous sources of instability, crisis and political and social conflicts justifying continuing hostile acts in cyberspace in a country the size of India. With its historical past, its tense relations with many neighboring countries, its desire for a dominating position in the region, as well its internal social divisions, India faces multiple conflicts often expressed in a violent way, and handled just as violently because they cannot be dealt with in a satisfactory way by politics.

3.3.2.1. *Internal sources of conflict*

Internally, threats to social peace are found in:

– confrontations between religious communities, mainly Hindu and Muslim, involving entire regions and resulting in thousands of victims. There were clashes between these communities in Gujarat in 2002;

– separatist uprisings of the country's northeast communities (Maoist extremist Naxalites and Bodos).

3.3.2.2. *International sources of conflict*

At the international level, crises and conflicts are found in:

– border squabbles with China, at the root of current tensions: these disagreements resulted in a war between India and China in 1962;

– the tense relations with Pakistan dating back to independence from British rule in 1947 have led to three wars: in 1947–1949 (regarding Kashmir), 1965 (involving Kashmir) and 1971. Pakistan's separation from India was never resolved in a satisfactory way, which is the reason for territorial conflicts. On the other hand, this neighbor acquired nuclear weapons with the help of China,[29] reviving the tensions and concerns in India as well as with the international community. The region

---

29. National Security Doctrine. B. Raman. Paper No. 578. South Asia Analysis Group. www.saag.org/papers6/paper578.html.

(India, Pakistan and China) has had nuclear power since 1998. India supports "no first use" (in that it is committed to only resort to nuclear power in retaliation) but this is not the case with Pakistan, with its "readiness to make first use" (i.e. having the possibility of using nuclear power as a means of attack). The starting point of a cyberwar with India as its victim can be traced back to May 1998, during Indian nuclear tests at Pokhran II. Soon after the announcement of the tests, a group of hackers (milw0rm) penetrated the Bhabha Atomic Research Center system (BARC), posted anti-India and anti-nuclear messages on its site, stole and defaced information, decommissioned eight servers and copied emails exchanged between Indian scientists. The hackers were clearly not targeting India any more than another country, but were defending a political anti-nuclear philosophy: the group subsequently declared that they could target Pakistan[30]. Four days after the attacks against Indian nuclear installations, the same group accessed a Turkish nuclear center, the Cekmece Nuclear Research and Training Center in Istanbul, followed by an Iranian nuclear research complex;

– relations with Pakistan on the question of the valley of Kashmir, previously an Indian state, which is today shared between the Indian Republic and Pakistan. The Pakistan question is one of the main sources of conflicts facing India. Pakistan, a military republic since General Musharraf's coup, now has over 165 million young residents (average age is approximately 20 years old) predominantly Muslim (97%). Less than 49% of the population over 15 years old can read and write. Only 7.5 million Pakistani have access to the Internet (2005 numbers). The India–Pakistan conflict is not only political, it is also religious. What makes this a major conflict in the context of the battle against Islamist terrorism is the fact that the region is predominantly Muslim and has been for centuries (since 1346), and Islamist insurgents want separation from India. Pakistan provides help to insurgents with weapons and serves as a base. The conflict is one of the most militarized on the planet (India, China, Pakistan) and the Indian army is losing thousands of men in this war. Sites[31] created by the Indian government to provide information on daily events in the valley of Kashmir were targeted. Hackers published pictures showing Indian military shooting Kashmiri militants with captions such as "massacre", "torture" and "illegal execution". The Indian government has often been denounced for its actions in Kashmir;

– the Kargil conflict in 1999: Several defacements of institutional sites were recorded during the Kargil conflict from April to June 1999 in India (and Pakistan);

– terrorism, a national and international problem that India cannot solve alone;

– relations with Nepal, which, according to Indian authorities, is being used for Jihad from Pakistan;

---

30. http://www.atoomspionage.com/opanderesites9.htm.
31. For example, see http://www.armyinkashmir.com.

– tensions with Bangladesh, who, according to the Indian government, also supports anti-Indian terrorist organizations.

The region's communities have many reasons for clashes, even though relations seem to have temporarily stabilized with China and Pakistan.

In this context, is information warfare a suitable method of battle, a form of war useful to the interests of India's enemies and of India itself to reach its political objectives?

These internal and external tensions can all be reasons for conflict or crisis expressed through information operations such as attacks on computer networks, hacker attacks and psychological operations (misinformation and rumor). But before confirming the existence of any official link between an information warfare operation and a political context, we must ensure that the attacks do not come from isolated individuals taking advantage of tensions to "have fun" with the situation.

3.4. Indian hackers

India is attacked but is not out for the count. Its hackers also attack foreign information systems. The Yaha Q worm (a variation of the Yaha worm) was propagated in 2003 by a group of Indian hackers, the Indian Snakes. The worm burrowed Pakistani sites (as DoS type attempted attack), especially government sites, the Karachi Stock Exchange and Internet service providers. An article published in "The Hindu" on June 9, 2003 maintained that the Yaha worm, launched by Indian hackers, paralyzed 200 Pakistani websites for several days and erased the contents of hard disks from government computers and from private company computers[32].

Computer hacking is illegal in India (under the Indian Information Technology Act, 2000) but that does not keep groups like the Indian Snakes, Indianspy and Indian Hackers Club from being created. However, hackers do not seem to constitute a real community. Recently, cases of hacker arrests have been reported on Indian soil[33], as well as elsewhere in Japan[34], and in the United States[35].

---

32. G. Anand, *Indo-Pak Hacker War Comes Here Too*, The Hindu, 9 June 2003.
33. Manu Joseph, Indian Hackers Scared Straight? http://www.wired.com/culture/lifestyle/news/2001/07/45569, 27 January 2007.
34. Steve Gold, Indian hacker marooned in a Japanese jail, http://securityblog.itproportal.com/?p=773, 20 March 2007.
35. U.S. charges Indian Hackers in Stock Manipulation Scheme, http://www.hackinthebox.org/, 13 March 2007.

Chapter 4

Japan

Which country besides Japan could symbolize innovation, technology, progress and information and communication society in this region of the world? An international heavyweight at the forefront of cutting edge technologies, Japan is not only the leader in the field of information technologies, but also a provider of these technologies. Which means that it controls all aspects. It knows what these products are made of when other countries settle for buying off the shelf. It may dominate technologies, which are at the service of information warfare, but its Constitution prevents it from acquiring methods of making war.

The recent changes in relations with the United States could modify this situation. But for now, Japan must maintain a defensive position. It does, however, have much to do in securing its cyberspace.

4.1. Japanese cyberspace flaws

4.1.1. *Theft of defense classified data*

In March 2007, three sailors were accused of stealing and divulging military secrets. The affair caused quite a stir. The scandal could affect the chain of command of the Japanese navy. The secrets involved the anti-missile Aegis system designed by the Americans.

4.1.1.1. *The offense itself*

The object of the offense concerned theft of files about an American anti-missile system, also adopted by Japanese defense systems: the Aegis system developed by the Americans in the 1960s. The Japanese adopted the system during the North Korean missile strikes over Japan. The theft involved precise data on calculating formulas for intercepting systems as well as for targets that the system can follow.

A more detailed investigation in May 2007[1] revealed that information stolen also involved anti-ballistic SM3 missile systems (Standard Missile-3 interceptors) and the Link 16 system, which is a highly secure data transfer system between ships and fighter aircraft, also used to exchange military data between the United States and Japan. This system is vital to the anti-missile defense system, notably because it makes it possible to safely exchange satellite data. Information relative to SM3 missiles and to the Link 16 system are classified under the 1954 law involving the protection of secrets in the context of the mutual assistance agreement between Japan and the United States.

4.1.1.2. *The players involved*

Several players were involved in this situation:

– three Japanese sailors accused of disclosing secrets, one of whom took a CD-Rom home (to Yokosuka, in the Prefecture of Kanagawa). It was a CD-Rom containing pornographic images and classified military data involving the Aegis anti-missile defense system. He pretended that he did not know he had copied sensitive data when he was copying pornographic images. The files were found on his personal computer's hard drive; did he send them through the Internet? Two other sailors, allegedly at least, copied the same information;

– accomplices, because the level of sensitivity of the data did not allow access from simple sailors. The investigation went all the way up to lieutenants;

– their chain of command, including commanders;

– students from the military academy of the Etajima fleet (Prefecture of Hiroshima) who copied data about the SM3 system[2]. Other bases were also investigated, such as military bases in the prefectures of Kyoto and Yamaguchi. Sensitive information was used as course material, and that is when students copied it;

– the Japanese Government, which must explain itself to the victim, the American Government;

---

1. *Japan military data leak wider than previously thought*,
http://www.computerworld.com/action/article.do?command=viewArticleBasic&articleId=90 20358&intsrc=industry_list, 22 May 2007.
2. *U.S. Missile Data Leaked in Japan*,
http://www.military.com/NewsContent/0,13319,136600,00.html, 22 May 2007.

– the American Government, victim of the data theft, expects an explanation;

– indirectly, the commercial partners and countries allied to the United States, acquiring American defense systems;

– an article[3] reporting the incidents added that one of the three sailors was married to a Chinese woman. The police were investigating her immigration status. It was during this investigation that police found the documents relative to the Aegis system.

4.1.1.3. The incident was not the only one

In August 2002, the Defense Department launched a large investigation into an event in which a sub-contractor involved in the computer systems of the Japanese forces stole ground and air forces information[4].

In February 2006, confidential information was stolen from the computer of a navy officer of the Japanese self-defense forces. It included information on military drills and personal information on several dozen navy members. The officer was in charge of communications aboard the Asayuki destroyer at the Nagasaki base[5]. The documents were broadcast on the P2P platform. Following the conclusions of the investigation in April 2006, instructions were given to not use file sharing software, 56,000 computers were replaced (!) and secured with data encryption systems, and personnel training was organized. Measures of dissuasion were also taken such as random controls and "secret defense" classification for documents which, until then, were classified simply as "secret", leading to greater sanctions for theft, loss or disclosure of this information.

In April 2006, information relative to a contractor (Mitsui Engineering & Shipbuilding Co.) from the Misawa air base, personal information and passwords were stolen over the Internet after one of the employees entered this data on his computer and used Winny[6]. It would appear that no American information was affected by this incident. Remember that the Misawa base receives Japanese and American troops. The base also hosted the Echelon surveillance network of the

---

3. *Porn-Swapping Japanese Sailors Leak Missile Secrets*,
http://www.spiegel.de/international/world/0,1518,476032,00.html, 6 April 2007.
4. http://findarticles.com/p/articles/mi_m0XPQ/is_2002_August_12/ai_90297163
Defense Agency begins investigation into leaked data, August 12, 2002.
5. *Secret information of Japan's MSDF leaked*,
http://english.people.com.cn/200602/24/eng20060224_245597.html, 24 February 2006.
6. Juliana Gittler, *Misawa Contractor Information Leaked*,
http://www.military.com/features/0,15240,94860,00.html, April 20, 2006.

NSA[7]. The base authorities claimed that despite this incident, security was not in question, which is obviously not true: passwords for secure zones were disclosed, and they had to be modified. If the theft had not been found out, passwords would not have been modified and security flaws would still have existed. On the other hand, information that theoretically must not get outside of military walls, does get out and apparently without any problem, via portable hard drives, USB drives and CD-ROMs. Security processes on military bases are easily penetrated. The military seem to have huge problems in controlling civilian intrusion. Whether the data is stolen from the military's computers, the personal computers of military personnel or from those of contractors, or from the personal computers of contractors' employees, the result remains the same: information is divulged.

In August 2006, a Japanese officer visited continental China several times without notifying his superiors[8]. Was the officer involved in espionage? According to the investigation, it would seem he was not. But the documents found in his home, copied on CD-ROM, involved classified documents relative to identification methods of foreign ships. During the same period, a Japanese diplomat, possibly visiting the same places as this officer, committed suicide (May 2004) after he was pressured to reveal defense secrets in connection with communications (Japanese version of the facts denied by China). The incidents accentuate the tensions between the two countries.

In November 2006, data concerning military operations of American troops in Iraq were stolen over the Internet[9]. The information was on the personal computer of a soldier from Japanese air force defense who used a file-sharing tool. Information involved transport operations and the deployment of American military troops in Iraq in June and July. Evidently, the precautionary instructions given to the military are not effective. Data relative to military drills of air forces in Naha (Prefecture of Okinawa) were also stolen. The officer was stationed in Qatar from March to August 2006 where the American military command for Iraqi reconstruction assistance operations was also stationed. The officer brought his personal computer on his mission and used it without authorization.

---

7. The Echelon project is designed by the United States, Great Britain, New Zealand, Australia and Canada. It is used to intercept private and commercial telecommunications (fixed and mobile telephony, satellite, fiber optic lines and micro-waves).
8. Japan says naval officer may have divulged secrets, http://www.taipeitimes.com/News/taiwan/archives/2006/07/17/2003175231.
9. *Data on U.S. military's Iraqi operations leaked onto Internet*, http://www.breitbart.com/article.php?id=D8LNDQ3G0&show_article=1.

In February 2007, a Japanese destroyer crew member sent sensitive military data that he had stored on his personal computer over the Internet by mistake[10].

4.1.1.4. *Reactions to the events of March 2007*

The Minister of Defense, Fumio Kyuma, denied SM3 missile information theft[11] and, at first, the American authorities (officially at least) showed solidarity toward their ally.

. A long and intense investigation was organized and lasted several weeks and led investigators to several military centers in Japan but it seems the location of the incident could not be found.

As a security measure, Japanese fleet commanders decided to move soldiers married to foreigners to posts where they would not have access to secret information to avoid leaking information to foreign powers. This decision, announced at the end of June 2007[12], may be linked to the information published in March about the presence of a Chinese spouse during the event. These moves began in August 2007 and involved ten officers in the first wave. 150 officers (including 100 married to Chinese women) were involved among the 40,000 people in the naval forces. This fact and the decision should be linked to the nationalist movement that seems to have been reborn in Japan, and to the fostered feeling of a Chinese threat to Japanese society, be it military or economic.

4.1.1.5. *Impact of the events*

Commercial relations between the United States and its allies could have suffered from these data disclosures:

– diplomatic relations between Japan and the United States could be damaged because of these serious incidents;

– the incidents delayed the 2007 deployment of new Aegis defense systems that Japanese naval forces were due to have. This program was intended to organize an anti-missile defense shield in case of possible attacks from North Korea. North Korea represents one of the greatest threats for Japan now, after the drills conducted on July 4, 2006, by Pyongyang (strikes of several ballistic missiles including one with a theoretical range of 6,700 km). These strikes were conducted in the Sea of

---

10. *Porn-Swapping Japanese Sailors Leak Missile Secrets,*
http://www.spiegel.de/international/world/0,1518,476032,00.html, 6 April 2007.
11. *Classified Data leaked widens to missile defense,* Japan Times,
http://search.japantimes.co.jp/cgi-bin/nn20070523a1.html, 23 May 2007.
12. MSDF Officers with foreign spouses to be moved from sensitive posts,
http://www.japantoday.com/jp/news/410685, 28 June 2007.

Japan, while the country was still traumatized by the missile strike that went over its territory in 1998.

4.1.1.6. *Analysis*

The key element in this event is… a CD-ROM. A simple device is sufficient for highly confidential data to exit their space of confidentiality and be found in a personal computer in an apartment with no security whatsoever, exchanged via the internet with no security protocol, eventually online on a website, or sent from a simple email to a foreign power.

A simple CD-Rom can hurt the most elaborate defense, protection, security, superiority of information and information space control doctrines. A simple CD-ROM can be the bridge between two information spaces (military and civilian).

Was there involuntary disclosure? Certainly not in this case. In view of information taken from press articles, what could, at first, seem like a simple additional anecdote (some articles make fun of the association of pornographic images and secret defense files) in the long list of incidents that Japanese forces of defense suffered, could also be well-orchestrated information warfare. We can identify several components of information warfare operations.

Intelligence first. None of the information we have enables us to confirm that we are looking at espionage for foreign interests. But the information was stolen, disclosed and copied; it was circulated and nobody knows the extent of where the files went, and there is no information to say if foreign powers could have been behind it, or if the stolen files were the subject of transactions. The fact remains that there was access to systems and secret defense files and that access to these files should involve a specific action: the intervention of people with authorized access. This secret defense information leak is similar to an intelligence action.

The event could also be perceived as a psychological operation. There could be different objectives:

– to discredit Japan and its defense program security, its security policies and obvious displayed ambition of becoming a model of security. In 1999, the Japanese government considered the implementation of new security policies. In 2000, it proposed an action plan for the protection of information systems against cyber threats, with the implementation of protection methods against cyber terrorism threatening sensitive infrastructures. The extension of the "e-Japan" program (2001) proposed security measures for government departments. In June 2006, the "Secure Japan 2006" report described the axes of the security policy of Japanese information systems for 2006–2009. The government displayed its ambitious project to make Japan a global model in terms of security. Repeated incidents in the most sensitive defense sectors have hurt this project. The government gave itself until 2008 to propose innovative solutions, but such a goal was quite impossible to reach, all the more so as beyond the security incidents linked to national defense, cyber crime on a grander scale keeps increasing each year in greater proportions. Internet monitoring methods (the Kari-no-Mail system, the Japanese version of the American application Carnivore) used by the police is not sufficient to stop the trend, neither is the allocation of specific methods to fight against cyber crime (creation of specific police units in 2001). The "Secure Japan 2006" report mentioned the need to train fighters against cyber terrorism, to analyze methods of attack and to evaluate protection measures. Despite the methods deployed, cyber crime progresses in Japan in spectacular and regular leaps. Virus infections multiplied threefold between 1999 and 2000. Internet crimes increased by 60% between 2000 and 2001[13]. In 2005, cyber crime increased by 52% compared to 2004[14] and by 12% during the first six months of 2006. Japan also invested in the creation of a legal structure contributing to the protection and defense of cyberspace. Globally, though, Japan is criticized for its lack of prevention for risks linked to networks and their fragile security architecture[15]. All these efforts focused on the fight against cyber crime are obviously not effective, and not useful for protecting security and national defense data against attacks;

– to discredit its capabilities in cooperating closely with the United States. In 1952, Japan approved a pact of mutual security assistance with the United States. The Japanese–American alliance is the major point of Japanese security; Japanese self-defense forces implement defensive operations, and the US army is responsible for offensive operations;

– to discredit the organization of the Japanese army when the country has just implemented a real Department of Defense (from January 7, 2007);

– to destabilize the balance of the Japan/United States alliance at a time when the country seems to move toward a new period that some call the post-Yoshida era[16]. 2006 marked an important turning point with the signature on May 1st of the "Defense Policy Review Initiative" (DPRI), agreement that redefines the U.S.–Japan Alliance for the first time since 1951;

---

13. *Japan sees big jump in cybercrime*, www.mail-archive.com/cybercrime-alerts@topica.com/msg00540.html, 9 August 2001.
14. *Japan cybercrime rises by 52 percent*, http://www.physorg.com/news11168.html, 24 February 2006.
15. Raisuke Miyawaki, *International Cooperation to Combat Cyber Crime and Cyber Terrorism*, Standford Conference, 7 December 1999.
16. The policy of Yoshida Shigeru, who was Prime Minister of Japan, was to revive the post-World War II Japanese economy, to the detriment of a certain diplomatic independence. We speak of the "Yoshida doctrine" to qualify this policy.

– to make Japanese–US relations tense concerning data exchanges, interoperability, sharing of methods, cooperation in intelligence and strategy coordination between American and Japanese forces. Because of this tension, the new alliance, and the new regional balance that Japan and the United States are trying to create in relation to the Korean threat or to Beijing–Taipei tensions, are questioned;

– to disrupt relations between the United States and its allies;

– to make it appear that Japan is extremely vulnerable to information warfare operations. Would that be a signal for potential assailants who could then clearly identify the weaknesses of the system, and analyze the reactions of the target?

– to conduct an operation to influence Japanese, American and international public opinion?

Psychological operations can use the sound box that is the Internet. Information goes around the world in a few minutes and continues to be used, interpreted and, of course, distorted.

The event can be presented as a form of physical attack against information and information systems. Even if there was intrusion via networks, if there was distortion of data, cracking of passwords or a software attack, there was also "physical" theft. The attack may have been done smoothly, without explosions or destruction but we can still consider that there was physical attack in some way.

We can also recognize a form of Computer Network Operation (CNO). The operation occurred via information systems, through access to data stored on a protected computer, and involved copying and disclosure of this data.

The operation could also be an economy of resources for electronic warfare. By knowing the information relative to missiles, "the adversary" with access to this information can use it in electronic warfare (in control of the electromagnetic spectrum).

If this event was an information warfare operation, who would the initiators be? Who are the enemies? Who benefits or could benefit from the crime:

– China? The presence of a Chinese spouse was mentioned. But the media gives no information on what role she played. We only know that she was the subject of an investigation in relation to her visa status. Must we suspect espionage from China? The risk of a possible leak of secret information to China is also mentioned;

– North Korea? The weapon systems involved (SM3, Link 16, Aegis) are used to build an anti-ballistic missile shield against the North Korean threat;

– Japan's enemies? Japan is once more perceived and presented as a threat to China or North Korea as well as to other countries in the region that see in the Japanese archipelago a potential military attacker, because of the resurgence of a certain warlike nationalism;

– United States enemies?

– the United States itself?

– Japan?

Who are the victims? The allies themselves? Is such an attack liable to put into question the conditions of the alliance and divide the allies over several vital points? This operation, deliberate or not, disrupts relations between allies which can only be favorable to their enemies in the end.

The problem of loss or theft of data comes under what Americans call "information assurance". A country can be at war and share information with its allies who are not directly involved in the war effort. But the flaws and weaknesses of our allies can be a new source of danger.

4.1.2. *Loss/theft of sensitive or confidential data*

The list of victims of theft or disclosure of confidential information in Japan is very long and involves more than just military boundaries.

Loss of data by viruses is regularly on the front page of the media and is put first before security problems on Japanese networks. Many Winny platform users were victims of the Antinny malware[17], stealing files on their computers and then opening them to the public on its platform. The Antinny virus, discovered in September 2003, was the first virus of this type in Japan able to exploit the characteristics of file sharing software. By June 2006, Trend Micro had identified 46 variations of the virus[18]. Access passwords to protected zones in 16 Japanese airports (stolen from the computer of a Japan Airlines pilot), data relative to police investigations, client information, commercial reports and lists of names have all been involved. The common point of this data is their confidential character. The victims are normal Internet users as well as mobile telephony companies, military (data involving drills conducted in Okinawa in 2005 with American troops), airline

---

17. *Computer virus highlights problems of Internet security, safety for Japan.* http://mdn.mainichi-
msn.co.jp/features/archive/news/2006/06/20060613p2g00m0fe009000c.html, 13 June 2006.
18. *Japanese virus shares private info,* http://www.mail-archive.com/isn@attrition.org
/msg05838.html, 13 June 2006.

companies and the police. The virus itself is not especially elaborate or destructive, but it does take advantage of the characteristics of the P2P platform and its popularity. Reactions have included orders to ban the use of the platform on machines dedicated for professional use, bans on processing professional files on personal computers, the necessity of changing stolen passwords, the necessity of changing computers and bans on the use of professional material for personal purposes. In the end, Internet users took the blame for not being able to use the Internet while respecting basic security rules. In 2006, the virus attacked a new platform; Share. Antinny is only responsible for a small part of virus-related incidents recorded over the 2005–2006 period but its nuisance factor is high. Basic questions remain unanswered. Can all incidents be attributed to the Antinny virus and to the Winny platform? Could there be other causes?

In the last few years, the P2P Winny platform and the Antinny virus caused numerous problems for companies, as well as for the military, police forces and the government.

4.1.2.1. *Data theft from sensitive infrastructures*

Sensitive data, possibly coming from national security, were stolen through the Internet and disclosed.

In June 2005, a Japanese nuclear power station lost 40 Mb of confidential data (pictures and lists of names) broadcast over Winny. The computer of an employee using Winny was infected by a virus[19].

In May 2006, sensitive security information (notably names and addresses of security engineers) of a thermoelectric power plant (Chubu Electric Power Company) was stolen in the same way: the share + virus. Four months earlier, the same company experienced the same problem with the Winny platform[20].

Confidential data of 8,800 patients from the Toyama hospital was also stolen in a similar fashion.

4.1.2.2. *Theft of police data*

In April 2004, 19 criminal investigation reports containing the personal information of people involved in the cases, as well as details on the crimes

---

19. *Peer-to-Peer network leaks confidential Japanese nuclear secrets*,
http://www.smoothwall.net/information/news/newsitem.php?id=799, 30 June 2005.
20. *P2P virus leaks confidential power plant information*,
http://www.smoothwall.net/information/news/newsitem.php?id=1021, 23 May 2006.

themselves and the names of suspects, were lost after a police officer from Shimogamo (Kyoto) used Winny on his computer, and was the victim of a virus[21].

In 2006, data from the Okayama police, including information on 1,500 people (among those, victims of sexual crimes) and files of over three years' worth of investigations, were also stolen via Winny. The computer of a police officer was involved.

In March 2006, information involving over 4,400 people was stolen from the computer of a police inspector in Matsuyama (Prefecture of Ehime), some of it going back to 1997[22]. Again, Winny was responsible. The information concerned a murder committed in Uwajima, an expert report on a DNA analysis, cell phone numbers and personal addresses of the people connected with the investigation.

In April 2007, personal data relative to police investigations were stolen over the Internet, in the prefecture of Aichi. The computer of a police inspector was infected by a virus after his son used it on the Winny platform. The file stolen contained specific information on people in connection with the investigation (names, addresses, and ages) and information on the crime investigated. The investigation dated back to 2002–2003, the theft probably occurred in 2004–2005 and in 2007, the national police agency declared that police information from the prefecture of Aichi was circulating over the Internet. Other thefts of this type were recorded in the police departments of the prefecture of Aichi[23]. It is quite easy to imagine the possible consequences of such disclosures, such as for example, blackmail or revenge.

In June 2007, 10,000 documents containing names and images in relation to criminal investigations were stolen through the Internet from the computer of a Tokyo police officer, who was using the Winny platform. It was the largest volume of information stolen from the police and included investigations, interrogation reports, victim reports (notably sexual assault), child abuse and suspicious banking activities.[24]

---

21. *Japanese finger virus for police document leak*,
http://www.theregister.co.uk/2004/04/07/japanese_keystone_cops/, 7 April 2004.
22. *NPA bans Winny after copious info leaks*, http://search.japantimes.co.jp/cgi-bin/nn20060308b7.html, 8 March 2006.
23. *Police probe data leaked over Internet from virus-infected computer*,
http://cc.msnscache.com/cache.aspx?q=8239378006704&lang=fr-FR&mkt=ja-JP&FORM=CVRE, 23 April 2007.
24. *MPD: 10,000 documents leaked / Data from police officer's PC uploaded onto internet* via *Winny*, http://www.yomiuri.co.jp/dy/national/20070614TDY01004.htm, 14 June 2007.

4.1.2.3. *Theft of lists of names in the commercial sector*

The Yahoo Broadband Company was also a victim of the loss of several million pieces of information: 4.5 million subscribers saw their data displayed for public view. Yahoo's partner, Softbank, was to blame because it had not secured customer databases[25].

In April 2006, the personal information of 66,000 subscribers of the Japanese Mainichi Shimbun national newspaper was stolen via the Internet, with the use of file sharing software[26], the *Share platform*. Data theft was made possible because an employee transported data to his personal computer where the *Share platform* was installed. A virus shared the hard drive.

In June 2006, NTT and KDDI, two of the major Japanese telecommunications operators, sustained significant losses because of intrusions in their systems. NTT lost the personal data of 30,000 clients, KDDI lost personal data of over 4 million clients.

In March 2007, Dai Nippon Printing revealed that the files of 43 client companies were stolen, including the addresses, telephone numbers and credit card numbers of the clients of these companies[27]. Data was stolen by the ex-employee of a sub-contractor. The ex-employee recorded the information on an external hard drive and sold the data of a finance company's 150,000 clients to a network of online criminals. The employee was arrested, found guilty and sentenced for the theft of the hard drive.

According to a study by Kyodo News, close to 10% of Japanese companies lose or divulge personal information concerning their clients, representing millions of records. A law enacted in April 2004 mandates companies to take appropriate measures to protect rights to privacy, but few companies seem conscious of the actual risks.

---

25. *Japon, les données privées de 4.5 millions de comptes Yahoo étaient en accès libre*, http://www.zdnet.fr/actualites/imprimer/0,50000200,39143347,00.htm, 27 February 2004.
26. Michael Ingram, *66,000 Names and Personal Details Leaked On P2P*, http://www.slyck.com/story1169.html, 29 April 2006.
27. *Huge Leak Revealed at Japanese Firm*, http://www.darkreading.com/document.asp?doc_id=119801, 19 March 2007.

4.1.2.4. *Theft of personal information in education*

In July 2007, information concerning over 14,000 students was stolen via the Internet from the computer of a teacher[28] in Ichinomiya (Prefecture of Aichi). The scenario was the same: use of P2P software and a virus.

From this same computer, a list of retired officers from the Kagamihara air base defense forces (Prefecture of Gifu) was also stolen. The 43 year-old teacher compiled this list at the request of his mother who had worked in the Japanese defense forces. He also compiled the lists of all the students in the establishments where he had worked for the last ten years.

4.1.2.5. *Japan is not the bad student*

Even though security incidents are the responsibility of each person, especially those in charge of national security, we must still insist on the fact that the accumulation of errors, of data loss and security breaches piling up in Japan are not, unfortunately, an isolated incident.

Announcements of massive losses of data are published all over the world: intrusions into information systems, or simply the theft of laptop computers, make it easy to access millions of records:

– In March 2006, information on 200,000 Hewlett Packard employees was stolen (laptop computers containing this information were stolen)[29].

– In June 2006, Ernst & Young lost a computer containing information on 243,000 clients[30]. Over time, the same company lost information on tens of thousands of employees from Sun Microsystems, BP, Cisco, IBM and Nokia.

– In March 2006, Hong Kong police lost information on 20,000 plaintiffs[31].

– In June 2006, Medical Excess lost information on close to a million people.

– In September 2006, a breach of security in the online virtual world *Second Life*'s servers led to the exposure of personal information relating to more than 650,000 users.[32]

---

28. *Students' information leaked onto Internet from teacher's PC*,
http://search.japantimes.co.jp/cgi-bin/nn20070701a8.html, 1 July 2007.
29. http://www.theregister.co.uk/2006/03/22/fidelity_laptop_hp/.
30. http://www.theregister.co.uk/2006/06/01/ey_hotels_laptop/.
31. http://www.theregister.co.uk/2006/03/28/hk_data_leak_rumpus/.
32. *Hackers Make Off With "Second Life" Data*, By Martin H. Bosworth;
ConsumerAffairs.com.,   10   September   2006,
http://www.consumeraffairs.com/news04/2006/09/second_life.html.

– In 2007, the British Government lost laptops which contained the personal data of over 25 millions citizens (40% of the population!).

– Data are stolen or compromised in several sectors (banking, hospitals, telecommunications, e-business, energy, education, police, national defense) in times of peace, crisis or conflicts.

4.2. The challenges of cyberspace security

4.2.1. *Relations between civilian and the military worlds*

The often serious attacks against information systems demonstrate how difficult it is today for a country that is as dependent of its cyberspace as Japan is to control all variables of the security equation in an environment that is so open.

The doors of access to data and systems multiply as the architecture constituting cyberspace gets more complex. The military defense systems themselves experience the same flaws, and because of the connections between civilian and military societies, it seems impossible to separate the two because the weak link is man. The soldier is a citizen coming home and communicating with the civilian world and expressing himself through blogs. He is not cut off from the world when he is at the service of its defense. All storage supports including USB drives, cell phones, laptop computers, MP3 players and CD-ROMs ensure this relation between both worlds of information. In the old days, soldiers would have to be bribed, spies would have to be sent and people would have to be paid to deliver confidential information. Today, access to the enemy's information can be quite simple. Anyone can become a spy despite himself, delivering secrets to adversaries in a transparent way, without being conscious of doing it. What are defensive doctrines worth in these conditions? The interpolation of civilian and military worlds in cyberspace is becoming predominant to armies who cannot work alone. They can use civilian satellites for their communications in wartime; their soldiers can even have to use their own cell phones during military operations. Commanders may have to exchange, communicate or collaborate with non-governmental organizations on the scene of operations. An increasing number of companies are defense service providers. There are therefore relations between both environments which can be a source of unsolvable problems.

4.2.2. *Cyber crime or act of information warfare?*

The second lesson to take from the facts related in the previous sections is that Japan is a victim of the flaws of its cyberspace security.

In February 2007, the national agency of the Japanese police published its 2006 annual cyber crime statistics. The numbers show a massive increase, up 40%, of the number of cases including 4,425 incidents (3,161 the previous year) of so-called "cyber crime" which were recorded and solved by the police. Although increasing, these numbers did not increase by the same proportions as in 2004–2005, when they more than doubled[33]. Since 2000, the number has quadrupled.

We can certainly fault security, which is not optimal. When sites can be defaced because of security flaws, when viruses penetrate computers from the military, police, lawyers or other players handling sensitive data through a P2P platform, there is obviously a flaw in security protocols. But the guilty parties are not the military, police or lawyers; the guilty parties are the authors of the virus, and all those attempting to steal sensitive data to exploit it. Must these culprits only be tried through the legal system? When cyber crime affects national security, it becomes more than just cyber crime (and by cyber crime we mean a counterfeiting offence, an intrusion in systems or frauds, for example. These acts of delinquency that are not intended to affect national security). The stakes are not simply to make more money or to attack individuals; we can suspect the existence of political interests meant to destabilize a country. Data theft thus becomes more aggressive. Besides technical and legal methods of protection, what other forms of reprisal, or appropriate response to these acts could Japan use?

4.2.3. *Optimal security?*

A third question for assessment is that in the event of a really significant aggression launched by a hostile nation, in the case of a cyberwar, is Japan ready to defend itself? Serious incidents (theft or loss of data, highlighting security flaws) recorded over the last few years put Japan's ability to protect itself into doubt. Who sponsors this security? Self-defense forces? The government? Police forces? The private sector?

4.2.4. *The challenges of non-traditional security*

While the outlines of defense relations between Japan and the United States are being redrawn, the debate mainly involving traditional military security is back at the forefront with new questions: how can information technologies change the alliance and enable the development of new methods of cooperation? What are the limits of interoperability of information exchange systems? Can exchanges through

---

33. *Japanese police confirms cybercrime growth trend*,
http://www.nnseek.com/e/boerde.lists.virus.avp/, 22 February 2007.

networks and NCW platforms balance the alliance[34]? This context raises new challenges for security.

4.2.4.1. *Site defacements*

Because of its political relations in the region, Japan is a target of choice for all hacktivists.

Through a series of attacks (psychological operations?), assailants want to demonize Japan by recalling war crimes, the rise of nationalism and the risk of the new emergence of a predominant power in the region. They try to strip away all credibility of Japanese security. The attacks are becoming more targeted, better organized and seem to be the extension of political, economic and diplomatic tensions. Site defacements are one of the preferred methods for attackers, as with many other countries. In the first decade of the 21st Century, the phenomenon has really taken off. Among the targeted sites, we note those of the Science and Technology Agency (STA) on January 24, 2000, and the Development Planning Agency on January 26, 2000. The attacks were signed "china", "Brazil p00 hackerz" and "Miracle" and include modification of the sites' data, defacement of home pages and insertion of insulting messages against Japan.

There are many objects of contention motivating the attacks:

– Japan refuses to recognize the massacre of Nanking perpetrated by its troops during the Chinese occupation of 1937–38, where 300,000 Chinese people died. In the early 2000s, the attacks against Japanese sites happened a few days after a group of Japanese extreme right historians questioned the reality of the massacre;

– Japan reaffirms the force of its relations with the United States;

– Japan claims possession of Senkaku islands (Diaoyu in Chinese). Over 200 Japanese (and Taiwanese) sites experienced attacks organized by Chinese hackers, at the instigation of the Chinese Diaoyu Island Federation of Defense after their website experienced a Japanese attack on 25 July 2004 ("Uotsori island belongs to Japan"). Among the victims were the websites of the foreign ministry, the national police agency, Japanese coast guards and the Japanese defense agency;

– refusal of Japan to recognize the war crimes of the Second World War, according to its neighbours. The Yasukuni temple website is the subject of regular attacks including defacing attempts and DoS-type attacks. The Prime Minister's

---

34. *Non-Traditional Security: the Transformation of Cooperation between the United States and Japan*, Seminar organized by The Japan Foundation Center for Global Partnership and The Maureen and Mike Mansfield Foundation, 19 July 2005;
http://www.jpf.go.jp/cgp/info/publication/pdf/mmmf/Non-Traditional_Security.pdf.

annual visits to the sanctuary of Yasukuni irritate the Chinese and make diplomatic relations between both countries more tense each time. The Chinese see in this attitude, and in the temple, the symbol of the rebirth of Japanese nationalism;

– Japan claims the property of Takeshima islands (Tokdo in Korean) occupied by South Korea since 1954. Japan is seen as a colonialist nation when it claims this property, making relations with Korea tense, and this was instantly expressed by website attacks from both sides. In 2005, the website of the Korean Voluntary Agency Network Korea (VANK) group was massively attacked by Japanese hackers (according to the Korean version of events) after VANK was able to modify "The Sea of Japan" to "Eastern Sea" on Google Earth[35];

– Japan also sees a serious threat in North Korea. Besides the missile tests in 1998 and in 2006, followed by a nuclear test, Korean attacks could take the form of cyber attacks because the country is presumed to have acquired sophisticated intelligence tools and an army of hackers all over the world (in South Korea, Hong Kong, Russia and Japan)[36].

4.2.4.2. Viral attacks

Japan is the subject of numerous viral attacks. The IPA[37], in 1997, recorded some 2,391 declarations[38] linked to viruses, 31,680 during the first quarter of 2004, 44,840 in 2006 and 9,544 during the first quarter of 2007[39].

All sectors of activity, without distinction, are affected by viruses including, and which is the most troubling, the departments responsible for Japan's security such as the army, police, emergency services and security software development companies (Trend Micro lost internal documents, and client information was disclosed over the Internet because one of its employees using Winny forgot to install an anti-virus program).[40]

In 2001, the call center of Japan's emergency service broke down under too many calls. At the root of the problem was a virus infecting the cell phones of 24 million users of DoCoMo i-mode. When a user opened his email, the phone automatically dialed 110, the local emergency number. Imagine the impact of such a

---

35. Google Earth Calls "Sea of Japan" the "East Sea", *August 19th, 2005, by Matt*, *http://www.occidentalism.org/?p=58.*
36. *N Korea's computer hackers target South and US*, www.ft.com, 4 October 2004.
37. Information technology Promotion Agency, Japan. www.ipa.jp.
38. Almost 90% of reports come from large corporations/.
39. www.ipa.gp.jp/security/english/virus/press/200703/virus2007-1Q.html.
40. *Trend Micro Data Revealed Due to Virus*, http://www.pcworld.com/article/id,125289-page,1/article.html, 3 April 2006.

nuisance on the rescue organization during an emergency (an earthquake for example).

4.2.4.3. *Terrorist threat?*

In Japan, the first decade of the 21st Century were the years when the country became aware of the risks linked to terrorism, in part because of the actions of the Aum Shinrikyo sect (author of the sarin gas attack on the Tokyo subway). After the attacks, the sect was not disbanded despite its leader's arrest.

The authorities discovered that not only did the sect pursue its activities, but it was contracted by Japanese companies and ten government agencies including the police department to develop software. The sect also built an information system connecting the networks of 20 military garrison forces to the Internet. The proximity of the sect to Japanese defense authorities is not a coincidence. A company in connection with the sect also stole personal information from thousands of employees of a large corporation[41]. The sect, like any organization, uses the Internet to communicate with its members.

4.2.4.4. *Bringing down Japanese networks*

Five minutes. That's how long it would take for a blackout on Tokyo's information systems to paralyze half of the country's information systems. These are the conclusions of a study presenting a model of the interaction between information systems and social infrastructures presented in September 2004 by Ichiro Murase[42], a researcher with the Mitsubishi Research Institute (Tokyo) during a conference entitled "Critical Information Infrastructure Protection"[43].

4.3. Information warfare: a specific Japanese approach?

The Constitution of Japan (1947), called the Constitution for Peace, forces Japan (notably in its Article 9) to abandon the idea of war and bans it from having any war potential. Japan therefore has no army *per se*, but has self-defense forces which were, until 2006, under the responsibility of the Japan Defense Agency (JDA). Since January 2007, they are coordinated by a new Defense department.

---

41. *Nippon: who's your software guru?*, http://www.atimes.com/japan-econ/BC02Dh01.html, Asia Times, March 2, 2000.
42. Ichiro Murase, *Vulnerability Analysis of Information Systems*, http://www2.gwu.edu/~usjpciip/MuraseI.pdf, September 2004.
43. http://www2.gwu.edu/~usjpciip/.

The Constitution limits these self-defense forces to an exclusively defensive role. They can only engage in the case of an aggression against Japan, on Japanese soil. Furthermore, Japan is restricted by its alliance with the United States.

Under these conditions, developing an independent doctrine, to include information warfare and distinct from the United States, would be difficult. Because of the ban on any potentially aggressive war, any information warfare doctrine would lose its aggressive component and have to settle for defense.

According to a report from the Rand Corporation[44], the Japanese government showed a specific interest in information warfare in its awareness of the risks that this type of conflict would represent for the national and global economy, following the serious crisis of the Yen in 1998. After an investigation, the fall of the Yen (22% of its value lost in just two days) was thought to be caused by a Trojan horse created by Chinese and Asian criminal organizations. If these conclusions are true, it means that a software program could have more effect than policies, a crisis or a war. But should we take this interpretation of the crisis seriously?

Sugio Takahashi[45], a researcher at the National Institute of Defense Studies, addressed the Japanese definition of the concept of information warfare, compared to the American approach. For the Japanese, Libicki's definition seemed too wide, confusing the new role played by information-in-warfare in the revolution of ICTs and traditional information warfare, such as deception. The development of operational concepts from Libicki's approach turned out to be difficult. Takahashi prefers to speak of cyber defense or cyber strategy instead of information warfare.

From a Japanese standpoint, information warfare includes methods that are not only based on ICTs, for example human intelligence (Humint). Operation information is not only centered on ICTs, is not network-centric as the communication, relational, human and psychological component is vital. One of the examples consists of information operations conducted by Japanese troops during their operations in Samawah in Iraq. The units first collected intelligence on local communities to find out who was influential. Then the commanders contacted these influential members of the community and built relations with them. Information on insurgents came from these people. This is a good example of non-technological information operations. This non-technological approach can be as important to Japanese forces as information operations centered on networks or based on technology.

---

44. Roger C. Molander/Andrew S. Riddile/Peter A. Wilson, *Strategic Information Warfare – A New Face of War*, http://www.rand.org/pubs/monograph_reports/MR661/MR661.pdf, National Defense Research Institute, RAND, 1996.
45. Please see [TAK 04] from this author.

The role of the military in cyber security is relatively limited, settling for protecting its own networks. The military controls information operations, but there is no interference of skills with the civilian sector. The national police department, General Affairs Ministry and the office of the Prime Minister share the responsibility of civilian cyberspace security.

From a military standpoint, the revolution in military affairs built on the foundation of the revolution in information technologies generally provides tools for information warfare, for network warfare, and for cyber warfare and network-centric warfare.

In Japan, reflections on the implementation of a revolution in military affairs really took off in July 2000, when top management of the Japanese Defense Agency was given the responsibility for this operation[46]. The following year, the Defense Agency proposed a program covering the 2001–2005 period[47], focusing on the integration of networks inherent to each service to improve the operation and efficiency of C2 systems. The question of information systems security was also included in this plan.

The reports and programs involving the modernization of self-defense forces converge into several points:

– the necessity of preparing self-defense forces for the new challenges of security, future conflicts and conventional and non-traditional threats;

– the necessity of securing military networks[48];

– the necessity of improving the quality of C4ISR systems;

– the construction of a modern infrastructure for a network centric war, still with a defensive logic, connecting the information systems of the three self-defense forces: the "G-Net" system of ground forces, the C2 systems of the navy, and the "BUGE" system of the air force;

– the development of CNO methods and the combination of CNOs with other methods (for example, precision weapons). Operations on computer networks cannot decide the outcome of wars, but must complement conventional attacks. A measure of CNO capabilities of the most advanced countries in 2003 put Japan

---

46. Information Technology Revolution of JDA/SDF, August 2000.
47. Mid-Term Defense Program (FY2001–FY2005).
48. Yukiya Yamakura, Network Centric Warfare: its implications for Japan Self-Defense Force, August 2005.

(after Singapore) in 14th place, on an equal footing with France (the United States was first, Russia 20th, and China 43rd) [49];

– the ability to inflict serious damage over short periods of time;

– limiting collateral damage. The concern for the respect of human life has become a major issue;

– the expression "information warfare" is not used but all its components are listed:

- inherent capacities (and no longer only based on American information) of intelligence, surveillance, reconnaissance: including participation in the Echelon network, observation satellites, sensors (wartime sensors, peacetime sensors, military sensors, civilian sensors, all provide data that must be integrated, processed and is liable to feed information useful to C2s in times of conflict), EP-3 spy planes[50];

- real time information processing and analysis;

- calculation capabilities;

- electronic warfare;

- information assurance (cryptography);

- precision weapons.

49. Giampiero Giacomello, *Measuring Digital Wars: learning from the experience of peace research and arms control*, http://www.iwar.org.uk/infocon/measuring-io.pdf, October 2003.
50. *Revelations on long Japanese ears*, (in French), at:
www.zdnet.fr/actualites/imprimer/0,50000200,2090345,00.htm, 29 June 2001.

Chapter 5

Russia

5.1. Estonia–Russia: information warfare?

The news early in 2007 was marked by the announcement of a series of attacks against Estonian information systems and presented by the international press as an example of information warfare against Estonia by Russia.

5.1.1. *Reconstitution of facts*

We will try to group the most significant elements from information that was published on different online information websites. The following documents were chosen at random, the way an Internet user would search, surfing the net and moving from one site to another:

– an article entitled "Hackers deepen Estonia–Russia rift" from 17 May 2007[1], published on the Aljazeera website;

– an article entitled "The cyber pirates hitting Estonia" published 17 May 2007 on the BBC News website[2];

– an article entitled "Estonia recovers from massive denial-of-service attack" published 17 May 2007 on the InfoWorld website[3];

1. http://english.aljazeera.net/NR/exeres/4434AB7B-00C7-4140-8234-1043635907FC.htm.
2. http://news.bbc.co.uk/2/hi/europe/6665195.stm.
3. http://www.infoworld.com/article/07/05/17/estonia-denial-of-service-attack_1.html.

– an article entitled "Estonia blames hack attacks on Russia" published on the website http://p2pnet.net/story/12262;

– an article entitled "Cyber Attack Vexes Estonia, Poses Debate", published 18 May 2007[4];

– an article published 19 May 2005, entitled "Estonia calls for NATO cyber-terrorism strategy"[5].

What image can we construct of the events from these articles?

5.1.1.1. *The context*

A statue paying tribute to soldiers from the red army killed in the Second World War against nazism was taken away from Tallinn, capital of Estonia. Estonians see in the statue the symbol of Soviet occupation. The Russians, and especially the strong Russian community living in Estonia, perceived the statue's removal as an attack against Russia. The statue's removal was a pretext for the start of hostilities between the Russian and Estonian communities in Estonia.

Some say that the real reason for the tensions between the two countries was Estonia's blocking of the building of a pipeline to Germany.

5.1.1.2. *The facts*

The incident translated into riots on the streets of Tallinn.

Massive attacks were simultaneously launched in cyberspace:

– DDoS attacks were launched against Estonia's information systems. The targets were government, banks and private companies' websites;

– in the first days of the attacks, websites usually receiving 1000 visits per day suddenly received 2000 requests per second. Some sites overloaded within a half hour;

– over a million computers in the world were used to launch the attacks. These were botnets used to launch DDoS attacks. Computers from the United States, Canada, Brazil and Vietnam were used. The Estonian Information Technology Center, an agency monitoring the government's computer networks, declared that the cyber attacks came from all over the world, including Russia. According to the Estonian Minister of Defense, instructions in Russian on how to attack websites circulated over the Internet;

---

4. http://online.wsj.com/article/SB117944513189906904.html?mod=googlenews_wsj.
5. http://www.telegraph.co.uk/news/main.jhtml?xml=/news/2007/05/18/westonia18.xml.

– the attacks also included site defacements such as redirection of Internet users, Soviet soldier images, speeches from Martin Luther King and a false message from the Estonian Prime minister apologizing and promising that the statue would be returned to its original place;

– the attacks started on 27 April 2007 and lasted over two weeks, each wave of attack being stronger than the previous one.

5.1.1.3. *Impacts and reactions*

In the context of the Estonian riots, observers, public opinion and the Estonian authorities estimate that the attacks were the direct consequence of the deterioration of political relations between the two countries.

Russians were instantly accused, albeit discretely, of being the authors of these attacks against the Estonian government information systems:

– the Estonian Minister of Defense declared "we have identified in the first attacks IP addresses belonging to departments in the Russian government";

– the Estonian government did not prosecute the Russian authorities, but posted a list of IP addresses as the origin of the attacks. Some of these addresses belonged to the Russian government and the Presidential administration. But there were also many from other countries;

– the attacks were likened to a terrorist act by the Defense Department. Regardless of who the terrorists were, Estonia, as any country who depends on its information systems (e-government, 98% of transactions made over the Internet), took measures. Protection methods were insignificant so the Estonian government decided to block access to the websites that were attacked.

Estonia did not want to consider this massive aggression simply as a wave of cyber crime, for which a legal solution could be found. Because of the scope of the attack and given the country's inability to find solutions alone, and because it considered such a large-scale terrorist attack an act of war, Estonia requested the help of the international community. Aggressions in cyberspace took on a diplomatic dimension. NATO sent an expert to help Estonia face the attacks against its government's websites.

Why did NATO get involved? Because an attack against one of its members is an attack against the organization itself. The situation took an international political turn. The debate changed levels: it was no longer about finding delinquent individuals but about defining the responsibility of a government, triggering a completely new debate on the political situation, diplomatic relations and regional balances involving cyber attacks. This wave of cyber attacks must have made governments question their way of viewing these attacks in the context of international law, and consider what the appropriate response should be.

We must also consider that Russia has also often requested the support of the international community in its fight against cyber crime. Rashid Nurgaliyev, the Interior Minister, called for the world to combine forces to fight against criminal groups operating over the Internet during an international conference in Moscow in April 2006. According to the minister, cyber criminals can cause as much damage as weapons of mass destruction.

The question is "can a government be behind the attack"? In more general terms, the question may be "is it possible to prove that a government is the author of a cyber attack against another government?"

In the case of Estonia, finding proof seems difficult. For now, it is one word against another. Estonia implicated the involvement of the Russian government; the Kremlin formally denied the allegation. The argument for the defense is of course the opposite of the argument for the accuser: according to the Russians, the Kremlin's IP addresses had been the victims of IP spoofing.

In order to conduct these attacks, there is no need for government. The anti-Estonian feeling was developed and maintained by government propaganda and was expressed through articles, blogs, forums and the press. Hackers were immersed in this general feeling and acted accordingly. Even if the government was not directly involved, the anti-Estonian hysteria may have encouraged nationalist hackers. On the other hand, launching attacks is simple, but there needs to be some basic expertise. Virus scripts, source codes and ready-made solutions are found over the Internet. Thousands of budding hackers can launch efficient attacks.

5.1.1.4. *Events as written in the press*

Does reading random articles found on the Internet among hundreds of publications on the subject answer the questions "could a foreign nation be behind the attack? Can Russia be guilty?" The articles, because of their number and repetitive use of identical information, can only highlight the absence of conclusive elements. An infinite combination of the same basic elements, the "ingredients" in the information, however, does contribute to creating an opinion which may be completely false.

What are the common elements, what are the "ingredients" in these articles, what is being said and what is generally ignored? Do we have all the conclusive elements to confirm that it truly is information warfare? What should we conclude from Russia's position?

A few lines from the article "Hackers Deepen Estonia–Russia Rift" from 17 May 2007[6], published on the Aljazeera website, are interesting because in a single sentence it presents the way things generally related to network attacks are reported: "NATO has sent an expert to help Estonia fight attacks on government websites, which the defense minister has said the Russian government was possibly involved in":

– a victim was named, Estonia in this case;

– the act was addressed. Government websites were attacked. The term "attack" was used, implying an aggression on the government instead of simply hacking (cyber delinquency);

– a guilty party was named: the Russian government;

– there is a reference from a relevant source, made in good faith: the Defense Minister;

– but at the same time, there is a large amount of imprecision ("was possibly involved").

There are enough variables here to start a rumor: a victim, the act committed against the victim, a named guilty party and a source that is highly credible. But we also find lack of proof and sources, and yet a level of precision in the narration of the facts (from a technical point of view, what attacks were conducted, how many sites were affected, etc.). In fact, nothing in this article, or in any other, enables us to confirm or deny the involvement of the Russian government.

The articles also imply relations between the different players and events:

– a relation is established *a priori* between Estonia and Russia, because the context (the events) is greatly slanted that way. However, what attests to the Russian involvement with any certainty? Could the attacks not come from another country and still use Russian systems?

– a relation is also established *a priori* between "hackers" and the "Russian government". Could the hackers not have acted on their own, with no official link to the Russian government?

– a relation is established *a priori* between the riots and cyber attacks. There were riots and cyber attacks. What connects the two? Can there not be two simultaneous events without instant connection?

The way in which incidents were reported, written and handled also shows:

---

6. http://english.aljazeera.net/NR/exeres/4434AB7B-00C7-4140-8234-1043635907FC.htm.

– the importance of subjectivity in the definition and especially the qualification of the incidents: do journalists know what they are talking about (what is a DoS attack? what is site defacement?)? Do they have reliable sources? On what basis do they speak of "information warfare", and what are the irrefutable elements of proof needed to accuse Russia instead of another player?

– the importance that the preconceived image of Russia can have on observers, and in general of any other player. Russia is commonly perceived as a country where cyber criminality rules, it is a country attempting to destabilize its close neighbors, a hoodlum state. In parallel to the growth of networks and number of Russian users, the number of cyber crimes keeps increasing. Cyber crime has multiplied from 2001 to 2005. In 2003, The Interior minister recorded 7,052 cyber crimes committed via the internet, 13,713 in 2004 including 8,000 that were intrusions in information systems[7], 14,810 in 2005 and approximately 8,400 in the first six months of 2006[8]. This Russian cyber crime is raging all over the world;

– the predominant place of uncertainty, ignorance, conjecture and suppositions. Observers have a hard time trying to reconstitute real facts for lack of time or resources, or because of a lack of technical expertise. The different views probably include truths, lack of understanding, false assertions in good faith and false assertions in bad faith. But this confusion only confirms the extreme difficulty in making a real accusation against a possible attacker. This attacker takes advantage of the vague nature of the attacks, of the possibility of hiding behind a fake identity, or of the impossibility of proving without a doubt the real identity of the perpetrator, to implement his operations. The denial of allegations from the Kremlin is proof of this difficulty.

The question of IP address appropriation is complex in that either Russia was a victim of identity theft and is not responsible, or the addresses from the other systems in the world used in the attacks were appropriated by Russia, in which case, they would mask their identity behind other governments. If the IP address is Russian:

– the attacker could be the Russian government;

– the attacker could be a Russian, or a group of Russians, with no link to the government, or maybe even have a link with other governments who would benefit from the accusations made against Russia;

– the addresses could be appropriated and the attackers might not be Russian. Or they could be Russian and have launched attacks by stealing Russian IP addresses.

---

7. *Russia: Authorities warn of Cybercrime Epidemic*,
http://www.rferl.org/featuresarticle/2006/04/7d821779-4411-43d1-bf7b-d19743879df6.html,
20 April 2006.
8. http://www.crime-research.org/news/02.11.2006/2327/, 2 November 2006.

But if the IP address is not Russian, that does not mean that the perpetrator of the attack (or the sponsor) is not Russian! An independent Russian attacker could appropriate a foreign IP address, and the same goes for the government.

The events in Estonia raise questions, but the Estonian case is minor in comparison to the scope of the real problem, which is how to protect the global Internet infrastructure from attacks that, as with the viral attack in February 2007, can block a part of the world's Internet.

5.2. Doctrines and components of the "information warfare" concept

Suspicions, allegations and accusations against Russia raise several questions. Is Russia able today to start significant information warfare operations[9]? Is there an official doctrine to that includes these operations? Who could implement such operations?

In the 1990s, the Federal Agency for Government Communications and Information (FAPSI) identified five major components:

– electronic warfare;

– intelligence warfare (i.e. search for information from radio signals, satellites and radars through interception and decryption of information flows);

– hacker warfare (cyberwar);

– psychological warfare;

– collection and processing of open source information.

For the Foreign Intelligence Service (SVR), information warfare is achieving superiority of information by controlling the information resources of other governments (i.e. by banning access to their own resources, introducing data in these resources and manipulating those resources), by hindering the development of information and communication technologies in countries perceived as potential enemies (which obviously includes all neighboring countries no longer under Moscow rule, but it can also include the whole world), by destroying enemy networks and information systems, and by developing information weapons and solutions to ensure the security of its own information systems. The approach is totally aggressive, offensive but contains a defensive component.

---

9. In order to better understand the reflection on the impact of the Desert Storm campaign on the Russian doctrine and understanding future wars, please refer to [FIT 92].

5.2.1. *The development of the Russian military*

5.2.1.1. *Aggressiveness*

Information warfare is a conflict in the information space. It is mainly considered a form of military operation that must be under the responsibility of the Department of Defense. The Russian concept is aggressive and offensive. The idea is to control and, in order to succeed, to destroy, disorganize and damage. Information systems and information (attack of C2 systems, cyberwar consisting of the use of hacker techniques), and individuals, in their psychological and physical dimensions, are the target of this aggressiveness. In 2001, Sergei Ivanov [see BIL 04], Minister of Defense, defined information warfare as the series of actions taken by a country to damage the resources and information systems of another country while protecting its own infrastructure.

5.2.1.2. *Type of Cold War*

In its strategic dimension, information warfare is perceived as a type of Cold War[10]. Cold War is defined as the implementation in peacetime of counter-measures between two governments, such as counter-psyops and counter-intelligence. The Russian military extends information warfare methods into peacetime, in the same way as the Americans did with their concept of information operations in the 1990s. Extending operations into peacetime also means that the military does not work alone in information warfare missions. Intelligence agencies, for example, may have to act in this context, since their role is to carry out counter-intelligence actions and collect open or hidden information on any potential enemy.

Information warfare is not a substitute for other forms of warfare. It complements them even though it is sometimes perceived as a totally new form of warfare, as expressed by General N.A. Kostin[11], and can be conducted in peacetime and wartime.

The expression, Cold War, obviously brings back the threat of a nuclear war. The link between the two types of war was established when Russia said it would respond with nuclear power if it was a victim of an information warfare type attack [THO 00].

5.2.1.3. *Strike at the right time*

Intelligence and counter-intelligence activities provide information on potential enemies and help us protect our own information and information systems against

---

10. Dr V.I. Tsymbal, a Russian analyst.
11. Quoted in [THO 00].

the same type of attempts from our adversaries. This accumulation of information will be useful when the time comes to attack or defend ourselves.

We have to be able to strike at the best time, with a single, fatal, "cyber blow". This idea is close to that of the Chinese. But to be able to strike such a blow presumes that the "mapping" of enemy resources and information systems was done beforehand, in time of peace. In order for that to happen:

– the enemy's behavior and the reactions of the opposing cyberspace must be studied;

– to do this, the enemy must be tested by attacking him;

– there must be an investment in intelligence, long term;

– all operations must be planned very carefully;

– the enemy's access to any relevant information should be blocked;

– we must be able to penetrate enemy systems without being detected before the beginning of combat operations.

During the attack, the enemy must:

– be isolated and unable to access any information;

– be deprived of access to, and use of, their C2 systems (destruction), along with any information system receiving, processing and storing strategic information for the military. These attacks against C2s may affect the enemy's allies;

– be cut off from their own financial resources, for without financial resources defeat is almost inevitable. Access to financial resources must be prohibited;

– be subject to sustained psychological operations (misinformation and propaganda).

5.2.1.4. Challenges, objectives and targets

Information warfare must have specific objectives. It provides the means and methods to reach these objectives.

The challenge is to be able to influence the information resources of the enemy (Admiral Vladimir Semenovich Pirumov)[12] while protecting our own. This is the approach traditionally adopted in the definitions of the American model. Beyond this basic challenge lies a specific objective.

---

12. Quoted in [THO 98A].

Information warfare therefore remains only a means, like any other, to reach one or more objectives, and it is not a substitute for other forms of warfare.

Influencing the information resources of the enemy must enable us to achieve our first objective, which is reaching and maintaining an advantage over information in relation to the enemy,[13] to the benefit of our own C2s. C2s must have the best quality and most precise information possible. There is a common idea: see first, see better and act before the enemy. The objective then is clearly to improve our own capabilities to close the OODA cycle while disrupting the enemy's. The observation and orientation phases require work before the conflict, with intelligence (acquisition of information on the enemy and allied troops), information counter-measures (blocking the enemy's collection and processing of information), information defense measures, deception and information sharing between both levels of C2. A government can not think about the improvement of these two phases when a war is launched. The advantage acquired will then be made a reality in the decision and combat action. According to the Russians, countries with superiority of information are more liable to use military force than in the past.

This advantage over information must be acquired by aggressive methods. According to Colonel General Valery Manilov, Chief of Staff of the Russian army (1996–2001), information warfare is a fight within or between governments, which must use very aggressive methods to damage or completely destroy the information space of the enemy camp. The information space here is meant in a wide sense and not only military. All spheres of social activity are included in this expression and submitted to this informational influence. The possibility of conducting information warfare within a government must also be considered.

The challenge is controlling what Russians call the space, or environment, of information, defined as a very large whole, not completely military or civilian. It includes everything, it is the sum of all a government's databases, infrastructures and methods of collecting, processing and broadcasting data, i.e. infrastructures of telecommunications, networks, terminals and satellites, everything that enables the interaction between information and organizations and citizens, and the satisfaction of their needs in terms of information [YUS 97]. It is a space that includes all the players in a nation (individual citizens, corporations and government organizations), who act on information (collect it, process it, manage it, use it and exchange it) in a space that is more than just virtual. Networks, infrastructures and communicating tools are the physical space that makes up the backbone of this informational space enabling information flows (transmission, storage, processing, interpretation, displaying, representation and perception). This information space is therefore a single entity and is global. Information resources are the raw material of this space.

---

13. Colonel S.A. Komov, Russian military thinker.

They include all the data acquired, processed and stored in all human activities including science, economics, politics, culture and information received daily by citizens and the government. We speak of resources because this data, once stored, can be delivered anytime and anywhere depending on the needs and requests of their users.

Within this information space and information resources, sub-spaces and blocks of resources are identified and must be the subject of specific security. All infrastructures and all sets of information do not have the same degree of strategic importance. Government C2s or those of the military, financial and banking systems, transportation and energy infrastructures and alarm systems, all are vital infrastructures and should be protected by higher security. The Global security of the information space remains one of its major problems.

Rafael M. Yusupov, SPIIRAS Director[14] estimates that the two major threats to this space are espionage and information distortion, two actions that can occur during times of peace. Other threats were identified by the government: intelligence gathering, electronic warfare, systems intrusion, terrorism, cyber crime and psychological operations – a major concern – via possible operations from foreign groups against Russia, or from internal propaganda activities against the government. We must not forget human error in sensitive information systems. There is no perfect solution for real protection of this information space.

The information space and information resources are the two major principles in the Russian doctrine of information control and information warfare. Space is simultaneously the key structure of a government and the target chosen to disrupt the global balance of power of that government. The concept of information control extends to the global control of information space and all resources, even overflowing from a period of crisis and conflict into a period of peace. There is no major difference with the American ideology. Any information can be strategic and sensitive; the information environment is global and its control can be problematic, but it is a major, given, challenge. But the desire to meet this challenge has only surfaced in recent conflicts.

There are a number of examples of the way the notion of "control of information" was handled in the conflicts conducted by Russia in the last decade. During the Chechnya conflicts [CASS 93] after 1994, Russia confronted an enemy that also had cyberwar capabilities and could use its capacities to dominate the informational world. In the first Chechnya war (1994–1996), meant to restore Russian order, Russia's strategy in terms of dominance of the information space

---

14. St Petersburg Institute for Informatics and Automation of the Russian Academy of Sciences, www.spiiras.nw.ru/index.php?nawlang=english.

focused on banning the press from following and reporting the conflict in the national and international media. It hoped to control all the information entering and exiting the space of conflict. Instead, Chechens used the media to spread their message across the international community. Information warfare in this first phase took the form of psychological operations, operations to influence public opinion through the media. Whilst the Chechens learned the lesson from the war conducted by the Americans in the Gulf, the Russians apparently did not. Not simply for this reason alone, the first Chechen conflict resulted in a Russian failure, but it illustrates the possibility of a digitally weaker adversary holding a superior enemy in check (in an asymmetrical war) by avoiding symmetrical confrontations, frontal attacks and by using the enemy's weak spots to strike. The information space was one of the weak points of the Russians during this first conflict, and Russian public opinion was one of Chechnya's preferred targets. Nevertheless, the Russians were still able to use information technology methods during the war: in 1996, Dzhokhar Dudayev, the leader of the Chechen rebellion, was located by the Russians through a call he made from his satellite phone and killed by a precision guided bomb.

During the second conflict (1999–2000), officially motivated by the fight against anti-terrorism, the Russians used the lessons learned from the past and information became one of the major tools for manipulating international public opinion. That opinion had to be won over to the Russian cause by demonizing the enemy, justifying war for a just cause. Those who received the information were certainly not fooled by the possibilities of manipulation that existed then. However, in the context of the global chaos at the time, it was difficult for public opinion to work out what was real from what was false, especially since the questions could not be addressed in such clear-cut terms; that was too simple. True information can be taken out of context, false information can serve a true cause, and information can be partially true and partially erroneous. We also have to consider the moment when information is broadcast, the way in which it is presented, who broadcasts it, who receives it, how it is duplicated, broadcast, modified and integrated into the environment of global knowledge. From the beginning of the conflict, the Russians carried out psychological operations. Foreign embassies and international organizations received videos showing Chechen cruelty. For the objective of psychological operations and military deception, information must be controlled, whether by traditional media (radio, television) or over the Internet. Strict instructions were imposed on journalists covering the events (the instructions are published on the "infocentr.ru" website created in 1999 at the start of the conflict. A decree (resolution 1538) from 7 February 2000 reinforced the powers of the Federal Security Bureau (FSB) which can now legally control journalists' access to Chechnya. Psychological operations were combined with electronic warfare operations to intercept communications from the enemy. The Russians were finally able to control the security of radio communications which were the strength of the Chechens in the first war. FAPSI launched a large surveillance operation of radio communications in the North Caucasus called "Experiment 99". The observation satellites launched before the conflict (notably Tselina-2) were vital to this electronic war. They were used during communication interception, location, control, decrypting and disruption operations of Chechen communications. Information warfare extended to the internet, a major vector of psychological operations along with hacker warfare. For psychological operations, both camps used websites to communicate their versions of events and demonize the enemy. This included denunciation of crimes and an escalation of violence in images, the broadcasting of videos of civilian assassinations, the killing of children, torture of prisoners and summary executions. Pro-Chechen sympathizers[15] supported this cause and websites hosted on foreign ground (the qoqaz.net website, for example, based in Malaysia and used as a relay for Chechen propaganda) began to be found. The websites proposed media reports, showed images of victorious operations conducted against Russian troops and interviews with war leaders presented as heroes. Conscious of Russian network war capabilities, pro-Chechen websites had several mirror sites in the world (.com, .my, .de, etc.). The Russians created their own websites and also created confusion by introducing false pro-Chechen sites or pro-Russian sites with domain names very close to the names of Chechen sites. For example, the Russian website kavkaz.com created confusion with the Chechen site kavkaz.org. Psychological operations also used the contribution of interviews with pro-Russian Chechen leaders on antiterror.ru and chechnya.ru. Hacker warfare attempted to paralyze enemy websites. Russian agencies were accused by Chechnya of attacking and paralyzing their kavkaz.org and chechenpress.com websites. After the official end of the conflict, the websites still exist[16], are still active, and support attacks (DoS attacks against servers). When pro-Chechen websites are attacked, they blame the Russian authorities[17].

In a more general way, and beyond the Chechen question, controlling information circulating in networks is a very significant problem for Russia, which is very sensitive to the possibilities of psychological manipulation of opinion. In 2006, Russia had close to 40 ultranationalist and extremist websites, a quarter of which operated from Russian providers. Ultranationalist sites and very active neo-Nazi sites ("web skinheads") operate freely using the Internet to coordinate their operations, maintain contacts between members throughout the country, and recruit new sympathizers.

---

15. kavkaz.org.
16. http://kavkazcenter.com/.
17. http://www.kavkazcenter.com/eng/content/2006/09/27/5731.shtml.

5.2.2. *Intellectual information warfare*

Control of psychology is a major component in the concept of Russian information warfare [BIL 04]. The objective of information warfare remains the acquisition and control of information, to gain an advantage in terms of information on the enemy. This objective is reached by exerting psychological influence on a government's decision systems, a system that includes decision-makers, all C2 players and the general population (operations of influence, as the Americans would say). This psychological warfare built around psychological operations covers actions such as deception, propaganda and misinformation of populations, armies and authorities. The objective is to distort the action phase in the OODA loop by disrupting the observation, orientation and decision phases. In order to do that, the opinions, intentions and decisions of all the players from both sides of a war must be influenced; this includes the enemy and our own camp.

5.2.2.1. *Russia as target of psychological operations*

Even though Russia is developing its offensive psychological warfare capabilities, it must also pay close attention to defensive capabilities. According to studies and reports published in Russia in the last few years, Russian society would be particularly vulnerable to psychological operation attempts launched by enemies.

This vulnerability comes from the cultural, ideological, political and economic shock that disrupted Russian society in the early 1990s, when the Soviet empire collapsed. The balance of the whole social model was in upheaval, starting a period of uncertainty and reassessment, making the population very sensitive to new ideas and to temptations from the West unknown until then. Thus, any information warfare conducted against Russia would attempt to capture this consciousness and undermine the morale of armed forces[18] in order to prepare for a real ideological invasion, to take control of the country's economic and political sectors. If we adopt this point of view, any country that is an ally can be a potential adversary; alliances are no longer possible and there is only one country against the world. The officer proposing this point of view on the dangers of information operations accused psychological warfare activities conducted by countries hostile to Russia of being the cause of all the country's woes. The psychological confrontation therefore becomes the main component of information warfare since it is the vector of the most strategic attacks. Russians call this psychological confrontation "psychological warfare" or "intellectual information warfare".

---

18. Colonel E.G. Korotchenko, in an article published in the review "La Pensée Militaire" in February 1996.

5.2.2.2. *Components and methods of intellectual warfare*

A permanent psychological confrontation mandates intelligence actions (the collection and analysis of information involving the capabilities of all potential enemies), to predict (from processed data) the nature of psychological operations that enemies or adversaries could conduct, and to evaluate the impact that such psychological operations could have on our own camp. This allows us: to adopt active, or even preemptive, defense measures to counter or prevent psychological aggression; to imagine solutions to neutralize the negative consequences of the influence of these psychological operations on the psyche of individuals in times of peace and times of conflict, and; to prepare forces (psychological information operations units) to conduct offensive psychological operations in times of crisis and conflict, as well as permanent operations on target populations in times of peace.

The Russian military certainly did not discover psychological operations in 1990 during the Desert Storm campaign! The possibility of manipulating the psyche of enemy troops has long interested Russia's military and its researchers. In fact, mind manipulation is the subject of the conditioned control theory developed by Ivan Pavlov, a 1904 Nobel prize winner. According to him, propaganda produced a subconscious association of ideas, which makes it possible to manipulate minds. What is the impact of psychological operations on the military and on civilians? How can we use information manipulation to affect the reasoning, values, emotions, beliefs, behaviors, decisions and actions of individuals or groups of individuals? How can we efficiently deceive the enemy, distract his judgment, divide, dissuade, suggest and pressure him? How can we affect the enemy's resistance capabilities? All these are objects of study interesting to the Russian military. Russians speak of "maskirovska" to describe deception and misinformation operations aimed at manipulating individual perceptions. We also speak of reflexive control to describe operations to influence decisions by manipulation of information.

Different actions can be launched against the psychological capabilities of individuals in order to affect their judgment, decision process and their behavior:

– Distraction, consisting of creating new real or imaginary threats to force the enemy to reexamine his decisions, changes his strategy or tactic, for example reviewing the allocation of resources or repositioning of troops. This operation is intended to force the adversary to make a decision that is detrimental to his camp.

– Overloading is a method consisting of saturating the enemy or adversary with a large volume of contradictory information. The possibilities offered by information systems facilitate overloading. It is possible to create contradictory information and send it through the multiple communication vectors within the information space (Internet websites, e-mail or saturating radars). This possibility shows how difficult it is to provide C2s with necessary, relevant, quality information, at the right time.

– Paralysis consists of selecting the main weaknesses of the target, developing the target's awareness of such weaknesses, and making the target believe that a threat might be able to use such weaknesses.

– Exhaustion consists of multiplying false targets, dispersing the enemy so that he engages in useless operations and launches actions with, if not exhausted, at least depleted, resources.

– Deception consists of misleading the enemy to make him take unfavorable decisions, reallocating his forces to the wrong place, for example.

– Division is intended to deceive the enemy into thinking that he must act against the interests of his allies or coalition troops. The objective is to isolate the enemy, make him be the one making a decision which will isolate him irrevocably, so that allied forces eventually have to confront each other, representing an economy of resources for their enemies.

– Pacification is a type of ruse, aimed at making the enemy drop his vigilance through a peaceful attitude. Pacification could take the form of cooperation, or exchanges with "partners" that we consider attacking. Pacification is maintaining that we are implementing strictly defensive methods, while we know that they can be used offensively. It is the famous argument of "nuclear power with strictly civilian purposes".

– Dissuasion is used to create an impression of superiority. The nuclear bomb is a dissuasion weapon par excellence. In cyberspace, dissuasion could be the threat of network attack capabilities through the use of an impressive arsenal of viruses. It is not as important to be superior as much as it is to give the impression that we are.

– S.A. Komov, the Russian military thinker, adds provocation to this list: leading the enemy to carry out actions unfavorable to themselves. This might consist of offering information affecting the enemy in a legal, moral, ideological or any other way; and of applying pressure, consisting of offering information encouraging society to discredit its own government.

5.2.3. *Control of an individual's physical dimensions*

The human, in his physical and psychological dimensions, is the major target that we want to affect in a conflict, with the help of methods offered by the capabilities of new technological weapons. These weapons include informational weapons, able to modify the psychology and behavior, as well as physical capabilities. Information warfare can in fact be intended to control the capacities of the human body.

Considering the human body as a data processor, a system of sensors and processors, it can, as with any technical system, be the subject of different manipulations, made easier as this system does not have protection [THO 98A]. The sensors and processors are hearing, seeing and the nervous system. The body is an open system permanently collecting data, processing it and storing it. We can imagine actions of manipulation, destruction, distortion of data and the processing system for this data, but can also imagine modifying the physical environment. Based on these assumptions, would it be possible to consider introducing "psycho-viruses" in this complex information system? Could a computer send out waves able to modify the behavior of its user? This type of study is being carried out at the Bauman Technical Institute in Moscow[19] by Dr Victor Solntsev.

5.3. Potential players of information warfare

Information warfare carried out in peacetime and in wartime involves the players responsible for security and national defense including intelligence agencies and the army. But it also involves hackers.

5.3.1. *Government agencies*

Following the failed coup against Mikhail Gorbachev, the KGB (Committee for State Security) was dismantled in 1991 into several independent security departments, one of which was the Federal Agency for Government Communications and Information (FAPSI).

This agency was the equivalent of the American NSA and its missions were to ensure the security of the State's encrypted communications, the protection of the government's websites against hacking and electronic intelligence (interception of encrypted communications and cryptanalysis) from its three centers spread over the Russian territory. From 1995, it had control over cryptography systems and was the only agency with the authority to grant licenses. More globally, it was responsible for all encrypted communications. It often unsuccessfully tried to gain control of the Internet.

During its operation, it collected, processed and stored large volumes of data in all sectors of social activity: political, economic, legal, financial and industrial. These resources were distributed between the Federal Security Bureau (FSB) and Defense Ministry after FAPSI was dismantled in March 2003.

---

19. www.bmstu.ru.

The FSB is Russia's secret police, born out of the ex-KGB. It inherited from FAPSI all activities involving telephone communications, mobile telephony, Internet, government secure communications, control of the system of electronic transmissions of election results (the "Vybory" system) and cryptography and encryption activities.

The FSB is considered to be the second most important army formation outside of the military itself.

5.3.2. *The military*

For Russia, the Desert Storm campaign was the confirmation of their predictions of the growing power of the American military, and of the capabilities now available to the military that chooses transformation by the introduction of information and communication technologies. That campaign paved the way for a new era, the era of wars based on information control. The Russian army also had to focus its efforts and reflection on the capabilities of information warfare, knowing that it did not have the same (financial) resources as the United States, especially since the country was not in a favorable period for investing in the military sector[20].

The war in Kosovo (1999) was perceived as the first contactless war, a virtual war during which superiority of information benefiting NATO ensured victory. Russia was not able to compete with the United States or with NATO forces. Because it was in a situation of technological inferiority, it could only rely on the asymmetrical option, notably asymmetrical information warfare. Solutions needed to be developed to affect the Achilles heel of greater military powers, disrupting the enemy's OODA cycle.

Modernization of armies is based on the creation of an integrated information environment, a single military standards system to transmit data. In January 2000, President Putin announced that from now on Russia had to increase the development of new high-tech weapons.

Is Russia very behind in terms of information warfare capabilities, by comparison to the West? That is not the conclusion of a report from the American Defense Science Board[21] which says that, on the contrary, Russia's information warfare capabilities are very high and include defensive cyberwar capabilities, development of software weapons (viruses able to break through IS security, to propagate and to defend themselves; reprogrammable memory chips, Trojan horses

---

20. See [FIT 94].
21. www.acq.osd.mil/dsb/reports.htm.

and remote attack tools), the development of electronic warfare capabilities (radars, jamming devices and espionage), hacking to steal information, development of guided weapons and electromagnetic power (EMP) anti-satellite weapons, more precise modern satellites, navigation equipment for soldiers, reconnaissance systems, automated air force control systems and C2 systems for nuclear strategic forces. The list is not complete but Russia is working on the development of specific methods for each component of information warfare.

5.3.3. *Hackers*

There are not many certainties in this field. The idea that a government can attack another government and that this aggressor uses hackers is based on assumptions, or even allegations.

Whether these hackers are part of the armed forces or of the secret services, or that they are paid "by the task", is irrelevant in the end. What is important is the threat, the aggression and the aggressor. Recently, the finger was pointed at Russia by the international community, not only because the whole planet sustained attacks from its spammers and other cyber delinquents for financial gain, but also for its "espionage campaigns" conducted against sensitive websites, as denounced by the United States. In February 1998, the Solar Sunrise affair emerged. Hackers penetrated the networks of the American Department of Defense. The guilty party named was Russia. An investigation revealed that in fact, it was two American teenagers living in California! In 2000, the Americans discovered that a wide espionage campaign begun in 1998 (and called "Moonlight Maze") affected 2 million computers in the United States. The Pentagon, NASA, the Energy Department, private universities and research laboratories, private American cryptography tools development companies, and the command center of space and naval war systems (Spawar) in San Diego were some of the victims. After investigation, Russia and the Moscow Science Academy were accused of involvement. But who were the sponsors? Was the Russian government involved? If so, at which level? The main characteristic of these network attacks is that it is extremely difficult to get to the real source of the aggression. The events in Estonia are nothing new; the questions that they raise today could have been raised a long time ago.

5.4. The Russia–Georgia conflict: new information warfare?

The *Ghost Recon* video game starts in 2008 with civilian problems in Russia. Ultranationalists have taken over power in Moscow and want to restore the Iron Curtain. Their first action is to secretly support rebellious factions in Georgia and in the Baltic States. During the first missions in the game, *ghosts* must fight against rebels from the North and South Ossetia regions in Georgia, who are harassing the legitimate government and its allies, as related in the Wikipedia[22] scenario of the *Ghost Recon* video game[23], distributed in 2001. In 2008, reality seems to have partially caught up with fiction. Trying to understand and analyze this armed conflict between Russia and Georgia as objectively as possible, with its complex international geopolitical and strategic stakes, has become all the more difficult as a strong information fog clouds the landscape. There was strong mention of information, misinformation and even information warfare in this conflict in the international media as well as from the authorities of both warring countries. There was a war of communications, propaganda and operations of influence. Information-in-warfare has always played a vital role. There were also cyber attacks in which both parties were victims. According to observers and direct players, cyberwar invited itself to the conflict, though denounced by the official political speech. These cyber attacks therefore should be analyzed, as should the civilian or military operations, to question their nature, origin and their place in the conflict.

5.4.1. *Operations in Russian and Georgian cyberspace*

From 8 August 2008, the date that we will use as the start of military hostilities for simplification purposes, many Georgian websites were defaced or paralyzed, their servers cracking under the weight of DDoS attacks. Amongst the sites affected from this date and during the following week, we find[24]:

– President Mikhail Saakashvili's website;[25]

– Foreign Affairs ministry;[26]

– The Parliament;[27]

– Ministry of Defense;[28]

– The National Bank of Georgia;[29]

– Rustavi2 television station;[30]

---

22. http://fr.wikipedia.org/wiki/Tom_Clancy's_Ghost_Recon., Video Trailer: http://www youtube.com/watch?v=7FTzbT99-KI.
23. Developed by Red Storm Entertainment.
24. Incomplete list.
25. www.president.gov.ge.
26. http://www.mfa.gov.ge/.
27. http://www.parliament.ge/.
28. http://www.mod.gov.ge/.
29. http://www.nbg.gov.ge/.
30. http://www.rustavi2.com.ge/.

– sosgeorgia.org (since then, the website has a flag to inform Internet users that it is the subject of massive attacks from Russian hackers)[31].

Georgia was not the only one affected by these website hacking operations however. The following websites were also hacked[32]:

– the skandaly.ru information website;

– the website Russian press agency RIA-Novosti;[33]

– The Russia Today information website;[34]

– South Ossetia information websites, osinform.ru and osradio.ru, where pages were replaced by those of the Georgian information agency Alania TV;

– stopgeorgia.ru;[35]

– Abkhazia government website.[36]

Georgian ISPs (Caucasus On-Line and GRENA[37]) started filtering the Internet (after a government request?) to block Russian websites, as a defensive measure, in the context of the state of emergency announced by the government.

We will not include a chronological table of attacks, because it would only be useful if all the facts were listed. A partial list would only show a false representation of the tempo of aggressions and classification of targets, information vital to the search of a possible attack/counter-attack type relation. On the other hand, such a chronological representation would not be satisfied with the analysis of facts that only occurred during the few days of the armed conflict. For example, were the attacks recorded against the Georgian President's website on 20 July 2008 and against osinform.ru and osradio.ru on 5 August early warning signs?[38]

---

31. On 12 September 2008 the text said "During the last three days we have sustained massive DDoS attacks. The degree of these cyberwar attacks is unprecedented and it is possible that they will continue and maybe intensify [...] it is not only an attack against our website, but war against all those who speak about the Kremlin [...]".
32. Incomplete list.
33. http://en.rian.ru/russia/20080810/115936419-print.html.
34. http://www.russiatoday.com/news/news/28835.
35. http://stopgeorgia.ru not to be confused with the stoprussia.org website, a pro Georgian site proposing an online petition against Russian actions.
36. http://abkhazia.gov.ge.
37. Georgian Academic and Research Network.
38. DDoS attacks targeted the Web.Caucasus.net server (62.168.168.9) hosting the President's website, as well as other Georgian websites such as Social Assistance and Employment State Agency (www.saesagov.ge). It is impossible to confirm that the Georgian President's website. was specifically targeted. The attack would have come from (or gone through) the 79.135.167.22 server located in Turkey, also used to attack Georgia's parliament website.

5.4.2. *The introduction of "cyberwar" and "information warfare" in the conflict*

Georgia's Ministry of Foreign Affairs published a few unequivocal lines on its blog[39] indicating that "a cyberwar campaign organized by Russia seriously disables numerous Georgian websites, including the Ministry of Foreign Affairs website. If you cannot access the Georgian government's official websites, please go to the following websites that will provide you the latest official information from the government of Georgia: http://georgiamfa.blogspot.com, the website of the President of the Republic of Poland, Lech Kaczynski www.president.pl (please click on the link 'information on the latest developments in Georgia')"[40]. The post is titled "Cyber attacks paralyze Georgian websites".

The website of Poland's President also states that "parallel to military aggression, the Russian Federation blocks Georgian Internet portals". It is to help Georgia, and at the request of Mr. Saakashvili, that the President of the Republic of Poland[41] agreed to make his own website available to broadcast information from the Georgian government[42].

The theory of massive attacks coordinated by Russia against Georgian information systems was relayed and supported by the words of Thomas R. Burling, manager of the American Tulip System host (a small company with a CEO, Nino Doijashvili, who is a Georgian expatriate): "We have accepted to host the President's website because Russian hackers paralyzed Georgia's Internet"[43]. The company also hosts other Georgian websites, including rustavi2 television[44].

"Information warfare" is the *raison d'être* of the very much talked about pro-Russia hacker website, stopgeorgia.ru. The site came live on 9 August 2008 and denounced information warfare operations from Georgia. It was mainly focused on

---

39. http://georgiamfa.blogspot.com/2008/08/cyber-attacks-disable-georgian-websites.html.
40. From 11 August 2008.
41. Remember that President Kaczynski was one of the parties involved in the liberation of Poland from Soviet rule. This hosting must be interpreted as an expression of the solidarity of Poland with Georgia. The fight of both countries is similar: the fight for freedom and democracy. Please see article http://www.latimes.com/news/nationworld/world/la-fg-media20-2008aug20,0,693386.story.
42. http://www.president.pl/x.node?id=479.
43. http://www.theregister.co.uk/2008/08/14/russia_georgia_cyberwar_latest/.
44. http://www.ajc.com/business/content/printedition/2008/08/17/tulip.html.

operations against enemy cyberspace and proposed a list of Georgian websites that must also be targeted [45].

Cyberwar and information warfare have penetrated official political views in wartime vernacular.

5.4.3. *Comments on "cyber attacks"*

5.4.3.1. *Media fad*

It is on the basis of these few official declarations and scant information relative to cyber attacks that, all of a sudden and all over the world, convinced they could see the premise of a revolutionary conflict, people in the press, on websites, in forums and blogs, used and developed this idea of cyberwar, of information warfare mercilessly fought between enemies.

Without irrefutable proof, mostly listening to their own opinions, admitting to taking the easy way out, succumbing to their fantasies, copying what others probably copied and relaying the official government speeches, hundreds of people all over the web have published their own "analyses" of the Russia–Georgia cyber conflict, proposing a vision of reality that reflects their own convictions, denouncing everyone in Russia (the military, government, intelligence services, organized crime – including the famous cyber crime network RBN[46]), in Georgia, the United States, Israel, Turkey, NATO, the real hackers, hackers in training, hacktivists, etc. The same information, for several weeks, turned around in circles without leading to a convincing analysis since the situation seemed to be so confusing.

The media frenzy in 2008 is a reminder of the one in 2007 during the famous "Russian cyber attacks against Estonia".

5.4.3.2. *The impact of cyber attacks*

Attacks against systems (telecommunications systems, networks, the Internet, etc.) that enable the transmission of official information occurred at the worst possible moment for Georgia, in the middle of the military engagement. They affected the most symbolic websites. We affect power when we attack the website of a President, a Parliament, a Ministry or a National Bank, and we affect freedom of speech, or even transfer power, when we attack the websites of some media. To deprive a government of its resources is limiting its communication capabilities,

---

45. http://stopgeorgia.ru/?pg=tar.
46. Russian Business Network. See http://www.zataz.com/news/17611/russe--georgie--conflit--geogia--russian--cyber-blocking.html.

isolating it, keeping it from seeing and being seen. But this was not the case completely. Georgia found relays, allies and alternative solutions. Its informational space was not cut off from the rest of the world. In addition to the Georgian government's websites being hosted in the United States and Poland, Estonia offered to host the websites of the Foreign Affairs Ministry, the National Bank and the Georgian Civilian portal[47].

Beyond the purely symbolic aspect of the targets involved, did these attacks really have a purpose, or give the cyber attacker a significant nuisance power? Similar attacks were recorded in Russia and Georgia before the conflict and will be recorded again after. What, then, was the added value of these operations in wartime? The texts displayed on the defaced websites do not convey any message on the inter-state conflict, on the events, on tests of strength, or on the way the action was supposed to influence the course of the war; they are non informational. The cyber attacker hiding behind those DDoS attacks and defacements reveals nothing about himself or the form of threat that he plans to use against either of the belligerents.

The attacks against information systems probably had a very limited impact on the capabilities of Georgia, because of its relatively low dependence on information systems. In fact, the network/telecommunications infrastructures of Georgia are not among the most well developed, national infrastructures are not as well linked as they are in the most advanced industrialized countries, and the population is not widely connected. Even though they are often questionable (what method was used, how were the measures defined, etc.), most indices and international classifications measuring the degree of development of nations in terms of networks, telecommunications and Internet agree on positioning Georgia among the worst students in the world. With a population of 4.6 million[48], and with only 7.49% of them being Internet users (2006 statistics)[49], the country is ranked 93rd out of 122 in the Network Readiness Index[50], behind Mongolia, Tanzania and Moldova. Estonia is in 20th position and the United States in 7th. If we refer to the series of indices published on the INSEAD website[51], Georgia is far from these model countries in terms of development of infrastructures and information and communication services. It is 100th in the E-Participation Index[52] which measures the quality and

47. "Estonia hosts Georgian websites after cyber attacks."
http://www.russiatoday.com/news/news/29544
48. July 2008, estimation https://www.cia.gov/library/publications/the-world-factbook/geos/gg.html.
49. http://www.insead.edu/v1/gitr/wef/main/analysis/showcountrydetails.cfm.
50. As stated by the World Economic Forum 2006-2007
http://www.weforum.org/pdf/gitr/rankings2007.pdf.
51. http://www.insead.edu.
52. Global Information Technology Report 2007-2008, http://www.insead.edu/v1/gitr/wef/main/analysis/showdatatable.cfm?vno=9.13&countryid=340

information effort made on government websites, and the services and online tools available for citizens. Georgia is ranked the same as Syria, Namibia and Burundi who are not necessarily recognized for their high level of ICT development. The "ICT Use and Government Efficiency" classification[53] (which measures the level of ICTs used by governments to facilitate interaction with citizens) positions Georgia in 96th position; Russia is 95th and Estonia is in 2nd position. The "Accessibility of public online services" classification[54] places Estonia in first position, Russia in 92nd and Georgia in 112th. The classification from the ITU[55] based on the bandwidth measure for 10,000 residents puts Russia in 73rd position and Georgia in 105th position out of 127 [56].

Even though Russia is only 70th in the Network Readiness Index[57] and 82nd for the E-Participation Index (equal to Lesotho, Mali or Kazakhstan!), it still has 18% of Internet users over a population of 140 million[58], has an oversized army compared to Georgia and obviously superior information warfare means.

The impact of an attack against information systems on a population and the organization of government services is not as immediate and profound for Georgia as it would be in the case of an attack against a country that is well connected.

On the other hand, if there was an impact on websites, it could be positive. The "publicity" created surrounding these attacks made these websites gain in popularity. Who, before these attacks, was curious enough to surf the website of the Georgian President?

But the defacement of some sites, as official as they may be, clearly cannot decide victory or defeat. Could these attacks have actually favored Georgia internationally by reinforcing its image as a victim?

5.4.3.3. *Cyber attacks before and after the conflict*

Attacks against information systems are not only focused on the conflict period; they also preceded the conflict. During the previous weeks, the Georgian President's website was already targeted, apparently from 20 July 2008[59]. The tensions between both countries have lasted for a long time, and the conflict was only an attempt

---

53. http://www.insead.edu/v1/gitr/wef/main/analysis/showdatatable.cfm?vno=9.11&countryid=340
54. http://www.insead.edu/v1/gitr/wef/main/analysis/showdatatable.cfm?vno=9.1&countryid=340
55. International Telecommunications Union. http://www.itu.int/net/home/index.aspx
56. http://www.insead.edu/v1/gitr/wef/main/analysis/showdatatable.cfm?vno=7.2&countryid=340
57. As stated by the World Economic Forum 2006–2007.
http://www.weforum.org/pdf/gitr/rankings2007.pdf
58. https://www.cia.gov/library/publications/the-world-factbook/geos/rs.html
59. http://www.shadowserver.org/wiki/pmwiki.php?n=Calendar.20080720
 and http://mypetjawa.mu.nu/archives/193591.php

through violence to solve the existing problem. As with any crisis situation, there were manifestations of the crisis in cyberspace during the previous months and years.

Cyber attacks then became part of the conflict, "accompanied it" as some would say. A few weeks after the military conflict, cyber attack announcements became rare. There is no reason to think that these attacks will not happen again; no real solution was found, no definite agreement between Russia and NATO was ever reached. All the conditions are there for the cyberspace confrontation to continue. But it seems that the vague attempts of hackers have slowed down after 15 August 2008. Be that as it may, if cyber attacks persist, there may not be as many people willing to report them as when all media attention was captured during the week of 8 August. Other CNAs[60] will probably happen in this crisis and in the post-conflict tension phase. Regardless of the reasons for this apparent decrease of cyber attacks, it will be interesting to take a step back and observe the volumes of attacks pre and post armed conflict.

5.4.3.4. *The impossible effect of surprise*

Similar actions (DDoS attacks, defacements) have been reported for a long time, in all countries of the region, as everywhere else in the world, especially where crises and conflicts are developing: between China and the United States, Japan and China, Russia and Chechnya, Malaysia and Indonesia, Israel and Palestine, etc. In April 2008, groups broadcasting pro-Kosovo propaganda defaced Albanian websites, and circulated lists of Albanian Internet website to target. In June–July 2008, 300 Lithuanian websites were defaced (with anti-Lithuanian slogans and Soviet flags[61]) following the adoption of a law banning public display of symbols dating from the Soviet era, or playing of the Soviet national anthem[62]. The recurrence of the phenomenon is such that Georgian or Russian authorities cannot invoke the effect of surprise in a context of extreme tension between both countries. There have been similarities in the processes, in the techniques used, in the logic (in a context of crisis and conflict), as well as in the nature of the targets: the website of the Georgian President was affected in July and August 2008, whilst in October 2007 the Ukrainian President's website[63] was also the subject of DDoS attacks[64]. In the United States, the Pentagon is constantly one of the major targets of all hackers worldwide. Political websites, as symbols of power, are obviously targets of choice.

---

60. Computer Network Attacks.
61. "Pro-Russian cyber-attack hits Lithuania". June 30, 2008.
http://www.mywire.com/pubs/AFP/2008/06/30/6809382.
62. Lithuania joined NATO and EU in 2004.
63. http://www.ukrainianjournal.com/index.php?w=article&id=5483 October 2007.
64. "Russian hackers cripple Yushchenko website". 30 October 2007.
http://www.ukrainianjournal.com/index.php?w=article&id=5483.

On the other hand, confrontations in the information space are not related to time or only limited to wartime. Information attacks[65] have been the subject of squabbles between South Ossetia and Georgia for a long time. An article published on the www.Civil.ge website on 14 January 2006, "S. Ossetia calls Tbilisi to Stop 'Information War'"[66], denounced information campaigns aimed at maligning the President of South Ossetia. The "information warfare" dimension, regardless of the components implemented, is part of the landscape of international relations. The element of surprise, therefore, cannot be invoked in this war situation. What can be emphasized, however, remains the state of helplessness against such operations, regardless of the author. How and why do the security systems of a government let themselves get overloaded by widely predictable cyber attacks?

The awareness of new deals in terms of information security and information systems exists in Georgia, since it is formulated in official texts, notably in the "National Security Concept of Georgia"[67], published on the web pages of the Defense Ministry site, specifically dealing with the question of information security in points 4.10 and 5.10:

– "4.10 – Information Related Challenges: Georgian national security may be put at risk because of the absence of a cohesive national information policy, weakness of infrastructure implementing such policy [...]. In addition, the existence of an unsatisfactory classified information protection system, the possibility of illegal access to state information systems with the purpose of acquiring or destroying information, and a likelihood of conducting large scale information attacks on Georgia from outside countries represent serious challenges to national security".

– "5.10 – Information Security Policy. [...] Georgia attributes considerable importance to the protection of classified information, legal regulation of security of information technologies, and protection of the critical information systems of the state. [...] the Georgian government is developing the legislative basis and infrastructure necessary for the improvement of the information technologies and secure flow of information. A Special Communications and Information Agency under the oversight of the National Security Council has been established. The establishment of the crisis management center with a situation room is under way at the National Security Council to facilitate unimpeded flow of information during the crises, inter-agency coordination and coordinated management of crisis or emergency".

---

65. Not only in "cyberspace", but also in the information space, in its totality.
66. http://www.civil.ge/eng/article.php?id=11511.
67. http://www.mfa.gov.ge/.

The awareness of the importance of the role of information space on security and national defense expressed in these few lines does not go so far as the definition of a real information warfare doctrine, or the outline of a security strategy.

In this text, we note:

– the assertion of a defensive attitude; nothing mentions the need or will to implement explicitly aggressive processes and structures;

– the awareness of the threat that superiority of information of potential enemies may represent;

– the identification of information warfare threats: CNA ("intrusions", "large scale attacks"…), ISR ("classified information", "illegal access"…), etc.;

– a methodology that gives the government control in terms of security and defense, but that does not seem to partner with the private sector (the text is probably too short to offer this direction).

5.4.3.5. *Unidentified authors*

Even though the attacks against Georgian and Russian information systems are part of the conflict, the identity of the (guilty) authors of these acts remains difficult to confirm. It would appear that accusing the direct enemy is legitimate, as the Georgian government is doing. The reality may be more complex but the accuser does not really have to worry about the validity of his comments, or the verification of the facts. The accusation must serve political, ideological and partisan interests.

The servers involved were in Russia, Turkey and the United States… Beside the military or governments, we could reasonably think that hackers driven by a patriotic feeling (hacktivists) were involved:

– Who is the famous "South Ossetia Hack Crew" claiming the defacement of the Georgian Parliament's website that nobody has ever heard about? Who is behind the "FeDeRer & Terrorists" signature claiming the defacement of the Interior Affairs Ministry police.ge on 5 August 2008? Who is "P47RICK" signing the defacement of the http://saagento.security.gov.ge website? Or who is SinqRonize, the author claiming responsibility for a simple "NO WAR! Fuck Russia:) For Türkiye…" the defacement which appeared on kavkazblog.com? Even if they are "signed", these actions remain anonymous because the signatures are worthless. They can hide an individual or a group; several signatures can hide a single individual, etc.

– Must we speak of Russian or Georgian actions? It is impossible to get precise information about the real identity of the authors of such CNAs.

5.4.3.6. *In the image of Nazism*

Defacements have mainly consisted of replacing official pages by photomontages associating the image of the Georgian President to Hitler. Such images are found on the Flickr.com website[68] and several forums in which there is not really a debate but rather where a bunch of scathing insults are exchanged. The war.georgia.su website, which denounces Georgian misinformation with videos as proof, presents the Georgian President as a Nazi. Saakashvili is said to use the same methods as the Nazis, wear the same clothes, etc. The website demonizes the enemy: "They have pity for no one, killing women, children and older people ... the wounded were struck with bayonets... some were burned alive in their homes...". A "genocide", a "holocaust" was committed, 3% of the population was decimated in one night, etc. Russian troops are presented as peacekeeping forces, Georgian operations as war crimes. This demonization has many effects including putting an enemy out to pasture in front of international opinion to weaken him, tarnishing his image, and clearly justifying the demonizer's own actions as well. Against enemies fearing neither God nor man, without morals, is everything not allowed? Hacker operations even seem legitimate, without even any questioning of the morals and legitimacy of their action.

Associating the image of authorities to 20th Century dictators is not peculiar to the Russian–Georgian conflict. There have been associations made of the images of Hitler and Mussolini to George W. Bush[69], of Hitler to Putin[70], etc. Armenia (pro-Russia) uses this comparison when it speaks of Azerbaijan. According to an article published by the Armenian website www.novarak.am[71], Azerbaijanis used the same methods as Hitler and Goebels: lying or telling the truth is irrelevant, the important thing is to be the first to talk, knowing how to manipulate national and international public opinion[72], being present in international organizations under the pretence of democracy, supporting information by reference to individuals with authority, whether they exist or not, institutionalizing the lie, changing the image of the enemy

---

68. http://flickr.com/photos/27074615@N06/2755219768/ and
http://flickr.com/photos/75255787@N00/2753053679/.
69. On http://www.thepeoplesvoice.org/cgi-bin/blogs/voices.php/2008/08/ see the image posted 3 August 2008.
70. http://www.flickr.com/photos/teonna/2756230123/ or
http://www.rgnpress.ro/Politic/Putin-=-Hitler.html.
71. www.novarank.am/en/?page=print&nid=1203.
72. Defining "public opinion" is a very difficult task. We just have to recall that for Pierre Bourdieu "Public opinion does not exist". Temps Modernes, 29 (318). January 1973. pp. 1292 – 1309. The text is available at the Website http://www.homme-moderne.org/societe/socio/
bourdieu/questions/opinionpub.html.

in the eyes of public opinion, etc. Azeris Day.az, ANS and APA press agencies seem to be the players of this institutionalized misinformation. We have been recording exchanges between Armenian and Azerbaijani hackers for many years now. In 2000, we registered the attack of dozens of Armenian websites located in Armenia and in the United States by Azerbaijani groups with names such as "Green Revenge", "Team of hijackers-187", etc. involving the Nagorno–Karabakh situation. Armenian groups were also active as "Liazor". Conflicts for the sovereignty of territories are the cause of these outbreaks[73].

5.4.3.7. *The idea of "cyber attacks" and "cyberwar" as communication tools*

The Georgian government chose to discuss the cyber attack aspect of the conflict, and to use these aggressions against its cyberspace to denounce enemy operations, accuse Russia, and thus reinforce its image as the victim (justifying self-defense) which it has circulated in its communication campaign directed at national and international public opinion. Although cyber attacks are no longer a new phenomenon in the context of international conflicts and crises, the condemnation of these operations and their use for communication purposes is significant. This methodology was used by Estonia in 2007, where that country widely denounced the cyber attacks against it, accusing Russia, and focusing the attention of the international community on its status as victim without providing more details on the nature of the attacks and the targets really affected.

The sentences in the texts published on government websites are structured similarly to what is written on Georgiamfa.blogspot.com by the Georgian Foreign Affairs Ministry: "Cyberwar attacks conducted by Russia disrupt Georgian websites; the Georgian government has implemented replacement sites". In the structure of this sentence, as in the others, we find the following information elements:

– action (cyberwar attack);

– author (Russia is the accused);

– impact of the attack: websites down;

– victim: Georgia;

– subject of the new action – reaction: Georgian government;

– action-reaction: solutions of substitution, compensating for damages (reaction to impact), verbal accusation (reaction to attack) and online publication of this short sentence (action, aimed at national, and especially international, public opinion).

---

73. www.infowar-monitor.net/modules.php?op=modload&name=News&file=article&sid=141 "Back files: computer specialists urge end to Armenian-Azeri hack attacks", 18 February 2000.

All the sentences are accusatory. The enemy is presented as the first attacker. Georgia is only reacting defensively. Cyberwar is not a theoretical threat, it is real. With very similar words and in a slightly different order, the texts published by the government, and the comments from the host Tulip System transmit the same message and contribute to building the image of a victimized state with its democracy being attacked.

5.4.3.8. *When cyber criminality benefits from the context*

Outside of the conflict itself, as with any extraordinary event, information is used by cyber criminals, taken out of context and used as a lure. Spamming using known information to lure the user is not new, and it is already detected by Symantec[74]:

– "Russia–Georgia conflict news used to hide malicious code in spam"[75]. Symantec identified a viral spam disguised in an information article involving the Russia-Georgia conflict. The subject of the message was "Journalists Shot in Georgia". The message contained an attachment with a password and instructions to download a file. The user was actually redirected to a payload identified as the Trojan.Popwin virus. This is using false information to attract the user in an operation that will be harmful. Protection against these viral spams involves using anti-virus software and common sense.

– Another example detected by the University of Birmingham (Alabama, USA)[76] is the viral spam that sends you, through a link, to false information from the BBC saying that the Georgian President is gay (19 August 2008). The spam servers were on Russian territory, one of the machines was even part of the Federal Education Agency. According to the article published in vnunet, the virus would add affected computers to botnets under pro-Russian control and would also contribute to the anti-Georgian propaganda[77].

5.4.4. *Isolated cyber attacks or information warfare operations?*

Information warfare operations can be conducted by an impressive range of players with the most varied potential, whether they are carried out by military or civilian players: States, the military, structured groups (terrorists, rebels, activists

---

74. http://www.symantec.com.
75. https://forums.symantec.com/syment/blog/article?blog.id=spam&message.id=111#M111 21 August 2008.
76. Related in http://www.crime-research.org/news/19.08.2008/3521/.
77. http://www.crime-research.org/news/19.08.2008/3521/.

etc.), isolated individuals, or simple computer "hackers". Their motivations can be political, economic, ideological, etc.

5.4.4.1. *Civilian operations?*

Were the actions qualified as cyber attacks only carried out by hacktivists? Are hacktivists always civilians?

The stopgeorgia.ru website calls for actions in cyberspace in defense of Russia: "We, representatives of the underground world of Russian hackers, will no longer tolerate Georgian provocation in any form. We want to live in a free world without attacks […]. We do not need to be guided by authorities or anyone, but act according to our convictions based on patriotism, conscience and trust by virtue of justice. You can call us criminals and cyber terrorists […] but we will fight in Cyberspace against the unacceptable aggression of Russia. We demand the end of attacks against information and government resources, and call for all media and journalists to cover the events objectively. Until the situation changes, we will stop the dissemination of false information […] We did not start this information warfare, we are not responsible for its consequences. We call for assistance from all those concerned with the lies from Georgian government websites..."[78]. The website offers a list of the main official Georgian resources[79] without publishing hacking tools. But by naming targets, the objective is to facilitate the job for hackers. The home page offers links to websites (war.georgia.su and www.stop-war.us) sharing the same concern for condemning Georgian misinformation. The "media-lies" section of the war.georgia.su website denounces the media manipulation, the doctored pictures from the Reuters agency, the distribution of false information from a press agency, and the use of this same false information by international media.

These websites and the individuals hiding behind them contribute to information warfare (giving their interpretation of reality[80], of the truth, or by feeding confusion), and to information warfare in its CNA dimension. They claim their independence, their freedom of action and speech. But as for their real nature, anything could be true. They may not be as independent as they pretend to be.

---

78. Text available on the home page of the stopgeorgia.ru website.
79. http://stopgeorgia.ru/?pg=tar.
80. On the concept of "reality" remember the work of Paul Watzlawick "La réalité de la réalité. Confusion, désinformation, communication", Le Seuil, Paris.

5.4.4.2. *Military operations?*

Were the actions qualified as cyber attacks carried out by the military? Was their use of information warfare methods to prepare confrontations, cut off enemy networks, blind the enemy, cover missions on the field by prior computer strikes? What military use was really made from information warfare in this blitzkrieg? Have the Russian and Georgian governments, beyond the regular psychological confrontation (information, misinformation), used network attack methods, interception of communication, or physical attacks against communication infrastructures to ensure control of the information space?

The Russia–Georgia conflict probably provided its belligerents with a field of use for their information warfare capabilities. But the absence of information from Russian and Georgian military operations prevents any definite conclusion and any methodical analysis. There is nothing to help us confirm that the attacks against Georgian information systems were a coordinated action by the Russian military in order to cut off the communication systems of the country and facilitate the progression of military operations. But there is nothing to enable us to deny it either. The few temporary site defacements and overloading of servers, to which replacement solutions were quickly found (mirror sites, website hosting from allied countries, etc.) do not add up by themselves to the concept of information warfare.

5.4.5. *Formulating the right questions*

It is probably too early now to rebuild the scenario of what really happened in the information space of the belligerents and draw conclusions.

Time will be needed for an investigation and methodical analysis that will prevent us from falling into the trap of the media fad, by focusing on the following questions specific to this conflict, and then to the more general and conceptual:

5.4.5.1. *The operations carried out*

– Could this "information warfare", as this is the expression used, be summed up as a few defacements and breakdowns of official Internet websites?

– What actions in cyberspace must be defined as acts of war, and which ones are only acts of delinquency?

– Do the confrontations reveal the existence of a cyberwar arsenal?

– Is it possible to reconstitute the tempo of aggressive and defensive operations from both parties and draw general conclusions on the role played by the 4th combat dimension in a blitzkrieg? Can this role be marginal or must it be central?

5.4.5.2. *The players in the operations*

– What actions were conducted under army or government control?

– Did the army really seize the information space, or cyberspace, to carry out this Blitzkrieg? What information warfare operations did the military really carry out? What is new in the way this war was conducted?

– Were citizens (Russian, pro-Russian, Georgian or pro-Georgian) involved in the cyber conflict? Could the "people's war" concept, dear to the Chinese, win the world? Could we eventually see a new type of citizen of the cyber combatant world? Nothing is more questionable. Hacktivists invite themselves to all crises and conflicts without their actions having any proven influence on the course of events so far. The masses of defacements are often the work of a few rare hackers who cannot alone authorize the use of expressions such as "people's war", supposing the investment of a significant number of individuals.

– Would the participation of civilians to conflicts be an asset or would it contribute to the increase of the information fog? If this participation proved to be harmful to success, would it be possible to contain it? Would the participation of civilians influence the international strategic balances of power?

– What are the relations, if they exist, between organized crime and war effort in cyberspace? Did the involvement of the RBN in cyber attacks against Georgia really happen?

– What would the relation be between civilian and military worlds in the 4th dimension of combat constituting the information space and particularly cyberspace? Could the States consider using Private Military Societies (PMS) to conquer the field of cyberspace? Could the experience acquired by cyber criminal groups enable a temporary conversion into cyberspace PMS? The expansion of the use of PMSs would then only be the extension of the privatization of violence. The reflection will then involve the role that PMSs could play in information warfare, as well as on risks that the States would incur with the uncontrolled use of such players, and on the acceptable limits of the challenge of the monopoly and the control of violence by the Nation-State (the Westphalian order).

– Does a "game-playing" dimension not appear in the war when simple hackers can benefit from a context of chaos to interfere, increase confusion by their actions, make the enemy think of acts of war, and take the appearance of great powers? Or when official war players (the military and governments) can make people think it was the action of ludic hackers to hide their operations?

– When server and site hacking does not disrupt, in a significant way, the operation of armed troops, does not penetrate and disrupt the C4ISR communication systems, does not affect the systems ensuring the operations of sensitive infrastructures, and does not jeopardize the communication systems ensuring the management of crisis and emergency situations, should we be worried about actions from hackers/hacktivists defacing or taking down general information, and even official, websites? In this conflict, hacking a few websites has taken on a media importance that is out of proportion, with no relation to the real consequences of the facts. Who has really benefited from the media sound box?

5.4.5.3. *The impact of operations*

– What has been the impact of defacements and decommissioning of official sites?

– Is the advantage gained by the offensive in terms of cyber aggression unstoppable?

– Must we give a strategic and political importance to operations that are not claimed?

– What dimensions of information warfare are real power intensifiers? Does information warfare confer an advantage leading to success?

– Isn't the control of the information space wishful thinking?

– Can a modern war, Blitzkrieg or long term, be won without using information warfare?

– To what does Russia owe winning the war? To its lethal kinetic actions or an information warfare advantage?

– Several categories of websites were affected: governmental, as well as hacker, commercial, media, etc. Is the impact on the conflict different according to the nature of the target?

– Must we know how to maintain hacking in peacetime to be able, when the time comes, to mobilize it with nationalist feelings? Can the hacker and hacktivist be manipulated?

– What alternatives exist in terms of cyberwar and information warfare to expensive American solutions? Is a cheaper cyberwar, far from the staggering costs involved in programming, planning and implementation of grandiose American cyberwar programs, possible?

Georgia is a nation that has too much vested in cyberspace for the few aggressions experienced (summed up as a few server and Internet website attacks) to appear as a massive information warfare operation. In this short period of asymmetrical war, Russia won a victory, but we still do not know, because of lack of information, the real importance that information operations have, and if the fight for the control of the information space is predominant. Of course, in the traditional sense of the term, there was information warfare, since warfare information and information-in-warfare were discussed, i.e. the use of information to recount events ("stories"?[81]), to play with opinion, influence, rally to its cause part of the rest of the world, denounce, i.e. conduct psychological operations. However, in terms of cyber attacks within the Russia–Georgia conflict, we would be tempted to conclude that they simply constitute a non-event.

---

81. "Storytelling, la machine à fabriquer des histoires et à formater les esprits", Christian Salmon, La Découverte.

Chapter 6

Singapore

In 1992, the terrorist movement Al Qaeda launched its www.alneda.com website. It was registered in Singapore[1]. The site was then hosted on servers in Malaysia and Texas. This affair is revealing of the problem that authorities have been facing for 20 years in every country. Cyberspace players defy regulations, controls, laws and borders, and the most voluntary policies in terms of security and defence have been, and will continue to be, helpless against actions that we could describe as common but able to bypass security and vigilance fortresses. The challenge is great for Singapore in this global context (which may actually be regional): to be able to secure its cyberspace and, if not to make it a tool of aggression as is the case in some nations, then to make it at least a space protected from unsettling attacks. Singapore, because of its wealth and central situation in the global economy, has been the object of great speculation, and for example, has attracted terrorism, economic warfare and cyber criminality.

6.1. Regional and global economic ambition

The Singapore economic model has many ambitions: becoming a modern day Venice, reinforcing its role as a vital global platform for trade, declaring itself the uncontested leader of Southeast Asia in the field of information and communication technologies (ICTs), and becoming the "hub of security" in Asia and one of the world leaders. In order to improve its leading position, Singapore must maintain an optimally secure environment.

---

1. Al-Qaeda's Extensive Use of the Internet. by Gabriel Weimann. In *CTC Sentinel*. Vol.1. Issue 2. page 6, January 2008.

Singapore is the image of a good student on the international scene. Small city-state in terms of its size (650 km^2), with just 4 million citizens, it is one of the giants of the global economy that commands respect. This old British colony that is now independent built its fortune on its decisive strategic position at the edge of Malaysia, at the crossroads of international commercial routes. The country is the largest global commercial port in Asia and the second biggest financial power after Japan in the region

Singapore has also become a global leader in the field of ICTs, through promotion and support for the sector for over 20 years by a government who have based the economic growth of the country on the development of information systems. This has been achieved through voluntary policies, pluriannual programs and massive investments in Research and Development, in the development of infrastructures and in training. Continuity, which is a guarantee for success, has been assured because of the stability of the single party in power since its independence.

The country was identified as "intelligent island" for the first time in 1990 by the British Broadcasting Corporation (BBC) in a televised program dedicated to technological developments.

In 1998, Singapore was the first country in the world completely connected to the Internet. The large bandwidth "Singapore One" network covered the whole territory in the same year. Singapore is planning the implementation of its new generation large bandwidth network by 2012, with throughputs of 100 Mb/s to 1Gb/s covering 85% of homes. A large bandwidth wireless network will cover the whole territory. Eight wireless service providers cover the territory today (1 hotspot/km2). In 2005, the World Economic Forum placed Singapore first in its "Network Readiness Index"[2], supplanting the United States. The 2006–2007 index placed Singapore in third position following Denmark (first) and Sweden (second)[3]. The 2008–2009 Networked Readiness Index placed Singapore in 4th position, following Denmark, Sweden and the United States; the United Kingdom was ranked 15th.[4]

---

2. In 2005, the World Economic Forum published an index called the "Network Readiness Index" ranking 104 countries based on their use of ICTs. Following Singapore in 2005 were Iceland, Finland, Denmark, the United States and Sweden. Asia was also in the top ten with Hong Kong and Japan. France was 20th, UK 12th. China came in 41st. http://www.forbes.com/technology/2005/03/09/cx_0309wefranking.html.
3. http://www.weforum.org/pdf/gitr/rankings2007.pdf.
4. http://www.weforum.org/pdf/gitr/2009/Rankings.pdf.

6.2. Challenges to security

The geographical position, ambitions and decisive economic role of Singapore make the country an almost ideal target. It has already had to face many challenges and crises during its turbulent history: wars, social and ethnic conflicts, epidemics and economic crises. Its emergence from the colonial period occurred under crisis and with ethnic confrontations. Singapore conserves a specific social structure from its past (a cultural, ethnic, religious and linguistic diversity) which is also a possible source of destabilization.

Today, Singapore gives the impression of a high-tech society relying on information systems for its development. At the same time, this reliance is its Achilles heel. As with all societies dependent on information systems, it has become vulnerable to all sorts of attacks against it. The information infrastructure is the architecture on which Singapore's activity is based. It is therefore its vital system.

Singapore's security lies in its economy and cyberspace on which almost all activities depend today. Singapore's security is also in its Strait and the Malay Strait, which in the last few years have recorded disturbing acts of hacking and terrorism. One quarter of global commerce and 50% of the global supply of oil go through these waters. Security is vital not only for Singapore's economy but for the economy of the whole world.

Singapore is certainly a country that is extremely dependent on networks and its cyberspace. But it is not necessarily at this level that the risks are greatest. Singapore has reinforced the security measures of its waters and its ports. Surveillance methods for ships, with the help of information systems on the movement of ships, were implemented; these are systems to electronically control the ships themselves (notably cargo ships) such as AIS (automatic identification systems).

In 1984, a defence strategy known as "Total Defence"[5] was implemented to face the different threats against Singapore. This concept allows for total mobilization of the population and resources in times of crisis and war, and provides a general framework for the development of integrated solutions to face attacks including terrorism, economic crises, epidemics and regional conflicts. By "integrated", we mean the combination of resources from the different state agencies, the private sector, civilian and military companies, the army and population around five predefined axes: military defense, civilian, economic, social and psychological defense. We speak of national coherence; these principles are promoted throughout the education program. Singaporeans do not suffer under this security culture;

5. http://www.mindef.gov.sg/imindef/mindef_websites/topics/totaldefence/home.html.

rather, it has become natural and is viewed probably not too far from the idea of "patriotism".

No one knows what would happen if Singapore was faced with a substantial attack. But the city-state has made itself a "poisoned shrimp"[6] for an invader. What is the poison? The military strike force, the developed forms of resistance, support of powerful allies, urban warfare tactics, strong economic interdependence with the rest of the world, or its capacity to conduct attacks through computer networks? Or perhaps, more importantly, it is a combination of all these possibilities.

6.3. Cyberspace and national security

Cyberspace is perceived as an inseparable whole. Whether we speak of the military or civilian information worlds, this cyberspace must be the subject of optimized security, since the risk of destabilization of the country can come from attacks or attempts against the civilian or military information spheres. The security of economic, social and cultural activities is a question of national security. The laws regulating the operation of information systems are a question of national security.

The cyberspace security strategy is based mainly on the Infocomm Security Masterplan program implemented by the Infocomm Development Authority of Singapore (IDA)[7] and the National Infocomm Security Committee (NISC).

NISC was created to formulate cyber security policies at the national level. It is presided over by the Permanent Secretary for the Coordination of Foreign Affairs, National Security and Intelligence. NISC includes representatives from the Interior Affairs ministry, Defence ministry, Communication and Arts Information ministry, ministry of Finances, Defense Science Organization (DSO)[8], national laboratories and the Defense Science and Technology Agency (DSTA). IDA provides the secretariat for the committee.

The *Infocomm Security Masterplan* program is aimed at protecting all the players in cyberspace, as cyber attackers do not only target government structures, but also corporations and citizens.

---

6. Singapore's first Prime Minister, Lee Kwan Yew, famously summed up this defensive philosophy many years ago as the "poisoned shrimp" strategy: Singapore may be small but it is also toxic to any regional power that seeks to consume it. For further details, see "Singapore, Inside the Lion City", by G.M. Greenwood, 14 September 2006, http://www.asia sentinel.com/index.php?option=com_content&task=view&id=159&Itemid=195.

7. http://www.ida.gov.sg/home/index.aspx.

8. http://www.dso.org.sg/home/about/about_os.aspx.

The government allocated 38 million Singaporean dollars from Singapore to the IDA in the 2005–2007 period to develop specific skills in the field of computer security and to form a pool of security, and fight against cyber terrorism specialists.

The "National Cyberthreat Monitoring Center" was also created to monitor and analyze threats, completing the activities of SingCERT which was created in 1997.

6.3.1. *Protected computers*

Important legal texts were enacted during the 1990s to protect Singapore from threats of cyber crime; amongst these, the Computer Misuse Act[9] is certainly the most important. This law, relating to the malicious use of the Internet and information technology in general, was voted in 1993 and developed from the British law of 1990, proving links to the island's past and cultural references inherent in this nation.

The law was modified in 1998 in order to include the evolution of techniques that opened the way to new types of information technology crime. Computers deployed for national security, the defense sector, international relations and financial services, vital economic infrastructures and health were covered by the notion of "protected computers", a notion that includes computers and the data that is processed, stored and transmitted by them. Protected computers have to go through a specific legal system, granting them high protection, under which any attack against them would be severely sanctioned. Penalties can be up to 20 years in prison, with fines of $100,000; on the other hand, hacking and web page defacement are "only" punished by three years in prison and $10,000. The purpose of the law is to protect information systems from any type of attack and, whether from inside or outside the country, the law would still be applied in the same way. Singapore's government is sure to pursue anyone in the world who attacks its information systems.

6.3.2. *Terrorism*

In 2003, a new amendment to the Computer Misuse Act reinforced this cyberspace legal protection tool, authorizing increased monitoring of the Internet and communication systems in the context of the fight against cyber criminality and, especially, terrorism, identified as one of the major threats to the balance and security of the country since the 9-11 attacks in the United States and aborted attempts in the city-state.

---

9. http://www.ida.gov.sg/idaweb/pnr.nfopage.jsp.

Information warfare takes the form of war against terrorism and cyber terrorism. An essential port of passage for a large part of international commerce, Singapore is certainly one of the most sensitive places on the planet, and any destabilization in this part of the world would have serious consequences for international trade exchanges. The threat level has justified the extent of powers given to the police, who now have complete power to intervene before the commission of an offense, from a simple suspicion or presumption, without a warrant[10]. The Minister of the Interior can authorize any person or organization to take any measure deemed necessary to prevent or counter any threat targeting a computer or information system, to defend national security, vital services, defense and international relations. The powers granted to authorities are not limited by law, and no safeguard seems to have been taken to protect against risks of abuse of power. Some even see this as a weakening of civil rights, the equivalent for cyberspace of the Internal Security Act (ISA), Singapore's interior security law, a law denounced by human rights organizations. This law is heir to the Emergency Regulations voted in the Malay British colony in 1948, the purpose of which was to protect Singapore against the communist threat. Today, the enemy is not the same, but the principle of defense remains the same. A legal context that comes to encroach upon individual freedoms should bring efficient protection against a threat to the vital interests of a state. Measures meant to be exceptional and temporary have a tendency to become permanent and ordinary. The principle of detention without conditions, or without a trial dates back from that era, when state security could be invoked. But we know that faced with vague threats, striking without discrimination and unexpectedly, Singapore, as all other nations in the world, has very few options. The fight against terrorism cannot settle for formal and intense investigations, restricted by a process of strict procedures; an emergency often decides the actions and methods to be used. This law enabled the arrest of 30 presumed members of the terrorist group Jemaah Islamiyah between 2001 and 2003 in Singapore. Without the wiretapping or surveillance without warrant powers granted to the authorities, would the same results have been obtained?

6.3.3. *Internet content as a source of threat*

Monitoring the quality of content circulating over the Internet is also one of the ways to monitor the maintenance of harmony and national stability. In this city-state, where ethnic groups with very different cultures live together in a limited space, any exacerbated tension could create an explosive situation and result in riots, as has happened in the past.

The Internet could be the ideal place for psychological attacks against Singapore, using the intensified ethnic conflicts in the country or region as a vector.

---

10. Article 16. Part III "Arrest by police without warrant".

Internet content is under the control of the Media Development Authority (MDA), created on 1 January 2003. Content is regulated by the Internet code of practice[11], a charter mandated by the MDA. The text has been much revised and came into force in July 1996. The purpose of the charter is officially to reinforce public safety and national defense (content liable to undermine public trust in Singaporean justice or government is prohibited), to promote racial and religious harmony (denigration or satire against races or religious groups are prohibited, as well as apologia for religious deviances or occult practices, such as Satanism) and to promote public morals (by prohibiting obscene, pornographic, sexual or violent content). A content provider must obtain a license prior to airing from the MDA according to the terms of the *Telecommunications Act (1999)*. The concern for content control was the basis of practices considered as abusive surveillance threatening individual liberties by human rights associations. In 1994, the country's only ISP, Technet (controlled by the state) scanned its subscribers' emails without notice, searching for pornographic content and viruses. In 1999, the SingNet provider scanned the computers of its 200,000 clients, also in secret, until the situation was revealed following the complaint of a user.

Singapore has specific constraints in terms of security that adversaries can use to their advantage. The country has the particularity of being a multi-ethnic and religious society: 77% of the population of Singapore is made up of Chinese (Buddhists, Confucians, Taoists); 14% Malay Muslims; 8% Indians (Hindus, Sikhs); and 1% other ethnic groups). Linguistically, Singapore has a mix of Malay, Mandarin, Tamil and English speakers. This extreme cultural diversity is a source of tensions. The different ethnic groups are very sensitive to circulating ideas and rumours. This situation makes the country vulnerable to possible psychological operations that could be organized in a region where economic and social stability entirely depend on maintaining this fragile balance between communities.

These tensions can be found on the Internet. Internet users can express their racial hatred. Chinese and Malay are often caught in verbal fights and the authorities maintain a watchful eye over the slightest verbal escalation. Any information warfare to destabilize Singapore could use "psychological operations" to fan underlying tensions.

The problem obviously resides in trying to control foreign content. Should Singapore Internet users be able to access the global Internet without filtering? Is the global Internet a source of danger? Singapore does not use technical filters much, unlike China, for example. According to a study carried out by the OpenNet Initiative (ONI[12]) only 8 international websites out of 1,632 tested (or 0.49%) are

---

11. http://www.mda.gov.sg/wms.www/devnpolicies.aspx?sid=161.
12. OpenNet Initiative. www.opennetinitiative.net/studies/singapore/.

blocked, and they involve drugs (cannabis), sex (Penthouse, Playboy, etc.) and religion, all strictly regulated fields.

It is mainly through the national Internet (.sg) and in the implementation of legal measures that control is undertaken. In 1998, SBA/MDA said it blocked 100 pornographic websites through the proxy servers of three ISPs (SingNet, Pacific Internet and Starhub). It was the first example in the world of outright censure over the Internet, but this block was justified by the necessity of making sure the content was compliant with Asian cultural (and the Nation's) values. Asian countries often invoke this threat to cultural values. Strengthened by their differences anchored in secular cultures, Asian people still fear seeing their values undermined by the influence of Western values. At least, that is the argument used to justify regulation, the limiting of access and Internet filtering policies.

6.3.4. *Data-mining to help security*

Four years after the American Congress had to fight attacks against the Orwellian project of spying on citizens' private lives, Singapore is under the spotlight. Now, Singapore is preparing to launch an even more ambitious version of the controversial Total Information Awareness (TIA) program created by Admiral John Poindexter, former National Security Adviser under President Reagan, later Director of the Defense Advanced Research Projects Agency (DARPA) Information Awareness Office, a project consisting of an attempt to collect data from government agencies in order to try and define threats to national security. The Singapore prototype is called Risk Assessment and Horizon Scanning (RAHS).[13]

The RAHS system was developed by the Singaporean National Security Coordination Center (NSCC) in cooperation with the Arlington Institute, Cognitive Edge, the Singaporean DSTA and national DSO laboratories.

TIA is one of the projects from the former Information Awareness Office of DARPA, the Pentagon's research project agency. Despite the closing of the Information Awareness Office and Poindexter's retirement, supporters of data mining (and Singapore in particular) have expanded his vision. RAHS is clearly different from TIA, but shares its spirit. The two major consultants for RAHS are John Peterson, from the Arlington Institute (Virginia), and Dave Snowden, scientific director of Cognitive Edge, based in Singapore. RAHS is presented as a system that monitors several sources of data, open and classified, to detect possible threats. It is a strategic tool linking the agencies in a wide network, permanently scanning the

---

13. http://www.wired.com/politics/onlinerights/news/2007/03/SINGAPORE?currentPage=all, 22 March 2007. "Son of TIA: Pentagon Surveillance System is Reborn in Asia".

horizon searching for low signals that may announce the possibility of a significant event that would have important implications for Singapore. The objective is to be able to detect these low signals that human analysis would miss. The fight against terrorism is one of the reasons motivating the RAHS project. But the SARS epidemic is what aroused interest for this type of technology.

As we were recently reminded during a symposium in Singapore in March 2007, transnational terrorism motivated by religion is only part of the problem. As was demonstrated by the SARS epidemic in Singapore, threats ever difficult to forecast such as pandemics can be even greater threats for entire societies than more traditional threats. The question is, how do national governments find out about these threats in a timely manner?

The current threat environment is marked by complexity and uncertainty, making traditional responses from national intelligence departments and security agencies less efficient than ever before. Today, thanks to what Thomas Friedman calls "democratizations" of finance, information and technology, many nations are vulnerable to a range of threats, including transnational terrorism, financial shocks and the fragility of the supply chain.

It is therefore vital to provide policy decision-makers with tools to be able to anticipate, predict, manage and decide in the contemporary context of the new nature of threats, risks, crises and conflicts. Modern and efficient intelligence tools and services are then needed in order to avoid repeating past errors, and not reproduce the situation where lack of cooperation and information exchange between agencies, or the inability of people to accept changes in working and thinking methods, made it possible for the 9-11 attacks to take place.

In 2004, the Singapore government introduced a new strategic framework for national security. The plan called for the implementation of a coordinated and networked approach to fight against the different threats. The RAHS project fits in to this program.

RAHS concepts and solutions could be applied to the social, economic and financial fields. Data-mining should find a favorable environment in Singapore. Implementing RAHS in all government agencies in Singapore would make it a more ambitious project for analyzing global data. Supporters of the project assure us that the application will use open-source information and that the data is anonymous.

6.4. Singapore armed forces in the information age

6.4.1. *Towards modernization of armies*

The process of army modernization experienced an important turning point in 1984 with the adoption of the concept of "total defense", according to which Singapore's defense strategy integrates national, civil, economic and social defense.

The modernization of Singapore's Armed Forces (SAF)[14], initiated in the early 1990s, is firmly part of the process of informatization, acquisition, development, implementation and absorption of ICTs into the global strategy of information control characterizing the economy and society. In 1990–1991, Singaporean forces recognized the importance of information systems for their capacity to change the way to fight a war. In 1991, networking the different military units was considered; information must be merged and shared. This transition fits in to the context of American troops demonstrating superiority in the Gulf.

Revolution in military affairs (RMA) was carried out. According to Singapore's approach, RMA and technological transformation will change the nature of war[15].

Singapore today has sophisticated combat forces, called third generation forces (3GF), focusing their efforts on networking platforms. Their strategy is based on the following basic principles:

– adopt a preemptive stance;

– try and fight as far away from the country's borders as possible;

– expand the range of actions;

– prepare to strike and fight as far away from the country's borders as possible.

In order to reach its objectives, the army acquired sophisticated C4ISR[16] and ILS[17] defense systems linking all surveillance capacities for decision-makers, giving them decision support tools for their operations and making it possible to launch

---

14. Despite the small population, SAFs are today among the best equipped and trained military in this region of the world, able to mobilize 350,000 troops during a conflict.
15. See the Singaporean reference document on this subject: "Defending Singapore in the 21st Century", Singapore; Ministry of Defence, 2000, 78 pages. http://www.mindef.gov.sg/ds21/.
16. Command, Control, Communications, Computers, Intelligence, Surveillance, and Reconnaissance.
17. Integrated Logistics Support. Integrated Logistics Support is intended to provide support for equipment and systems in order to ensure operational availability and long term operations, easily and at lower cost.

precise actions on determined targets. C2[18] systems were among the world's most evolved systems in the middle of the 1990s.

But Singapore is a territory with limited dimensions and its forces are not engaged in conflicts enabling them to test the systems in place at full scale. Simulation and experimentation are therefore very important in army training. In November 2003, the SAF Center for Military Experimentation (SCME) was inaugurated. SCME has three laboratories (the "Command Post of the Future" laboratory, Battlelab and the C4I laboratory) and their mission is to test scenarios and imagine operations, concepts and new doctrines.

Investments in the field of military defense are made possible by the economic growth of the country in the last 30 years. As with China, Singapore's economic growth supports army modernization through significant investments. Again, as with China, the armies' technological development was in part accomplished through acquisitions of material and weapons (aircraft, submarines and missiles) from foreign powers (mainly France, the United States and Israel). But at the same time, Singapore also developed its own military–industrial complex relying in part on civilian industry. All the players involved in defense activities, whether it is the army, civilian industry, government research agencies and universities, constitute a real defense ecosystem. Specific efforts are made to develop dual use technologies, and some effort is dedicated to the needs of the armed forces in the context of informatization: high performance calculators, simulators, C4ISR systems, military communication protection systems and defense infrastructures for information warfare.

6.4.2. *IKC2: Singapore's version of network centric warfare*

A key element in Singapore's revolution in military affairs is IKC2: "Integrated Knowledge-based Command and Control". The implementation of this concept is at the heart of the process from acquisition of information, its management, comprehension, manipulation, decision and action (the OODA[19] loop). The objective is to ensure that we can go through the loop faster than an adversary, ensure that we can disrupt the enemy's loop and, more generally, keep superiority in controlling and processing information: seeing before the adversary, seeing better, understanding faster, deciding faster and acting decisively. IKC2 is organized around the management of networks and knowledge, for better efficiency in C2s. IKC2 is Singapore's version of network centric warfare.

---

18. Command and Control.
19. Observation, Orientation, Decision, Action.

The term "integrated" actually means "integrated systems for integrated warfare". An integrated operations warfare strategy was enacted in 1994. According to the definition of the American Department of Defense, integrated warfare is the conduct of operations where forces use unconventional weapons in combination with conventional weapons[20].

According to the underlying logic of this concept, the greater the optimization of the universe, the more optimal is the solution. The object is to develop an environment in which any department can develop plans based on the capacities of the whole of SAFs and not from only one department or unit.

"Knowledge-based" means that implicit knowledge must become explicit. Knowledge is integrated in decision support systems. The objective is to help command, and to focus more deeply on judgment than on technical analysis.

6.5. Players in information warfare

6.5.1. *Defense sector agencies*

6.5.1.1. *Defense Science and Technology Agency*

The DSTA[21] was founded in 2000 and is an agency placed at the core of the Defense Department with the responsibility of acquiring weapons systems and developing military infrastructures.

It is responsible for developing C4ISR architectures and software systems. Through a specific program, it also supports start-ups whose technologies may have military applications. The applications then go from the civilian sector to the military and vice-versa, depending on needs.

Within this agency, Research and Development activities are carried out in themes that can come directly from the systems used in information warfare:

– advanced platforms;

– advanced material;

– sensor technologies (radars, surveillance techniques);

– network technologies;

– advanced communication systems (cognitive radio, ad hoc wireless networks);

20. http://usmilitary.about.com/od/glossarytermsi/g/i3157.htm.
21. http://www.dsta.gov.sg/home/index.asp.

– command, control and cognitive systems: modern armed forces are highly mobile and geographically dispersed, connected through networks and share information. They also have to have shared knowledge of the battle space with the use of relevant information, updated in real time, that must be accessible and usable intuitively;

– decision and planning systems considering cognitive aspects (consideration of the human mind models, and internal and external motivation factors) and must be able to support the decision process in a critical situation, to help in a collaborative decision;

– planning and surveillance techniques and systems, appropriate to uncertain and quickly changing environments;

– adaptive and dynamic multi-sensor algorithms and techniques, which can extract and interpret information and knowledge from text, speech, images and video in different environments, to acquire shared knowledge;

– visualization and knowledge representation systems, automatically adapting to user needs;

– human sciences to develop strategies to manage the deterioration of physical and cognitive human performances linked to fatigue, and to help in the development of technological solutions centered on the human to improve the decision process in network situations;

– detection technologies for the fight against terrorism (for the detection of dangerous products);

– electronics and optoelectronics (high power lasers);

– signal and image processing;

– information assurance to design new cryptographic systems to protect from attacks against quantum computers;

– technologies for detecting presence.

This agency published an annual "DSTA Horizon" report focusing on questions of defense, and notably on the defense ecosystem within which knowledge sharing must be maintained and developed. The articles published in the 2007 edition involve data sharing in the context of warfare conducted by joint forces, cognitive radio and an environment of combat modeling and simulation (in JEWEL laboratories: *Joint Modeling and Simulation Environment for Wargaming and Experimentation Labs*, currently used as a training platform for SAFs)[22]. Other questions are addressed such as managing intellectual property involving

---

22. See "Evolution of Modelling and Simulation in the Singapore Armed Forces", by Victor Tay Su-Han, *Pointer: Journal of the Singapore Armed Forces*, Vol. 32, No.4, 2006, pp.33-43.

procurement in the defense sector, the implementation of a framework of safety management and a culture of security in the defense community, an article on how to develop MASINTs (*Measurement and Signature Intelligence*) to increase intelligence collection.

The DSTA is also responsible for the C4I program[23] (*Command and Control, Communications, Computer and Intelligence*).

The Infocomm Infrastructure of the Defense Department, SAF and DSTA is a network of very complex systems supporting all IKC2 systems. Its objects are the establishment of a standard operations environment for over 20,000 client computers of the Defense Department and SAF, of a system of identity management for the Defense Department and SAF (securing applications and reinforcing authentication) and a system of secure email for the government.

6.5.1.2. *DSO national laboratories*

The history of DSO laboratories goes back to 1972. The Defense Minister at the time, Dr Goh Keng Swee, perceived the need to equip Singapore with technological research and development centers to prepare armies and defense for the future.

The first efforts were focused on electronic warfare methods through the Electronics Test Center (ETC). In 1977, the DSO was formally created. The research team was made up of sixty people. In the 1980s, the DSO was working on the development of solutions for SAFs, notably C2 systems. The existence of DSO was only made public in 1989. In 1997, the DSO became DSO National Laboratories and changed status to become a corporation, currently with over 600 researchers.

6.5.2. *Universities and defense*

The *Temasek Defense Systems Institute* is the result of cooperation between the DSTA and National University of Singapore (NUS) as well as the Nanyang Technological University (NT.U). This cooperation was a significant step in the efforts carried out by Singapore to reinforce its technological defense capacities. Temasek Laboratories are dedicated to carrying out research in the selected fields of science and technology, critical for the defense and security of Singapore: aerodynamics, computer security, signal processing, computer modeling and simulation, microsystems and radar systems.

Singapore makes its significant potential in the field of Research and Development, particularly in ICTs, available to its security, its armies and its IKC2

---

23. http://www.dsta.gov.sg/home/index.asp

concept. The policy consists of preparing the armed forces to engage in warfare in the information age. The country's security is not only focused on the risks linked to information systems in a country that is greatly dependent on it; identified threats also lie elsewhere and, in terms of terrorism, protection against (for example) a biological attack must also be taken into account. The approach is therefore global, complex and integrated.

6.5.3. Training for information warfare

Training for information warfare is given by the Singapore Manufacturers Federation (SMA)'s School of Management, through its Masters of Information Security and Intelligence[24].

The SMA is a federation in the corporate sector grouping 2,800 members from 11 industrial groups (chemical products, food, medical technologies and electronics) and works closely with government agencies such as the Economic Development Board of Singapore (EDB) to promote investments, the International Enterprise Singapore (IE) to develop the export market, Infocomm Development Authority (IDA) to help in the development of a global telecommunications industry standard, and Singapore's Productivity and Innovation Board (SPRING) responsible for supporting competitiveness of companies. The SMA created excellence centers which include the School of Management, in partnership with foreign universities, notably Australian and American. Training in information warfare is provided by the Edith Cowan University (Australia). Training is addressed to those in the economic and defense sectors.

6.6. International cooperation and cyberspace protection

Threats have globalized. For a city-state the size of Singapore, the threat field is huge. It cannot alone have all the answers to the challenges that it faces in terms of defense and protection of its cyberspace. The Singapore police is working with Interpol in questions of cyber criminality and with legal departments all over the world. In 2004, it was involved in an important joint operation with the FBI, the Fastlink operation[25], to dismantle groups of pirates organized in international networks. In order to ensure efficient follow up of threats, specifically to network security, SingCERT and the National Cyber-Threat Monitoring Center worked together with their international counterparts.

---

24. http://www.sma.edu.sg/programmes-p040.asp.
25. www.newsfactor.com/story.xhtml?story_title=Cyber_Cops_Arrest_Trio_in_Piracy_Crack down&story_id=23809.

On a military level, Singapore has developed a network of alliances all over the world. Singapore favors integration with a network of alliances as one of the keys to its security (for example, the Fire Power Defense Arrangement (FPDA) created in 1971 which links Malaysia, Singapore, Great Britain, Australia and New Zealand).

Perhaps because of their similarities (the smallness of their territory surrounded by other much larger States, and their low level of population), Singapore and Israel have developed close connections. From a military point of view, recommendations from the Tsahal[26] have been feeding Singapore"'s defense strategy for many years:

– conscription, adopted in 1967, is on the Israeli model. Today, the SAF has over 50,000 active troops but 300,000 can be mobilized (called Operational Ready National Servicemen (ORNS)) for a population of 4.6 million;

– the preemptive stance, in the image of Israel, adopted by Singapore who reserves the right to intervene in case of a threat;

– the defensive stance strategically, and offensive stance tactically.

But Israel is just one of several other partners on whom Singapore is relying to generally develop its security, and thus cyberspace has now become a major component of society (cyberspace is ranked as one of the critical infrastructures of a country).

In November 1999 a hacker defaced Singaporean governmental websites[27]. The authorities stated at the time that no important systems were exposed to any risk. The message which replaced the official texts on the sites was "Site edited by flipz. Why? Because I can". Of course, this website defacement was not the first incident recorded in Singapore and is not an isolated one. The hacker "flipz" was already well known at the time for being the first person to have defaced the Microsoft website in the USA (in 1999).

Ten years later, hackers can still deface websites in Singapore. More than 50 ".sg" Internet sites were defaced during the course of July 2009 alone[28]. Five of these sites (10%) had already been defaced during the period 2004–2008; 43 defacements were classed as mass defacements. This demonstrates that Singapore was not targeted specifically, but was touched all the same. We should note that no governmental sites were in the list of these attacks, which can be classified as minor.

---

26. Tsahal = Israel Defense Forces (IDF).
27. Hacker breaks into Singapore govt site, 2 November 1999, http://www.indianexpress.com/res/web/pIe/ie/daily/19991102/ige02057.html.
28. Statistics compiled from archives on website defacements published on the site www.zone-h.org.

Eight groups of hackers were the instigators of these defacements: 4 revealing themselves to be Turkish (or pro-Turkish) hackers, one defending the cause of Azerbaijan. Of course, these defacements alone do not make up the entire threat to cyberspace: we must not forget intrusions into IT systems, information theft, the loss of sensitive information, each of which have their place and a significant international dimension. Like all connected countries, Singapore can thus be involved in political questions about which it perhaps has no direct interest. The management of cyberspace security certainly imposes an increased awareness of international political considerations, as each standpoint taken on a sensitive subject is from then on susceptible to provoking attacks on national cyberspace.

Even if there has been no major incident (for the moment) on the functioning of institutions, these acts of website defacement seem to be just an insult to the security and can put a great strain on the pride of a country, such as Singapore, which makes security one of its fundamental policies, one of the foundations of its development.

Of course, the examples of website defacement, even when they concern government sites, are essentially a matter of cybercrime and not really information warfare (putting the sovereignty of a state in danger or under attack, or being part of a confrontation between states). However, the faults shown up by the exploits of hackers demonstrate well the difficulty, if not the impossibility, of securing cyberspace perfectly. Singapore is no exception to this rule.

However, over the course of the last decade, important means have been deployed for cyberspace security, and particularly since 11 September 2001, in the scope of the fight against terrorism:

– the security of the industrial sector has increased;

– the security policy of critical infrastructures has largely been applied to cyberspace;

– security has benefited from the Infocomm Security Masterplan (first plan in 2005, second plan launched in 2008);

– the army has resolutely entered a phase of informatization;

– no major cyber incidents have occurred in Singapore (at least, no incident has ever been revealed).

So, how can we explain that an excessively secured cyberspace is open to attacks which often rest on rudimentary technologies? Maybe because Singapore, like the rest of the world, does not seem to call into question the persistent application of the fortress paradigm.

Next to the fight against cybercrime, information warfare thus remains, as elsewhere throughout the world, a sensitive question for Singapore, as progress in security has not been as great as it should or could have been, not enough in any case to achieve the desired level of security. Now neighboring countries all have the abilities needed to launch their own cyber attacks.

It will thus be interesting to observe, over the course of the coming months, the choices that will be made by the country with regard to cyberspace security, and particularly to watch the results of a strategy for bringing together the civilian and military, public and private sectors. Like the USA (who in July 2009 launched an appeal – the *US Cyber Challenge* – for candidates to become cyber warriors[29]), could Singapore engage itself in a call for increased militarization of cyber security, and perhaps even create official cyberwar units?

---

29. "The US Cyber Challenge is looking for 10,000 young Americans with the skills to fill the ranks of cyber security practitioners, researchers and warriors", http://csis.org/uscc, July 2009.

Chapter 7

Identifying Aggressors and Acts of Aggression

During 2007 and 2008, so many cyber attacks were reported all over the world that it was possible to speak of real "waves" of attacks. This type of event had been recorded before but their nature and intensity seems to have changed significantly, suggesting a gloomy future for cyber security.

2007 was rich in events that threw the world of computer security and the national defense and safety of the largest nations in the world into turmoil.

During April, consecutive waves of cyber attacks targeted Estonia. The attacks lasted several weeks and affected public institutions, banks and corporations. They were the immediate extension of a conflict that broke out and degenerated into riots between the country's Russian and Estonian communities.

In June, the United States declared it was the victim of attacks against the Pentagon's information systems.

In August, it was Germany's turn to announce that the government's information systems were hacked.

France came next in August and September when the nation's information systems were affected and the national defense department spoke of a "serious situation".

Between September and December 2007, the United Kingdom reported being the victim of large scale attacks, affecting the systems of large corporations, banks and the country's security services and other departments.

In September 2007, New Zealand was also affected by the phenomenon (intrusion attempts, information theft and taking control of machines).

During October, the United States again denounced coordinated attacks against sensitive laboratories, including the Oak Ridge and Los Alamos National Laboratories.

In May 2008, India and Belgium were also the victims of similar attacks.

During the conflict involving Russia and Georgia in 2008, both countries denounced information warfare maneuvers.

In November and December of the same year, the Pentagon was again victim and accused China.

This is obviously only a few of the "attacks" that have affected information systems all over the world in consecutive waves during that time.

China also noted that it experienced permanent attacks during this period.

All these acts of aggression have reached a new level on the scale of dangerousness, in terms of nuisance, as well as in terms of the power of the media. However, no attack has yet reached such power that a nation has been brought down to its knees.

The events of 2007 and 2008 provide us with much information on the nature of crises and conflicts at the start of this new century, and on the state of peace under constant attack in which we live today.

The victimized nations have all denounced their guilty party: Estonia denounced Russia, as did Georgia. The United States and European countries (France, Germany, the United Kingdom and Belgium) have all accused China, without really checking first before acting. Do we really have victims on one side, a group made up of Western and European nations or their allies, and on the other side the culprits, a group made up of China and Russia? There seems to be a trace of the cold war here, of a dualistic vision of the world. On one side the capitalist bloc and, on the other, the communist bloc: a confrontation of values. Is the information space anchored in the paradox of balances that we thought were long gone? Or has the bloc mentality never really gone away, despite the emergence of new enemies in the global arena? It is highly improbable that the aggressions only target one of the blocs. The Chinese information systems, for different reasons, were also the target of attacks. Dissidence, anti-communism and defense of human rights are all ideals, rights, values and claims motivating aggressive operations against this nation. The relation between the "blocs" most probably consists of a permanent game of scrimmage, with defensive and aggressive operations. This is more a system of mirrors than a balance of power because the players share the same weapons and flaws. What A does to B, B can do to A; what A experiences, B can also experience; the flaws of A are those of B, and it is possible that both can be aggressors and victims at the same time, etc.

There is not a modern nation today that is not connected, or that cannot conduct aggressive actions against the interests of another government (if not by itself, then at least via someone else). Could the "victims" then have been attacked by India, the Middle East, Latin America, Africa, Australia, by close neighbors, or even by aggressors located in the same country? The question is very difficult to solve. Where is the aggressor? A report published by Riptech in 2002 concluded that, in 2002, most cyber attacks came from the United States and Israel[1], not China or Russia. But the world of insecurity is changing in cyberspace and a new map is liable to emerge from month to month, to such a degree that we can question the map of the balance of power today without too many problems.

The reactions of the "victims" provide just as much information as the methods of aggression used, the strictly technical considerations, and the aggressions themselves. At the top of the list of reactions is the accusation. The United Kingdom, France, the United States, Germany, Belgium and New Zealand spoke of espionage; Estonia, on the other hand, talked about attempts to destabilize and about attacks against its sovereignty. In the first scenario, the motivation suggested is to penetrate systems to steal strategic information; we are faced with a logic of intelligence, or even of economic warfare. In the second suggested scenario, the attack is presented as an attempt (even though directed via economic infrastructures) more to paralyze than to destroy. Attacking to steal, or attacking to paralyze or even to destroy. These are the two methods that have, or may have, immediate consequences in the relations between nations, in economic, political and diplomatic terms, creating crises or conflict situations. But, as with CNAs[2], accusations and the way they are presented can make these relations more tense.

Extreme reactions and quick accusations made without proof demonstrate that targets were affected. The players are destabilized and disrupted. We are never as extreme in our reactions as when we feel weak, or at fault. Who is at the root of aggressions against Estonia? The Estonian government chose to accuse the Russian government. Overcome by the violence of the aggressions, Estonia called on NATO, asking them to intervene in the resolution of the problem (mainly to attempt

---

1. www.usatoday.com/tech/news/2002/01/28/security-study.htm.
2. Computer Network Attacks.

to stop the problem, find a culprit and involve NATO military forces). The excessive character of initial reactions is felt more greatly after the fact. For example, when, one year later, in January of 2008, the arrest of Dmitri Galushkevich, an Estonian student born in Russia, was announced for his involvement with the cyber attacks that paralyzed Estonia's Internet sites. He was only found guilty of his involvement, but his punishment (of 1100€) is in stark contrast with the claims (one year earlier) from the Estonian government requesting the military involvement of NATO. There is a wide gap between the threat perceived in 2007 and the image of the condemned student, between the sanctions requested and those applied, and between the heated political interpretation and the realities emerging after an investigation.

The attacks seem to take the victims by surprise. But how can this element of surprise still be possible? Measures seem to have been taken to secure systems, to face risks or at least make it so that attacks are only aborted attempts. For years now, the number of reports insisting on and denouncing the vulnerability of systems responsible for sensitive infrastructures keeps increasing, confirmed by tests and simulations. The 2007 and 2008 CNAs were preceded by many more. The incidents multiply, and each generates its own tests and reports. Remember the Moonlight Maze (1998)[3] and Titan Rain (2003)[4] events, two major waves of attacks experienced by the United States? CNAs with varying degrees of importance (what is an attack, really?), with different motivations (ideological, political, economic), involving different types of players (hackers, hacktivists, terrorists, etc.) have probably now affected all the web-connected nations.

All this reminds us that flaws exist and that the fault is not so much that of the attacks and the attackers as much it is the worm that slipped onto the fruit during the creation of the computerized world. Despite warnings, awareness and the billions invested in security, systems and experts still seem to be overwhelmed, caught off guard and red faced with helplessness, if not incompetence. As with a ship taking in water, a house on fire or a nation crumbling, the advice is "run for your life"! Who or what will be able to protect us against "coordinated" and "massive" aggressions penetrating the doors of our secure systems? Not that many, it seems. But the answer must be found quickly. That our security leaders or our governments admit to the world that they were "victims", all almost at the same time, all in similar conditions, is a confession of helplessness, an acknowledgement of vulnerability and lack of control, and this is all confusing instead of being reassuring. There is no doubt that the real attackers are gloating, and we can even imagine their impatience

---

3. http://archives.cnn.com/2001/TECH/internet/05/10/3.year.cyberattack.idg/.
4. http://www.silicon.fr/fr/silicon/news/2005/08/26/operation-titan-rain-attaques-massives-chine.

to do it again, better, after having carefully observed the reactions to and effects of the initial attacks.

A dense fog of information prevents us getting a healthy vision of the real situation and making clear decisions. The impossibility of determining the origin of the attacks with any precision, investigations that may never reveal conclusions, the lack of proof, and the problems measuring the true scope of real damages (who was affected, from when, until when, what was stolen or destroyed or distorted?) constitute a flare of uncertain information, hypotheses, probabilities and inaccuracies. None of this prevents specific accusations being made (against the Chinese army or the Russian government, for example) which are, in the end, only pure allegations.

Does this very public victimization not offer "victims" the opportunity of trying to take advantage of the situation? Making good use of the attacks experienced is obviously an obligation. Full-scale aggressions enable the victims to identify their own flaws, to better understand their adversaries and know the potential of attackers. This is the positive side of being the victim of a cyber attack. Beyond that, victims could use attacks as an excuse for political, economic or strategic actions, or even take advantage of the confusion to, in turn, conduct their own aggressive or preemptive information operations.

Some of the attacks mentioned so far fit within the context of conflict (between Russia and Georgia in 2008, for example) or crises (the riots in Estonia). The expressions "information warfare" and "cyberwar" have been used in specific cases. But other attacks are only motivated by confrontations between hacktivists, as is often the case during a crisis or a conflict. Are the "attacks" (the term is in quotation marks because of the necessity to be careful in qualifying the actions recorded) against France, Germany, Australia, Belgium and India (to use just a few examples) attacks against industrialized countries, against NATO, against capitalism, or against wealthy countries that need to be destabilized? Are they really "attacks", or are they only "cyber criminality" or "cyber delinquency" type operations, intended to take over computers in order to distribute viruses, worms and spam, or to allow phishing or fraud? If so, it could be that we need to distinguish between information warfare type "attacks" and cyber criminality type "attacks" (where the major goal is often only financial gain).

The boundary between peacetime and wartime is becoming blurred. This means that in times of peace, "aggressions" and "hostile acts"[5] can occur in cyberspace. The problem, then, is to accurately define an act. In the case of site defacements or

---

5. A hostile act is intended to weaken, paralyze, destroy, destabilize and take over one or more adversaries.

attacks against government computer systems, how can we work out if an attack is a real aggression by one nation against another, an act that can be qualified as an act of war, or just a "simple" incidence of cyber crime?

The answer to this question could eventually even determine the reaction of a victimized nation, or even justify preemptive actions such as political measures, economic sanctions or military intervention, whilst reactions to cyber criminality can be found in law and legal cooperation.

Do the statistics of incidents reveal strong enough clues to distinguish acts of aggression (act of war) from organized cyber criminality or ordinary delinquency? Do the players (attackers, sponsors and victims) have specific profiles? What strategies and tactics can be characteristic of the aggressions?

The responses to these few questions will make it possible to draw analysis and interpretation grids to better understand security incidents in cyberspace. Before announcing to the world that a cyberspace war has broken out between two or more countries, we must be sure that it really is a war.

7.1. Statistical data

Is it possible to read the clues (clearly or between the lines), or even to find the obvious and conclusive traces of acts of war from the information in simple statistical data? The data chosen to try to answer this question was published by the Computer Emergency Response Teams (CERTs) of a few Asian countries over the period between 2000 and 2005. This sample can be separated from the one involving the more recent 2007 period which marked a significant turning point in the methods of attack against the world's information systems. From 2007, more massive and coordinated attacks emerged, notably using botnets for DDoS attacks.

In conclusion, these statistics do not pretend to display, by themselves, a faithful picture of the situation in terms of insecurity/security of the networks of a given country. They cannot be because the data is only based on the incidents that were known and reported to CERTs. These statistics may only be the tip of the iceberg, showing only a small part of the danger to the ship's captain; the worst might be hidden under the water. The available statistics, based on deliberate declarations, cannot reflect reality and we need to extrapolate data. The proof of this is in the results of an investigation carried out in 2005 involving 36,000 American corporations, the results of which were published by the American Justice Department in September 2008. Of the 23% of the companies who responded to the survey, 67% reported having detected security incidents, 91% experienced losses, and only 15% of this last sample turned to justice for assistance. This survey only involved companies who knew about incidents; but for every known and recognized incident, how many are never detected?

7.1.1. *China: CNCERT/CC reports*

CNCERT/CC (The National Computer Network Emergency Response Technical Team/Coordination Center of China) was created in October of 2000 and has been a member of FIRST (*Forum of Incident Response and Security Teams*) since August 2002, as well as being on the Steering Committee of the Asia Pacific Computer Emergency Response Team (APCERT). It is under the responsibility of the Chinese Domestic Ministry. Some 31 branches of CNCERT/CC cover 31 provinces of continental China.

2003 was marked by viral attacks, notably including SQL SLAMMER, Deloader and MSBlaster. In January, SQL SLAMMER caused significant damage to the Chinese network, interrupting it on a large scale. In March, the Deloader worm paralyzed networks in many regions. In August, a significant infection was caused by Blaster/Blaster Remove, provoking a drop in network throughputs in many regions. DoS attacks have also targeted government portals, Internet service providers and important Internet websites. Several cases of site defacements and Internet fraud targeting the commercial and banking sector were recorded. 13,295 reports of security events were transmitted to CNCERT/CC (against only 1,761 the previous year), and over a million attack attempts against network computers were recorded. The largest number of incidents recorded involved external intrusion attempts, a category of incidents responsible for a jump from 1,761 to 13,295 reports, the single source of most of the increase (10,873). Spamming accounted for 2,201 cases.

2004[6] was marked by the SASSER worm that infected close to 1,400,000 computers worldwide, as well as by Trojan horses (23% from Taiwan, 17% Hong Kong, 18% the United States, 11% Russia, 6% Korea, 5% Japan, 4% Canada, 2% Germany, and 14% from other countries).

The surveillance of website attacks identified 1,024 foreign servers frequently attacking China. Attacks come from the USA (38%), Korea (16%), Japan (10%), Brazil (8%), Taiwan (8%), India (3%), Hong Kong (3%), Canada (2%), Holland (2%), Indonesia (1%), Thailand (1%) and others (8%).

CNCERT/CC received 64,000 reports of security incidents during 2004 compared to 13,295 the year before.

---

6. CNCERT/CC Annual Report 2004. www.cert.org.cn.

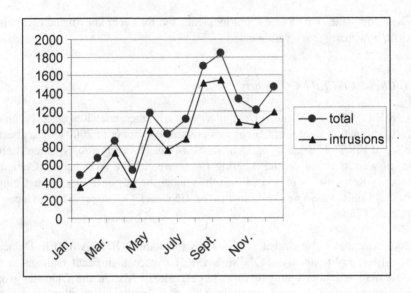

Figure 7.1. *Graph (taken from data in the 2003 CNCERT/CC Annual Report) showing the monthly number of incidents. The upper curve represents the total (viruses, worms, spamming, intrusions), whilst the lower curve represents only intrusions*

Incidents that CNCERT/CC handled, by type, are distributed as follows: site defacements, 74% (2,059 sites); phishing, 20%; malware (worms, viruses). 3.50%; DoS, 0.80%; and others, 1.7%.

DoS/DDoS type attacks paralyzed the operation of the websites and jeopardized the economic activity of the corporations involved. The report describes an attack by a major BotNet that was obviously intended to decommission the victim's site and destroy a competitor. The DoS attack was presented as an economic warfare weapon.

Site defacements in 2004 are shown in Figure 7.2.

In 2005, CNCERT/CC monitored 28 Trojan horses on the most popular websites and reported that 22,500 addresses were contaminated. The computers affected were mainly in seven provinces: Guangdong (21%), Shanghai (15%), Jiangsu (10%), Zhejiang (9%), Beijing (7%), Fujian (6%) and Hubei (4%). The remaining 28% were located in the other provinces.

When monitoring 30 types of spyware, 700,000 contaminated computers were identified. Spywares were delivering private information to servers based elsewhere, mostly in the United States and South Korea.

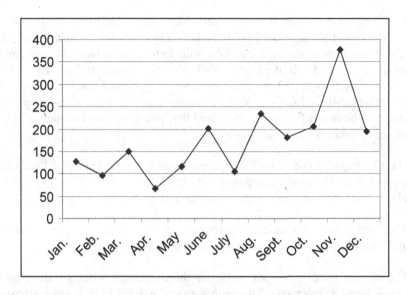

Figure 7.2. *Graph showing monthly number of incidents recorded by CNCERT/CC in 2004. (Taken from data in the CNCERT/CC 2004 annual report)*

A study of the most frequent attacks recorded 220,000 foreign computers launching regular attacks against Chinese websites. Attacks came from the United States (40%), Japan (11%), Taiwan (10%) and Korea (8%).

13,700 website pages were defaced in China during 2005, of which 22% were government websites. This ratio is very high when we consider that government websites only represent 2.2% of Chinese websites.

143 botnets in over 5,000 machines were also recorded. The largest, Diablo BotNet had 157,000 machines. In 2005, botnet DoS attacks caused significant damage in China. The report describes an incident in January 2005 leading to an investigation that resulted in the arrest of the author of the attack which had paralyzed a corporation.

In 2005, CNCERT/CC received over 120,000 incident reports. Of these, 53% involved site defacements and 11% phishing.

Following the publication of an article in the Hong Kong press, Chinese hackers planned attacks against Japan, by way of Korea on 15 August 2005. CNCERT/CC worked in cooperation with the Japanese and Korean CERT to monitor possible malicious activities, but nothing happened. The CERT declaration on this point seems to demonstrate that Chinese authorities were concerned about blocking attacks that could be launched against neighboring countries as much as possible, and thus cooperated to show their collaboration in terms of network security, and to demonstrate the good will of a China which does not support hackers. The fact that no event occurred (officially at least) would also demonstrate that the rumors about China are generally unfounded. We often attribute aggressive tendencies to China, but that may be unjustified; the report noted that "we have found no sign of actions organized by hackers".

On 17 October 2005, CNCERT/CC received a report from SURFnet CERT saying that 290,000 Chinese computers had been infected by W32/Toxbot and were members of a wide botnet of 1.2 million computers all over the world.

The 2005 report also mentions phishing activities carried out from China and against which Chinese authorities took quick measures.

The conclusions of this report show that threats change. Viruses and worms are no longer threat number one. The main dangers in 2005 were botnets, spywares, identity theft, and site defacements. DoS attacks, phishing and spamming were still important and worrying. There were also several incidents correlated to political events. The complexity of attacks was also one of the major trends.

The most severe incidents discussed in the 2006 CNCERT/CC report involve site defacements, notably of government websites, and critical information systems, phishing and DDoS attacks targeting commercial companies. The number of vulnerability alerts published by CNCERT/CC increased (+16% compared to 2005), as well as the number of IP addresses affected by Trojan horses (+100% compared to 2005). Over 10 million computers held client bot code; 33% of bot servers were located in the United States and 10% in South Korea. Reduced size botnets (less than 1 million computers) seemed to be preferred by attackers with determined targets. CNCERT/CC recorded an increase of 100% compared to 2005 for defaced pages, including 24,477 defaced sites on the Chinese continent (13,653 in 2005; 2,059 in 2004; and 1,157 in 2003).

The most important incident involved the Worm.Mocbot worm which infected over a million computers.

CNCERT/CC recorded over 200% more reports compared to 2005. This regular increase in the number of incidents is explained by the extension of networks throughout China and the increase of the number of Internet users, whether individuals or companies.

7.1.2. *Hong Kong: HKCERT/CC report*

The HKCERT/CC was created in 2001 by the government of Hong Kong. In 2005, the HKCERT/CC received 2,223 incident reports, including 846 that involved viral attacks and 1,375 security reports (spywares made up 64%).

Security incident reports now outnumber viral incident reports.

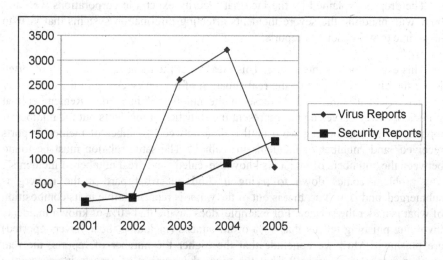

Figure 7.3. *Graph drawn from data published in the 2005 HKCERT/CC annual report*

Both superimposed curves over such a short period show a clear trend: the regular increase of security incidents. Viral attacks greatly vary from one year to the next.

The report described that hackers were motivated by financial reasons. Is there nothing ideological, then, in security attacks such as spyware, spamming and phishing? Such assertions are based *a priori* on the fact that Hong Kong is a financial and commercial place, and so it would be targeted for that purpose. Phishing and spamming attacks first disrupted the heart of Hong Kong activity, including economic activity and corporations. Other attacks attempted to steal information and divert money. The precision given in the report is not completely founded, however. Viral attacks could just as well attempt to destabilize some targets with a goal other than a strictly financial one. A more detailed study (of attack dates, origins, nature of targets, and their possible connections with Beijing) would probably enable us to have a better understanding, and maybe reformulate, in other terms, the report's assessment.

7.1.3. *Japan: JPCERT/CC reports*

The JPCERT was created in 1992, well before its Asian counterparts. In 2002, the JPCERT received half as many reports as in 2001 and 2003. What explains this drop in 2002? Does this mean that Japan experienced fewer attacks? No, on the contrary, they may even have experienced more.

The drop is explained by the fact that security experts in corporations were too busy with handling the severe incidents affecting information systems that year to have time to write incident reports.

This explanation is interesting. This means that the number of incidents reported is not the direct reflection of the real situation of networks. A dip in the curve may in fact reflect a significant increase in the number of incidents. Remember that statistical CERT curves do not represent the statistics of incidents but the number of reports. What relation can we establish then between "number of incident reports received" and "number of incidents in reality"? The same relation must be found between the "numbers of incidents known/revealed" and "real number of incidents". The problem comes down to trying to find out what part of the iceberg is submerged, and if the part that is out of the water is representative in its composition of what is under the surface. For example, does saying that 40% of known incidents involving phishing tell us that 40% of all attacks (including those never reported) are phishing? Must we conclude that the higher the number of reports, the real number then also increases? That the more the number of reports increases, the more the experts are aware of the usefulness of writing these reports? Would the experts, who write incident reports and consequently feed the statistics, be more inclined to report some forms of attacks than they would others? We might imagine that experts are more sensitive to viral attacks than to a site defacement, or conversely. Some incidents are more sensitive than others and deserve more publicity, more support, communication and coordination.

The greater the number of incidents, the less the experts have the time to handle them technically, and the less time they have to write reports. It is therefore a proportionally opposite relation that is established here. As there are fewer reports recorded by statistics, the number of incidents may be higher. Conversely, as the number of reports increases, that may mean that experts have time to write them and therefore, in reality, the number of incidents may be going down slightly. Trying to read a curve then becomes difficult. Drawing immediate conclusions becomes impossible.

Interpreting the curves must obviously be done in light of other data, such as the fact that networks keep expanding in industrialized or developing countries. The number of users and computers keeps increasing. It is therefore natural that statistically, in raw data, the number of incidents increases proportionally. More connected computers means more entry points, flaws and probabilities that security holes exist. More users also means more potential hackers. But that does not mean that the number of Internet users/number of incidents ratio must also increase in proportion.

7.1.4. *South Korea: KrCERT/CC 2005 report*

Incident reports are classified into two categories: reports involving malicious code and reports relating to hacking (spamming, phishing, intrusions, site defacements, etc.) The KrCERT/CC received 16,093 reports involving malicious codes (including 10,764 worms, 746 Trojan horses and 611 viruses) and 33,633 hacking reports.

The report describes an increase in incidents compared to previous years. There were more incidents relating to codes, which were now in second position (in terms of number of incidents). How can we interpret this simple information? What conclusions can we draw?

– That the malicious code attacks really reached second place:

    - because the number of worm, virus and Trojan horse attacks was really decreasing, while others were increasing;

    - or because the measures of protection were more efficient?

    - because other forms of attacks were diversifying and multiplying. Spamming did not exist a few years before, neither did phishing and imagination in this field is only limited by technical methods. New methods of attack will appear in the next few years and will add to the existing ones or replace them;

    - because codes were/are becoming more discrete? Because they are less detectable? Which explains why we don't report them as much?

    - because malicious code is not always destructive and does not always justify reports or particular attention?

– or that events linked to phishing or spamming were now reported because the commercial sector was more affected, because there were financial stakes, because security managers and victims were more sensitive to this type of attack than to viral attacks. The number of reports received would then reflect more a behavioral change, how some attacks were perceived, rather than material reality.

The first interesting piece of information, at first glance, is in the change, the reversal of trends, and the reversal of balance of power from one year to the next.

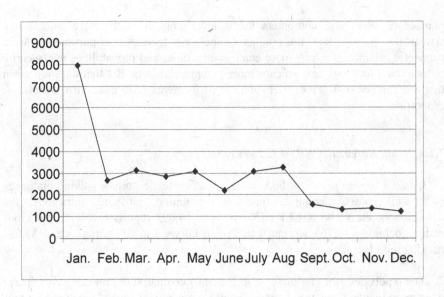

Figure 7.4. *Graph taken from data published in the 2005 KrCERT/CC report*

Interpreting the curve of incidents classified in the "hacking" category quickly reveals a peak in January. "Peaks" are another interesting phenomenon of evolutions. "Peaks", "dips" and "reversals" are three phenomena that can retain our attention in the interpretation of statistical curves.

The annual sums of categories of incidents are not always the reflection of the trend; two or three peaks are enough to inflate totals. We must analyze the peaks.

The January peak is explained by a wave of site defacements. Close to half of site defacements occurring in 2005 (16,692 in the whole year) happened in January (6,500). And site defacements represent 50% of the "hacking incidents" category in the year. The major phenomenon is therefore site defacements. The January peak was isolated. Why? What does it represent? The KrCERT/CC report writes: "the massive defacements of website home pages are the work of a few groups of foreign hackers". In order to reconstitute significant information, and possibly to conclude to the existence of information warfare maneuvers, we must consider the following questions:

– the moment in time: why in January?

– the nature of the victims: who are they?

– painting a picture of attackers and attacks:

- through contents defacing the websites: political or ideological slogans?

- are there many? A massive attack is not synonymous with a large number of attackers;

- the response will have to consider the nature of the victims and defacement contents.

January was a victim of the mass defacement phenomenon. Hackers took advantage of vulnerabilities shared by many websites, or by websites hosted on the same servers, to expand their attacks. It is, then, more by opportunism that attacks became massive and not deliberate attacks against each of these victims.

In other countries, the examination of statistical curves of incidents reveals similar phenomena.

In Malaysia, March recorded a peak in the number of intrusions (this category includes website defacements); the number is close to ten times higher than the other months in the year. MyCERT 2005 reports explain that intruders took advantage of security flaws. They were opportunistic intrusions, then, conducted by hackers not searching for technical difficulties. May until August experienced an (abnormal) dip in statistics relative to spamming (approximately ten times less than the other months in the year).

SingCERT (Singapore CERT), in 2005, recorded an increase of 100% of the number of incident reports, mainly caused by the increase in spamming.

The number of reports received by TWCERT/CC (Taiwanese CERT) presents a regular curve in 2005, with a tendency to decrease, but with an important dip in August.

In conclusion, therefore, we must be careful in interpreting these numbers. The doubling in volume of attacks recorded is not synonymous with doubling of the number of attackers. The volume of attacks alone does not help us determine an offense, a crime or an act of aggression that would be politically motivated (an act of war).

We should always be able to connect a curve over time to events. We must, then, interpret with precaution possible cause and effect relationships. For example, in month x the curve recorded a peak of website defacements. The calendar indicated that during month x a diplomatic incident opposed the victim country to the attacker's country. Was the victim then targeted in this context of diplomatic crisis because it has a direct relation with the crisis situation or the interests of one of the parties? Was it instead swept in the wave of defacements by coincidence? Or was the attack actually connected to another context, and was it simply a coincidence? The curves do not answer all these questions.

It is impossible to confirm from the statistical curves alone that what seems like a massive wave of attacks is an act of aggression of one nation against another.

7.2. Attacks against personal information and information warfare

No continent is safe. Attacks against personal information indiscriminately affect companies, public and private institutions, and civilian and military players, revealing the existence of significant flaws in the organization of systems and data security processes. Personal and sensitive data are attractive to cybercriminals because of their specific nature and because of their inherent value. An analysis of the most significant events in terms of attacks against data highlights the characteristics of this type of offense. But one question remains: could these attacks, commonly classified as acts of delinquency, not be qualified as "aggressions" or "information warfare operations", at the same level as the waves of attacks that information systems in many nations around the world experienced just over the previous months?

As the major objective of all information warfare operations is the acquisition of superiority of information, information domination (American doctrine), control of information (the French approach)[7], it seems immediately obvious that in this wide information space, personal information will play a central role.

The simple question then will be: are attacks against personal information a manifestation of information warfare operations?

7.2.1. Characteristics of attacks against personal information

Convention 108 of the Council of Europe defines personal data as "any information relating to an identified or identifiable individual ("data subject")"[8]. Directive 95/46/CE clarifies that "an identifiable person is one who can be identified, directly or indirectly, in particular by reference to an identification

---

7. Livre Blanc sur la Défense et la Sécurité. June 2008. http://www.premier-ministre.gouv.fr/information/les_dossiers_actualites_19/livre_blanc_sur_defense_875/livre_b lanc_1337/livre_blanc_1340/.
8. http://conventions.coe.int/Treaty/en/Treaties/Html/108.htm Convention for the Protection of Individuals with regard to Automatic Processing of Personal Data. Chapter I, article 2 of Convention 108 of the Council of Europe.

number or to one or more factors specific to his physical, physiological, mental, economic, cultural or social identity"[9]. The field of personal data also includes:

– Last name, first name, date of birth, age, data directly concerning the person and which, alone, do not confer the one holding this data any specific power. This data is relatively public.

– Information that can be linked to the individual, such as the address, social security number, telephone number, car registration number, banking information, IP addresses (yes[10] or no[11]), passwords, email address or information on educational or professional program, marital status, etc. This data associated to the first category defines the individual, profiles him, describes him, reconstitutes his social networks, makes it possible to steal his identity and is considered "sensitive".

Attack against personal data is the malicious use of this data for criminal purposes, including theft of data, distortion of data, use of data to steal the identity of an individual for fraudulent purposes, access to other information, places or services and taking his place.

Attacks against personal data are in reality often the result of two offenses: first, we must access data in an illicit manner, whether it is by stealing the peripherals for this data (laptop computer, USB drive, cell phone, CD-ROM, etc.), by intrusion in a system, by buying data illicitly; then the available data is used, either by modification, distortion of data stored on a server, by identity theft or by reselling the data.

The simple loss of a peripheral containing personal data is another form of attack against personal data[12]. The computer or USB drive was lost: who took it? Can the data be accessed and exploited? What sort of data was on the peripheral? All questions with no answers, but questions which trigger a feeling of insecurity in individuals and expose their data to any use.

---

9. Directive 95/46/CE from the European Parliament and Council from 24 October 1995, relative to the protection of individuals with regard to the processing of personal data and on the free movement of such data. Chapter 1, article 2, paragraph a) http://eur-lex.europa.eu/smartapi/cgi/sga_doc?smartapi!celexapi!prod!CELEXnumdoc&lg=fr&numdoc=31995L0046&model=guichett.

10. http://www.cnil.fr/index.php?id=2244.

11. http://www.01net.com/editorial/358706/l-adresse-ip-n-est-pas-une-donnee-a-caractere-personnel/.

12. The loss or theft of computers and storage devices was the largest cause of violations to personal data in the second half of 2007, according to the Internet Security Threats Report Vol. XIII by Symantec. http://eval.symantec.com/mktginfo/enterprise/white_papers/b-whitepaper_internet_security_threat_report_xiii_04-2008.en-us.pdf.

Some constants emerge in the family of attacks against data recorded in the world enabling us to describe this type of offense:

– the events all involve a large chain of players, and an attack against data is mostly a series of effects and consequences;

– low security of data, lack of control over data processing, attitudes toward laws and rights, a feeling of threat from the inside, are all revealing of the attitude of the different players managing data against risk;

– due to time factors and the problem of finding proof, there is a low probability that victims will ever know the truth and be master of the situation: the nature of the incidents and they way they are carried out mean that, the more time passes between the incident and its discovery, the less chance there ever is of knowing the authors of the attack; and, finally,

– the question of cost (of data and the consequences of the attacks) and the question of the dimension of losses recorded, involve measures of evaluation and assessment.

7.2.1.1. *The victims*

An attack against data involves a long list of players such as the criminal(s), the victim(s) (data processing manager, employees, contractors and individuals), the hierarchy, external partners, the third party discovering the theft or data loss (monitoring Internet websites, associations, etc.), the legal system, the media, the public, human rights associations, consumer associations, right to privacy associations, corporate security managers and legislators.

But who is the real victim in all these incidents? Is it the corporation from whom the computers were stolen, lost, experienced intrusions or whose data was targeted? It is the employee responsible for losing his computer, or who has had his laptop stolen? Or the individual whose information was stolen and whose identity may be stolen? Or even the whole industry because of a consumer lack of confidence?

Evidently, in view of the long lists recording personal data, it seems that the phenomenon affects all sectors of activity and in significant, if not troubling, proportions. The 2008 Identity Theft Center (ITRC) annual report recorded 35 million citizens who were victims of the loss of their personal information and 656 losses of files in the United States alone.

Any player processing personal data is liable to take on the status of victim. The mission of managing databases or processes is much more difficult than it seems. The public and private sector, civilian or military, including those responsible for defense, security, justice and health, are all involved.

The economic sector is often on the front page of the media. In 2006, hackers stole private data relating to 650,000 users of the online virtual world *Second Life*. In May 2008, data from the clients of over 40 international financial institutions were found on a server in Malaysia[13]. In December 2008, over 400,000 client files from the French Internet service provider Orange could be freely accessed over the Internet because of a flaw in security. In January 2009, the American Chekfree company alerted its 5 million clients because it was unable to identify the 160,000 clients whose information was exposed to an attack.

Another sensitive sector is health. In January 2007, St. Mary's Hospital (in Leonardtown, Maryland, USA) lost a laptop computer containing information on 130,000 patients (names, social security numbers, etc.)[14]. In February 2007, in Birmingham (Alabama, USA), a computer was stolen which contained medical information on 530,000 patients[15]; concern comes from the fact that the data was stored on a hard drive with no encryption.

For the security sector (police) remember the examples mentioned in the chapter about Japan: incidents within the Kyoto, Okayama and Matsuyama police among others, with losses of criminal investigation reports, names of suspects, victims, DNA data and lists of yakuza gang members[16].

The field of defense is also particularly sensitive to these attacks. We have already mentioned the major incidents that occured in Japan. They continued in 2008, as if past incidents could not help in controlling the situation. On 11 January 2008, a computer was stolen on the Camp Foster base on the island of Okinawa (Japan), containing personal information identifying 4,000 members of the American military, government services and personnel from Okinawa bases. This data was made up of names, ranks, social security numbers, dates of birth, names of children and email addresses. In Afghanistan, in 2006, computers containing sensitive information from the American military were found for sale in markets in the city of Bagram. In May 2006, a computer containing data from 26 million United States military veterans or active duty personnel was stolen from the home of a US government employee. The British Royal Navy have lost computers containing sensitive data during the last few years. In 2005, an intrusion in the information systems of the US Air Force resulted in the theft of 33,000 files containing officer names, addresses and personal information relative to their careers.

Although personal data losses and thefts in the commercial sector raise significant problems (attacks against individual rights, banking risks, feeling of

---

13. http://reclamere.com/headlines/index.php "Crime Server Held Personal Data". May 7, 2008.
14. http://somd.com/news/headlines/2007/5358.shtml.
15. http://www.chicagotribune.com/news/local/bal-te.nih25mar25,0,7029580.story.
16. http://www.theregister.co.uk/2008/08/14/russia_georgia_cyberwar_latest/.

insecurity, loss of trust and shortfalls), the incidents recorded in the more sensitive sectors, i.e. those involving vital infrastructures, and security and national defense, are much more disturbing and lead to questions in terms of the level of data and systems security, in terms of the organization of national information infrastructure, and the risk management inherent to these losses.

According to a study by Symantec, it seems that administrations and government agencies are the most vulnerable to the problem of data theft, representing 60% of the volume of personal data affected during the second half of 2007. But this proportion is subject to great variation since it only represents 12% in the first half of 2007[17]. All accessible statistics, taken by different institutions around the world, are only based on the analysis of tight samples and have a hard time presenting a real image of this global phenomenon.

The behavior of the "victims" is interesting. We can observe quite a consistent will to minimize the scope of the losses experienced: "we think that the author of the offense was not searching for the information on the computer or did not even know of its existence", maintained the financial manager of Stanford University (United States) where a computer was stolen in June 2008, which contained the personal data of 72,000 employees. "Often, such thefts are only crimes against the assets and the hard drive is erased before being sold"[18]. These comments only reflect the will of the people responsible for data files to justify their actions, and shirk their responsibilities.

The victims must also often confess their ignorance of the facts. The characteristic of these types of attacks actually resides in the possibility of being an unknowing victim. Data can be stolen, exploited without anyone finding out, or finding out too late.

But the victim may also deliberately try to hide his state because it may be preferable to absorb the shock in silence than to take responsibility for the consequences of the disclosure (confronting the media, human rights associations, lawyers, trials, damages and the effect on a reputation).

7.2.1.2. *The culprits*

Guilt often slides from the real culprit (the one that penetrated the system, the one that stole the laptop or the one who stole the data) to the one who was the vector of the problem because of his carelessness, his lack of awareness for his

---

17. Internet Security Threats Report, Vol. XIII. Symantec.
http://eval.symantec.com/mktginfo/enterprise/white_papers/b-whitepaper_internet_security _threat_report_xiii_04-2008.en-us.pdf.
18. http://reclamere.com/headlines/index.php (10 June 2008).

responsibility, or his mistakes concerning security rules. In the United States, an institution or corporation sometimes deliberately points the finger at the employee at the origin of the incident, the one who had his laptop stolen, giving his name to the media. The culprit is the one to whom the offense happened or was made possible because of his negligence. Pointing the finger at the employee has the appearance of a shift in responsibility from the management of the institution or company to their subordinates.

As for the author of the offense, it is difficult, if not impossible to track him. This type of criminal invisibility makes him impersonal and elusive. A police investigation may last several weeks, or even several months without ever reaching conclusions. The solution to the problem is not the arrest or identification of the author of the offense.

It seems that accessing online information systems is a relatively easy act in many cases, and presents many advantages:

– The systems are not very well defended. The target generally offers little resistance. When it is hit, we do not always know it. When we know, we do not always react, either because we do not have the means, or we do not want to acquire those means. When we react, the operation quickly reaches its limits: assessments, evaluations, difficult investigations and cascading problems to handle.

– The systems can contain or give access to huge masses of data. This data can potentially result in thousands, if not tens of millions of victims.

– If the systems do not retain records of the events, the culprits can act with impunity. The act can remain relatively transparent.

– The managers of systems and data can take weeks, months or even years to find out about an offense. Enough time for the criminals to take advantage of the stolen data. In 63% of cases, the delay between an attack and its discovery can be measured in months[19].

7.2.1.3. Weak data security

The access path to the data is often punctuated by weak technical (data not encrypted) and human (who respects rules and regulations?) security barriers. Personal data, then, seems extremely vulnerable to attacks, suffering from a long list of vulnerabilities including software (non encrypted data during its transfer or storage, unsecured servers, unsecured Wi-Fi networks, lack of firewall as was the

---

19. CSI 2007 report. Page 22.
http://www.gocsi.com/forms/csi_survey.jhtml;jsessionid=UEJRSTMXLUOGYQSNDLRSK HSCJUNN2JVN.

case in the TJX[20] event revealed in 2007), hardware and human vulnerabilities, or because of corporate strategies (BPO – Business Process Outsourcing – is a potential source of risk for data):

– In a major episode of personal data theft which, in 2007, involved the American TJX company, the culprits used war driving[21], taking advantage of the lack of security of the Wi-Fi network, and then took advantage of the lack of data encryption during the transfer process to intercept[22].

– Individuals themselves have, often unintentionally, become the providers of large volumes of personal data in unsecured spaces, such as in virtual communities, discussion sites or online meetings, subscriptions to services and forums now proliferating over the web. By not knowing how to hide their true identity, millions of individuals reveal themselves and their most intimate confidential information.

According to the 2008 Verizon Business report[23], 90% of data breaches could be avoided if reasonable measures of security had been taken. But what about the remaining 10%?

7.2.1.4. *The lack of data processing control*

Control of data consists of its security during processing, implying knowing what data is where, and when. Which is far from the case in practice. It seems that the players are completely overwhelmed by the volume of data processed. Questions keep coming back in relation to personal data loss or theft:

– what data was on the stolen/lost computer?

– how long was the data on the machine?

– what data was accessed during intrusions?

– what data was protected (encrypted)?

– who has access to data, since when, for what purpose and under what rules?

– how may intrusions occurred?

– for each intrusion detected, how many intrusions are not?

---

20. http://somd.com/news/headlines/2007/5358.shtml.
21. War driving (also called access point mapping) is the act of locating wireless networks, e.g. while driving around a city.
22.
http://www.informationweek.com/news/security/showArticle.jhtml?articleID=197001447.
23. "2008 Data Breach Investigation Report", 27 pages,
http://securityblog.verizonbusiness.com/2008/06/10/2008-data-breach-investigations-report/.

Data processing managers can often only admit to their lack of control:

– TJX[24] was a victim of multiple intrusions in its information systems during the 2003–2006 period. Hackers accessed the data from CB transactions in TJX stores, without the company finding out or being concerned. Intrusions and loss of data were only revealed in 2007. Senior managers declared that they did not know who was responsible for the action, whether there was one or more culprits, or if it was a continuous intrusion or multiple separate intrusions[25].

– 66% of the events analyzed in the 2008 Verizon Business report involve data that the victim was unaware was on their system[26]. According to the report, the lack of control extends to the detection of attacks. In 75% of cases, attacks were discovered by a third party, not the victim. Is this loss of control or a deliberate lack of control? How can we explain that 83% of attacks were considered not difficult to make, according to the same study? That 85% of attacks are the result of opportunistic attacks? And that 87% of attacks are considered avoidable with simple measures?

The lack of control extends beyond the incident:

– The data can be divulged over the Internet, sold and copied many times.

– The author of the offense himself has no real control on the data stolen once the information is disclosed. The data itself is only an image of the data that is actually stored. There cannot be any real "control" of this virtual object called data.

– Even if the author of the offense was arrested, it would not mean that the attack was over.

7.2.1.5. *The connection to rules and regulations*

We notice that in many data attack events, the connection to rules (charters, security rules) is one of the sources of insecurity. Laws are ignored: TJX stored customer credit card and bank card numbers and expiration dates when this is prohibited by the Payment Card Industry (PCI)[27].

Rules are forgotten, unknown, inefficient, not applicable and not respected. At TJX, encryption (etc.) rules were "generally" applied [28]. In May 2006, in the United States, the loss of personal data linked to more than 26 million American military

---

24. http://somd.com/news/headlines/2007/5358.shtml.
25. The TJX Effect, 11 August 2007. http://lists.jammed.com/ISN/2007/08/0024.html.
26.   *2008   Data   Breach   Investigation   Report*,   27   pages, http://securityblog.verizonbusiness.com/2008/06/10/2008-data-breach-investigations-report/.
27. https://www.pcisecuritystandards.org/.
28. http://lists.jammed.com/ISN/2007/08/0024.html "The TJX Effect", 11 August 2007.

veterans and active duty personnel, resulting from the theft of the hard drive of a computer[29], caused quite a stir. This loss highlighted the problem of data security in national defense/security. How could so much data be stored on a single private computer for three years without the simplest authorization? In this case, security rules did exist (it was prohibited to take this personal data home), but they were not respected.

As for justice, it does not always result in responses expected by the victims:

– In Japan, 43 company clients of the Dai Nippon Printing company were the victims of data theft. Beside the fact that almost half of the victim companies were not informed, the culprit, an employee of the corporation, was only sentenced to a $200 fine for stealing the hard drive, and not judged for the stolen information on 9 million individuals[30].

– The notion of "privacy" and human rights is not considered on all continents and the lack of laws can sometimes be the result of economic lobbying pressures that have no interest in regulations. In Malaysia, the Personal Data Protection Bill that was supposed to be in effect in 2001 has since been constantly delayed because of the pressure of several influential lobbies, including banks. Malaysia waited until 2008 to recognize the right to privacy for individuals.

7.2.1.6. *Internal threat*

According to the annual 2007 report from the Computer Security Institute[31], companies' feelings of insecurity have increased due to the internal threat, "the Insider Threat", now above viral attack risks. Could enemy number one, the thief, the spy that we cannot detect, be among us?

This sense of risk, a purely subjective vision, seems to be contradicted by the 2008 report published by Verizon Business[32]. On the contrary, the report says that in 73% of cases, attacks against data are external and 39% even involve commercial partners. We should search elsewhere than within our own walls for the source of major risks.

7.2.1.7. *Time factors*

Discovery of facts, reactions and slow implementation of security measures following incidents, often significant delays between the theft and awareness of the

---

29. http://www.washingtonpost.com/wpdyn/content/article/2006/06/06/AR2006060601332.html.
30. http://www.infowatch.com/threats?chapter=148831545&id=207784672. 29 March 2007.
31. The 12th Computer Crime and Security Survey: CSI Survey 2007. 30 pages. http://i.cmpnet.com/v2.gocsi.com/pdf/CSISurvey2007.pdf.
32. *2008 Data Breach Investigation Report*, 27pp., http://securityblog.verizonbusiness.com /2008/06/10/2008-data-breach-investigations-report/.

facts by managers and the police, and finally by the victims (the individuals) often informed as a last resort in the chain of problem handling, the time factor seems to be a major component in personal data attacks. Several days, weeks or even months can go by between the event and notice to victims, between the event and the result of the investigation. Sometimes, even, the individuals will never know, the investigation will never end:

– In June 2006, the Department of Energy (DOE, USA) revealed that the names and other personal information of 1,500 employees of the National Nuclear Security Administration (NNSA) were stolen during a network intrusion two years earlier. The NNSA discovered the breach over one year after the events.

– The PC of a consultant at Neiman Marcus, USA, was stolen on 5 April 2007. It contained data stored for two years, including 160,000 files on the company's employees. The CEO was informed of the theft on April 10th and informed employees on April 23rd. This delay, which may seem short with regard to other events of this nature, was imposed by the police who wanted more time to carry out their investigation before announcing it to the employees[33].

– In the event involving TJX revealed in June of 2007, data breaches occurred during the 2003–2006 period[34].

– In Aichi (Japan), information from investigations was stolen from the computer of a police officer between 2004 and 2005, and broadcast over the Internet where it was discovered in 2007.

– In December 2007, the University of New Mexico (United States) was involved in a disclosure of personal data on the pages of its website. A teacher had, carelessly and by ignorance of computer tools, uploaded 31 files containing information on 333 students (social security numbers, email addresses, etc.). The files were online from 2001 and, in 2007, the SSNBreach.org website[35] and Liberty Coalition[36] found them.

– The breach of information from the Bank of Ireland containing account numbers as well as medical information, life insurance, and names and addresses of over 10,000 clients was only reported to the Irish Commissioner of information protection in April 2008, whilst the four laptops containing this information were stolen a year earlier[37].

---

33. http://www.unbossed.com/index.php?itemid=1480.
34. *The TJX Effect*, 11 August 2007. http://lists.jammed.com/ISN/2007/08/0024.html.
35. http://www.ssnbreach.org.
36. http://www.libertycoalition.net/.
37. http://reclamere.com/headlines/index.php "Four Unencrypted Laptops Stolen". 22 April 2008.

– A computer was stolen in December 2007 from the Staten Island University Hospital (SIUH) (United States), containing data from 88,000 patients; the latter were informed on 11 May 2008[38].

– American, Japanese and British military have revealed loss of hardware and data over the last few years. The British Royal Navy lost computers containing sensitive data (events revealed early in 2008 though the losses occurred after 2005)[39].

– On 23 February 2008, the laptop of an employee of the federal National Institute for Health (NIH) agency (United States) was stolen[40]. It contained the results of medical tests on 2,500 patients, as well as their names and addresses. Even though the police was alerted in the hour following the theft, the patients were only informed in May of 2008; management was not certain that the computer contained personal information.

– In the spring of 2005, an intrusion in one of the US Air Force systems resulted in the theft of 33,000 files of officers containing names, information on careers, birthdates, social security numbers, number of children, etc. Three years later, no result was ever made public. Must we then conclude that no investigation was ever completed?

Storage time for data is also part of the temporal dimension of the problem: in October 2007, the University of Akron (Ohio, USA) alerted its 1,200 students from the class of 1974 that a microfilm containing personal data had disappeared[41].

The events can carry on over several months or even years. The attacks can occur over several years before being discovered, followed by phases of system updates, investigations, reparations for the harm experienced by the victims (even if only moral), and of discovery of damages following the exploitation of stolen data [42].

The time factor is not specific to personal data attacks however. Other large scale incidents, notably security issues, were only discovered and revealed much later. In the Titan Rain event[43] (United States), intrusions lasted two years before being discovered, and, in the end, with accusations made against China.

---

38. http://reclamere.com/headlines/index.php "Staten Island hospital waits for months to notify". 2 June 2008.
39. http://www.timesonline.co.uk/tol/news/uk/article3227172.ece "Three military laptops with secure data missing". 21 January 2008.
40. http://www.chicagotribune.com/news/local/bal-te.nih25mar25,0,7029580.story
41. "Educational Security Incidents (ESI) Year in Review – 2007". 12 February 2008. page 154.
42. http://www.boston.com/business/globe/articles/2007/08/15/cost_of_data_breach_at_tjx_soars_to_256m/
43. http://fr.wikipedia.org/wiki/Tom_Clancy's_Ghost_Recon.

7.2.1.8. *Investigations and problems with proof*

Usually, in IT investigations, it is obvious that a crime was committed: paedophilic images are found on a computer or a server, a rootkit[44] is installed, etc. In the case of an intrusion in a database, it seems at first glance that nothing is wrong. The "prima facie" evidence is not there, data may have been stolen but only a copy can be made and the original is still there[45]. The relative invisibility granted to the culprit works in his favor during and after the offense.

7.2.1.9. *The value of personal data*

Personal data, because of their value, are attractive to cybercriminals. Legally, they can be transferred and sold. Illegally, they feed parallel markets. This data has a price, because of what it says about an individual and their environment:

– Stolen computers and other peripherals from the American military were sold locally in Bagram (Afghanistan)[46], containing sensitive information including information on Afghan informants spying on Al Qaeda and the Taliban, amounts paid, information on intelligence methods, images of torture, personal information from American troops, etc.

– Symantec[47], in 2007, provided a list of fees for data sold from underground forums and websites: from \$5 for a listing of 29,000 emails, an identity including US bank accounts, credit card number and birth date was sold for between \$14 and \$18, a PayPal account for \$500, a Skype account for \$12, and a World of Warcraft[48] account for \$10[49]. Even the black market is regulated by the market and it would seem that, recently, prices are lowering considerably because of the volume of goods on offer. In its last report in 2008, Symantec indicated that the cost for a complete identity is now between \$1 and \$15.

---

44. A rootkit is "a backdoor Trojan horse hiding behind or within processes and files that can provide crackers remote access to a compromised system. Besides being the name of a specific software tool, the term rootkit is often used in a more general sense to describe a tool providing system administrators access privileges to snoop while avoiding detection," according to http://www.yourdictionary.com/hacker/rootkit.
45. *Oracle Forensics Part 5: Finding Evidence of Data Theft in the Absence of Auditing.* David Litchfield. 10 August 2007. http://www.ngssoftware.com.
46. "Stolen Military Data for Sale in Afghanistan". April 13, 2006. http://www.msnbc.msn .com/id/12305580/ Times could not verify the authenticity of the documents and was not able to confirm the accuracy of the information.
47. Symantec Internet Security Threat reports http://www.symantec.com/business/theme.jsp? themeid=threatreport.
48. World of Warcraft, aka WoW, is a MMORPG (massively multiplayer online role-playing game).
49. Data from http://blog.washingtonpost.com/securityfix/2007/03/stolen_identities_two_ dollars.html

Beside the gains from personal information transactions, the costs incurred by the victims must also be considered:

– In the TJX event, 45 million credit card numbers were stolen. The cost for the company was estimated at \$256 million in August 2007[50], made up of fees for securing the computer system, problem resolution, investigations, lawyer fees, legal fees and informing the victims, to which should be added the millions of dollars in damages for clients who were victims.

– Attacks against information cost companies an average \$182 per compromised data[51], according to a study published by the Ponemon Institute in 2006. This amount includes the services offered to clients, fees for informing clients, loss of productivity, as well as client turnover including the problem of finding new clients. The cost of implementing new security measures can be added to those fees: for the panel of companies observed in this study, that cost was an average \$180,000.

7.2.1.10. *The size of losses*

Attacks against information seem greater each year in terms of volume of data:

– In 2003, an America Online engineer admitted having stolen and sold 92 million user names and email addresses, triggering an avalanche of 7 billion unsolicited emails[52].

– In 2007, the British government had to explain the loss of hard drives containing personal information on 25 million citizens (40% of the population and almost all children under 16 in the country!) receiving family allowances, including an unknown number of bank account identifiers. It was the third time in the same year that the British administration was involved in personal information loss events[53]. The data was not encrypted.

– In June 2007, a computer was stolen from the vehicle of an employee of the government of Ohio. First assessments reported that 75,000 files were lost. But the numbers were quickly revealed to be much higher. In July 2007, the New York Times spoke of 786,000 individuals and companies involved[54].

---

50. http://www.boston.com/business/globe/articles/2007/08/15/cost_of_data_breach_at_tjx_soars_to_256m/.
51. http://www.computerworld.com/pdfs/PGP_Annual_Study_PDF.pdf "2006 Annual Study: Cost of Data Breach", The Ponemon Institute, October 2006. The cost analysis is based on the study of 31 victimized companies.
52. http://bak2u.blogspot.com/2007_11_01_archive.html.
53. http://bak2u.blogspot.com/2007_11_01_archive.html Data Leak in Britain Affects 25 Millions.
54. "Ohio: Data Theft is Larger than First Thought". http://www.nytimes.com/2007/07/12/us/12brfs-

– In the TJX attack, 45 million client files were lost[55].

– In the United States, information from 26 million American military veterans or active duty personnel was lost in May 2006 during the theft of a hard drive in the apartment of an analyst from the Department of Veterans Affairs[56]: the data included information on 645,000 members of the reserves, 430,000 members of the national guard, 1.1 million military personnel, etc.

The PrivacyRights[57] evaluates at close to 234 million the number of American citizen files affected since 2005. The Identity Theft Resource Center (ITRC) announced an increase of 69% in the number of attacks against personal information recorded in the first half of 2008 compared to the same period in 2007[58]. In Russia, 93% of data stolen in 2007 was personal information[59]. A specific measure of the global scope of the phenomenon seems difficult to evaluate:

– Recordings and statistics are based on inaccuracy of accounting units. Are we talking about a million files (an individual can be represented by several files) or data relative to a million individuals? The few statistical studies on personal information attacks sometimes highlight the problem of this inaccuracy, but do not resolve it[60].

– The recorded facts are, of course, only the facts reported. How many events remain hidden, deliberately or not?

– The volume of data affected in a single attack often remains impossible to evaluate accurately. Nobody knows how many files were on the stolen peripheral (laptop, disk, etc.), or how many files were copied, etc.

– The ITRC estimated that in the first nine months of 2005, some 56 million files from American citizens were exposed. But one case, CardSystems International, represented 70% of this data. Furthermore, three cases represented 84% of the data affected. The statistics deserve closer examination because a few large incidents are not necessarily significant of the general trend[61].

theft.html?ex=1341892800&en=9fc00eaf37020e25&ei=5088&partner=rssnyt&emc=rss July 12, 2007.
55. http://lists.jammed.com/ISN/2007/08/0024.html "The TJX Effect", 11 August 2007.
56. http://www.washingtonpost.com/wpdyn/content/article/2006/06/06/AR2006060601 332.html.
57. http://www.privacyrights.org/ar/ChronDataBreaches.htm.
58. http://www.idtheftcenter.org/artman2/publish/lib_survey/ITRC_2008_Breach_List.shtml.
59. http://www.viruslist.com/en/analysis?pubid=204791995.
60. "Educational Security Incidents (ESI) Year in Review – 2007". 12 February 2008. page 2. http://www.adamdodge.com/esi/files/Educational%20Security%20Incidents%20Year%20in% 20Review%20-%202007.pdf.
61. Numbers cited in "Toward a Rational Personal Data Breach Notification Regime". Michael Turner. June 2006. www.infopolicy.org/pdf/data-breach.pdf.

If statistical data recently increased in the United States in a significant way, it may be because of the law mandating that all data breaches must be reported when personal data is involved, as imposed by the California Database Security Breach Notification Act, Senate Bill 1386[62]. To date, almost all American states have adopted a legal framework in this case. Similar laws do not necessarily exist elsewhere, making incident reporting that much less likely. Undetected attacks are obviously not reported, attacks detected are still not all reported because of ignorance of the law or reticence to make public events that may have an impact on a company. Finally, only events that cannot stay hidden too long anyway seem to be reported.

7.2.2. *Personal data in information warfare*

In 1994, Winn Schwartau in his book "Information Warfare" [SCH 94] divided information warfare into three categories: personal information warfare, commercial information warfare, and global information warfare. Global information warfare involves industry, spheres of political influence, critical computer systems and an entire nation by disrupting its systems (transport, energy, information...). Commercial information warfare is our contemporary economic warfare. As for personal information warfare, it groups attacks against data involving individuals and privacy including disclosure, corruption, intercepting personal and confidential data (medical, banking and communications information among others). This separation of the "information warfare" concept has not become the norm, but it is interesting because it gives personal data a significant place in a context of conflict, and not only in cyber criminality.

Information warfare confers to the information (including personal information) three major characteristics: it becomes desirable (it is the information that we must acquire), it is vulnerable (information peripherals and vectors are vulnerable; information is therefore vulnerable), it is formidable (where propagation is favorable to one camp and harmful to another). Personal data has these characteristics because:

– It can become a target;

– Since the systems and resources containing this data are fallible, with little or no security, they constitute an easy point of access to the information systems of a player. Personal data often constitutes the weak link in the chain of data processing;

---

62. http://info.sen.ca.gov/pub/01-02/bill/sen/sb_1351-1400/sb_1386_bill_20020926_
chaptered.html Coming into force , 1 July 2003.

– Data is accessible in large volumes and can provide considerable amounts of information, sending the victim into a state of disruption, thus in very high state of vulnerability. An adversary then only has to observe the behavior of his victim to get other useful information;

– It offers a better, tighter and more "intimate" knowledge of the adversary. It can be a weapon used to benefit the one holding the data, and be used as a lure (identity theft);

– Even if the representation of W. Schwartau did not stand the test of time, personal and sensitive data integrates perfectly into today's concept: simultaneously a target, weapon and privileged instrument of information operations;

– Personal data can be used for ISR (Intelligence, Surveillance, Reconnaissance) purposes. Access to data would make it possible to modify or use the information on soldiers on the field, analyzing the masses of data to map the capabilities of a target or access secure locations;

– Personal data can be used for PSYOPS (Psychological Operations) type operations. Imagine for example the consequences of obtaining and using information on the health of a military commander;

– It can be used for CNA type operations (by revealing the flaws in security systems, by using identity theft to penetrate a sensitive system, etc.);

– A massive attack against personal data can be the result of Effect Based Operations (EBOs) in that they involve a chain of victims and reactions that can have a much greater impact than the attack against the initial target alone.

Personal data and associated processing systems are one of the centers of gravity of a target's adversary.

7.2.3. Attacks against personal data as a method of aggression

Personal data is specific data, the value of which comes from its relation to the person, information that it reveals about him, the capacity it offers to those who have the information to know, make more vulnerable and manipulate individuals, and through them institutions, structures, organizations and processes.

In terms of an offense affecting personal data, the terms "attack" or "aggression" are not, or not much, used. Incidents are rarely linked to the notion of "cyber attack" or "CNA"[63]. Reporting of incidents only shows acts of negligence (losses), delinquency, cyber criminality (intrusions, fraud, organized networks and black

---

63. Computer Network Attack.

market), whereas they could turn out to be more strategic, political, ideological, military and security-based, and come from operations conducted by information warfare players.

Victims of attacks against personal data do not have the same reactions and considerations of the events as when faced with cyber attacks. Faced with the CNA affecting several nations recently, victims have quickly attributed the coordinated and substantial acts to Russian[64] or Chinese[65] governments and armies, accusing them of conducting espionage operations or destabilization attacks. The massive attacks against personal data, however major, are normally not attributed to a foreign power, whereas they can constitute, as with intrusions, as with the propagation of viruses, attacks against the information space of a nation. The victims can be quite accusatory, when involving CNAs, bringing the events to an international level. In the case of massive attacks against personal data, they look toward cyber criminality or even prefer to adopt a more shut off attitude, looking for fault internally ("the insider threat").

Regardless of the victims' attitude, the observation and analysis of their reactions remains a source of interesting information for the aggressor.

The reasons for this difference in handling these different events probably involves, partially at least, the perception that we have of the events:

– These acts are primarily perceived as attacks against privacy despite their intrusive and aggressive character in an information system or information space;

– These acts seem less massive, organized and coordinated than CNAs by botnets for example, and are very often presented as acts of negligence, flaws or human error;

– Attacks against personal data are not claimed by the authors, as website defacement operations conducted by hacktivists can be.

Would the nature of data and players involved in many recent events (for example in the defense sector) not deserve that the qualification of these events be reconsidered as aggressive operations? The numerous attacks against personal data involving the fields of security and defense are not always due to coincidence or human error. How can we not legitimately question when data processed by sensitive sectors such as defense, energy (nuclear power plants), transportation and health (hospitals) are misused because of the loss or theft of their peripherals (computers, CD-Rom, USB, cell phones, etc.), or intrusions in the systems? How

---

64. Cyber attacks against Estonia early 2007.
65. Cyber attacks denounced by the United States, France, Germany, United Kingdom, New Zealand and Belgium since January 2007.

can we not question when, in May 2008, a security audit revealed that in the American State Department, close to 400 laptop computers of employees disappeared from circulation? These computers contained secret data involving American diplomatic relations[66] as well as information on the anti-terrorist assistance program[67] managed by the Bureau of Diplomatic Security of the Department of State[68] responsible for the security of the networks of the Department, sensitive equipment and... the vanished computers.

Attacks against personal data can be part of a method of information warfare in time of peace, crisis and conflict. The volume of accessible data, low reactivity of victims, the invisibility of acts, the processing capacity of the masses of data offered by data-mining tools, can serve operations of observation, analysis, destabilization of a target, by using the weak link of the information space which is the individual. On the other hand, we should mention that there is an exponential increase of attacks against personal data globally, while waves of CNAs also multiply. Without immediate proof of the relation between both phenomena, we still should not reject the possibility of actions with the same logic and with the same objectives of destabilization of an adversary by controlling the information space.

7.3. Classification of CNA type aggressions

7.3.1. *Problems and limitations of attacks*

Does an attack against information constitute an efficient strategic instrument? Paralyzing the servers can block an enemy, but then what? An attack can send viruses, and then? On paper, theoretically, it may seem efficient and powerful. But these attacks have their limits in terms of usefulness/efficiency, and they have problems:

– we must plan the interactions triggered by an attack. For this, we must first have collected information through intelligence actions open source knowledge analysis. In the absence of such measures, an attack against information could be very unpredictable;

– attacks against information require that we possess high quality information and knowledge of the target. We must constantly analyze potential targets (how a system works, where to attack it and how it will resist). This requires preparation.

---

66. http://reclamere.com/headlines/index.php "Four Unencrypted Laptops Stolen", 9 May 2008.
67. State Department's Anti-Terrorism Assistance Program. http://www.state.gov/m/ds/terrorism/c8583.htm.
68. State Department's Bureau of Diplomatic Security (DS). http://www.state.gov/m/ds/terrorism/c8583.htm.

Efficient CNAs must rely on information operations carried out in time of peace during which the necessary information is collected;

– an attack can only be conducted by country A against country B if B has information resources. This also supposes that B is an intelligent enemy. A will have to think about the way to eliminate the countermeasure obstacles of B (firewall, security systems, duplication of information, duplication of systems), and consider forms of retaliation;

– attacking a vulnerability is not necessarily a good strategy;

– attacks against information systems must target the will of the enemy, his capacity to fight, force and dissuade. But they do not offer the possibility of controlling a territory;

– are information systems as vulnerable as we like to think? They have become quite complex, have their own protection system making an aggression difficult, with random results, maybe even inefficient (because backup or mirror systems are undoubtedly ready to get to work). Not hiding our protection can be a way of sending a message to a potential assailant that yes, they must attempt to strike, but it will be difficult and will have no impact. And even if the target was affected, there would still be a capacity of resistance;

– modern societies develop protection against aggressions that are not only technical, but also psychological. Societies have developed high resistance levels against all types of attacks. Modern societies in the 20th Century displayed highly significant resistance capacities at high and spectacular levels of aggression (global wars, substantial attacks, epidemics and natural catastrophes). This resistance finds a partial explanation in the phenomenon of resilience, which is the capacity to rebound after a trauma. In the case of a terrorist attack, for example, the most important factor is the psychological effect on populations (maintaining the feeling of fear, panic, destabilizing the organization of a society), more so than the level of destruction achieved. The effects are clearly perceptible. Following the London attacks, the number of bomb scares in good faith increased by 600% in Brussels [HEN 04]. But despite these fears, populations learned to live, and continue to live, normally. In what measure can an information attack actually "wipe out" a target? Weaken it perhaps? Make it tremble? What would be the impact of a real aggression on a society?

– in the end, regardless of the level of force of the attack, the assailant is not the one who decides if he won or lost. The victim is the one who decides if the losses experienced exceed the stake of the war and then surrenders, conquered. In this way, an attack, even if it is very destructive, does not guarantee victory as long as it does not kill the will to fight. It is therefore the will that is the real target, an unattainable target. The failure or success of an aggression depends on the final decisions taken by the enemy. Could it be possible to bend the will of an enemy by an information attack, when bombardments and massacres do not succeed?

– we must also get rid of the idea that a computer attack is easy and cheap. If that was the case, wouldn't the computer "Pearl Harbor" have happened by now? This does not hide the great power of nuisance of these attacks;

– information warfare, computer warfare, is not a universal form of war, the only type of war adapted to any conflict. No weapon or strategy has that universal quality and guarantees victory. Each conflict has its constraints, its strategies and forms of operations that must be adapted and measured. There is no magic formula.

7.3.2. *Methods of attacks*

Attackers have a well equipped toolkit: trapdoor operations, mass dialing systems, email attacks, trojan horse attacks, worms, viruses, spoofing, Van-Eck radiation, destructive microbes (at the nano scale, introduced into circuits could attack the critical components of hardware systems), hacking (penetrating networks and computers, and once in, taking control, destroying, modifying and distorting data). These attacks can happen:

– without the possibility of identifying the attacker;

– without there being collateral damages;

– in a very planned way;

– without prior declaration of hostilities;

– as a demonstration of strength, with the intention of dissuading and intimidating.

7.3.3. *Being able to define the origin of attacks with accuracy?*

Being able to define, with accuracy, the origin of an "attack" constitutes one of the major challenges for the targets affected. We cannot be satisfied with suspicions to conduct a counter attack, retaliation or legal or political actions. Today, for example, China is one of those scapegoats that we image behind every attack, which we can only denounce before any verification, when a network security event occurs.

This can be a first recourse when we want to mask a flaw in our own security systems (when it exists), or when we absolutely want to extend the list of offenses of a player to incriminate his general attitude. Such denunciations therefore fit in a more global, generally political, context, when we try to demonize an adversary, weaken him, cut him off from relations with new possible partners, marginalize him from the community.

The technical phenomena such as attacks by rebounds, attacks that we can conduct by taking over a computer that is in another territory, and the importance of botnets make identification increasingly difficult and seem to make certainties impossible.

Attacks against information systems can be grouped into three categories:

– "physical" attacks consisting of physically destroying servers, routers, cutting communication cables and destroying communication satellites with the help of conventional weapons (bombs, fire, etc.);

– "syntactic" attacks through viruses, worms, DoS and DDoS attacks and flooding are intended to disrupt, saturate, damage or ban the operation of networks, computers and information systems in a generic way;

– "semantic" attacks, which modify information (site defacement, semantic hacking) broadcasting false information. A semantic attack is combined with a syntactic attack, because to modify the content of web pages, for example, we must first penetrate the system.

7.4. The players in CNA type aggressions

Military doctrines usually distinguish two forces in the presence of a crisis or conflict: our own camp, that must be protected and the enemy's that must be attacked and conquered. Doctrines relative to information operations, information warfare, and the different operations that make up psychological operations and computer network attacks have long relied on a bipolar vision of the world: us, including all friendly forces, our allies and others, against the enemy.

Blue against red. Good against evil. An eternally divided representation of the world. But it would seem preferable to detail the players and their respective relations. We can distinguish:

– our own camp, that we will call A;

– the enemy, the adversary, who we will call B;

– allies of A, that we will call C;

– allies of B, that we will call D;

– third parties, designated by E, neutral in the A-B-C-D relationship.

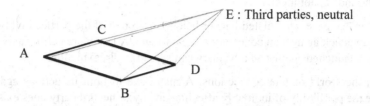

Figure 7.5. *Players in the information sphere in a conflict situation*

Therefore, there are three classes of relationship:

– "enemy/adversary". This is the A-B relationship;

– "ally". This is the A-C and B-D relationship;

– "neutral". It is the relationship that E has with all the parties present.

What is the nature of the C-D relationship? "Enemy"? Are my enemies' friends always my enemies? When an "ally" relationship is not possible, can we not imagine a "neutral" relationship? C can bring its support to A, and D its support to B, without necessarily having a relationship of adversary between each other.

Similarly, what is the nature of the relations between A and D, B and C?

The doctrines studied previously seem to only be in two blocks, one grouping A + C, and the second grouping B + D, i.e. each camp with its own allies. The relations can be very complex in reality:

– E is a third party, neutral but... a network attack by computer virus can be launched from E. This attack can affect A, B, C or D without discrimination. Without there being a political connection between E and the others, the action emanating from him can still momentarily serve the interests of one of the parties in the conflict. Imagine a hacker launching from E, of his own volition or on the orders of specific interests, a massive attack against the military information systems of one of the belligerents. E is politically neutral but finds itself involved. On the other hand, because of the interdependence of the nations, interdependence of their economies, the structure of their communication and exchange networks, it is not likely that a cyber environment nation can boast of being totally neutral;

– C and D and their allies are all agents with which A and B respectively share a common understanding in a way. The alliance can be a power intensifier, or a preventive measure (avoiding being attacked by the ally) or dissuasive (by allying with a strong party, we dissuade others from attacking us, we reinforce our own positions and capabilities);

– in cyberspace, an isolated hacker belonging to one of the parties involved can launch an attack against an adversary or against an ally (!), either deliberately or not. An attack launched against an adversary can spread (a virus) to allies;

– in the world of interconnections, A may have to limit its actions against B, because the possibility of indirectly affecting an ally or neutral party does exist;

– in cyberspace, rebound attacks can create an erroneous vision of the origin of attacks;

– allies are most often an array of allies. Which increases the complexity in view of constraints of the interconnection and interdependence of the players;

– the phenomenon of sympathizers to a cause, as seen over the Internet, reinforces and makes relations more complex at the same time;

– adversaries are often undeclared, notably in the context of out of bounds or fourth generation warfare. If identifying our adversaries is difficult, identifying our allies becomes impossible;

– positions are certainly not established. A player can go from stage B to C, C to B, etc. The landscape at moment T can quickly change.

Is the solution for controlling this complexity really absolute superiority of information? If I dominate my adversaries, allies and neutrals, is that the solution to all my existing and potential problems?

What are the consequences that I should take away from this quick representation of the complexity of the relations between cyberspace players in a context of conflict?

First, when facing an attack, the victim must always ask questions before naming an alleged guilty party:

– what is the context?

– who are the players in this context?

– where is the victim located in this context?

– what relations does this victim have with the players (alliances, enemy, neutral)?

– what are the possible, probable and credible scenarios?

Second, he must consider that he may have been a victim of an attack from an ally or a neutral player. He must also consider that he may not have been the target, but simply the victim of the side effect of an attack launched between two parties (effect of interdependence).

7.4.1. *The hacker*

Right in the middle, between sponsors and targets, because he is the one acting, implementing, controlling the attack, the one who can launch it, stop it, the one with the skills and who knows how to develop his weapons is: the hacker. How can we classify the hacker? How can we draw his profile? The attacks take multiple forms, motivations are numerous and the impact of their actions is variable.

What criteria should we analyze to distinguish the hacker who should be ruled by cyber criminality laws from the one that would carry out an act of aggression against a nation? Here are some criteria making it possible to draw a profile of computer hackers and imagine a classification. Hackers could be cataloged:

– according to their age?

- the adolescent described as a computer genius, on the front page of the newspapers, for his talent in penetrating the information systems of banks and the military, later becoming security consultant or employee in companies using his services. Couldn't the adolescent, relatively protected by laws, be used as cover for large-scale criminal actions?

– based on their propensity to remain discrete, secretive, behind the scenes, or conversely searching for celebrity, the limelight, signing each action, granting interviews to journalists, all the way to giving an email address to be contacted;

– according to their motivations?

- the game, technical exploit;
- test technologies;
- display their power, their capacities;
- threaten, be feared;
- destroy;
- steal;
- blackmail;
- financial gains;
- defend ideals, claim;

- spy;
- be recognized by their community;
– according to their nuisance power/the impact of attacks?

- insignificant attacks, without consequences;
- deface a few websites;
- deface thousands of websites;
- be able to penetrate systems and paralyze them;
- attack highly secure systems;
- program viruses;
- copy turnkey procedures: "script kiddies";
- cause light/heavy financial damages;
- cause light/heavy technical damages;
- trigger diplomatic, political, regional, national and international crises; risk the provocation of crises and conflicts;
- encroach upon the power of Nation states;
- encroach upon the power of the military to declare war;
- psychological impact: influencing the men, behaviors, decisions and have an impact on more than just the technical systems;
- cascading effects (an attack paralyzing a system followed by others, the speed of propagation of a virus, etc.);
– according to the nature of their sponsors?

- nations;
- military;
- private companies;
- terrorist organizations;
- criminal organizations;

– according to their degree of freedom;
- act according to their own individual desire, for fun, as a game, or to defend ideas;
- can be compared to snipers, working alone, knowing how to wait, aim and fire whilst remaining invisible to the target;
- act on command because it is their job (in the military, defense or intelligence agencies);

- act as "mercenaries" and do the bidding of sponsors[69];

- free or paid action;

- relations with criminal or terrorist organizations;

– according to targets?

- local, national and international;

- political, military, industrial, civilian, universities, Research and Development centers, atomic centers, sensitive or non sensitive infrastructures;

– according to their degree of relation with other hackers?

- limited or wide area networks, collective organization, mode of communication between members, long term or fleeting active cell;

- national or international communities;

- solitary, isolated;

– according to their reactivity?

- capacity to take advantage of flaws before the others do;

- capacity to reorganize, chase and re-launch an attack once the victims react;

– according to their capacity to think and follow a strategy?

- isolated attacks;

- coordinated attacks;

- consecutive attacks;

- react to political or social events;

– according to the technical level of attacks?

- simple (script kiddies);

- complex (undetectable, intrusion in secure systems).

7.4.2. *The sponsors*

In cyberspace, the list of players liable to sponsor attacks against another nation, in time of peace or war, is almost as long as the list of all players present in cyberspace.

---

69. Some hackers are picked up by the intelligence agencies of some nations, who would go so far as to pay them to deface enemy websites.

By sponsors, we mean all those who want to launch an attack but who cannot do it themselves (because of a lack of technical knowledge, for example), have it done by a third party (a hacker) who is convinced to act by paying him (mercenary), by recruitment or by ideology. This list of sponsors could include organized crime, government services, corporations, the military, activists/patriots, insurgents and terrorists.

7.4.3. *Targets*

An assailant attempts to affect the center of gravity of the target. The center of gravity of an adversary (military, economic):

– is its major strength;

– is unique (each adversary has only one center of gravity);

– depends on the nature of the war;

– is defined by strategy.

The list of targets is not different from the list of assailants/sponsors. It can be a nation, a corporation, an organization, an institution, an individual or a group of individuals.

The targets of information operations are data/content (information), channels/media (systems) and players, including leaderships, commanders, support (financial, suppliers), sympathizers, soldiers, populations, international opinion or opposition.

The target can be real or contrived, in the case of honey pots for example (computer decoys).

7.5. One weapon amongst others: the virus

Computer viral attacks can hit cyberspace and all peripherals including computers, PDAs and cell phones. There are many vectors of infection: disks, USB drives, CD DVDs, networks, email file attachments and websites. Protections seem to have a hard time guaranteeing global security.

Viral attacks have a negative impact on the victim:

– cost (restore, restart the activity, loss of revenue due to the break in the activity);

– activity paralysis;

– loss of data, distorted or modified data;

– attack against confidentiality;

– emphasise the vulnerability of systems;

– possible material destruction;

– access to blocked resources;

– increase of dependence on third parties (to restore systems and data);

– dependence on the attacker who may impose his conditions (threats and blackmail), or who may paralyze, block, or disrupt the victim's actions.

Viral attacks have a negative impact on the victim's environment:

– loss of access to data;

– lack of activity (loss of jobs, paralysis of activities);

– delays in services;

– viral contamination.

Even though the negative impacts of viral attacks seem more obvious (intuitively, even if we do not know the real consequences and damages that viruses can have, even a novice can feel fear, if for no other reason than their analogy with biological viruses, the term "virus" has a menacing connotation), a viral attack can also have positive impacts for the attacker and for the victim. For the attacker:

– an attack can be interesting not for its power of nuisance, but because it will reveal the reactions of the victim. The attack has a strategic advantage;

– it can become a weapon of dissuasion. Having the capacity to launch a viral attack can dissuade potential enemies;

– after a few attacks and after showing his power, the attacker could launch threats (and launch a stronger attack if his demands are not satisfied);

– hackers know the software flaws to exploit. These flaws are the bargaining chips. Hackers threatening to exploit the flaws request money from software developers;

– it exercises forces of opposition.

The attack can have a positive impact on the victim's third parties: economic gains (anti-virus providers, restore data, offer consultation and training).

The attack can have a positive impact on the victim when it leads to awareness of our vulnerability and the deployment of security solutions, and the implementation of adapted reaction measures. The attack can be positive because it can serve to request additional methods, be an argument to denounce an adversary and confirm suspicions.

When we want to compare the balance of power between two nations, numbers are usually put side by side. We count ships, airplanes, satellites, men, bombs, the range of weapons and reserve forces. The annual report to the American Congress "Military Power of the People's Republic of China 2006" shows such a list (page 48), comparing the Chinese and Taiwanese potential. But are these numbers enough? The quantity of weapons has not been a criterion for a long time now, their quality and capabilities are more important. Today, other factors are added such as information, information technologies and information warfare capabilities. The comparative China–Taiwan list is not involved in this exercise. But the question is raised about the evaluation of the information warfare potential of a nation. What should be counted? The number of computer specialists that a country has? The number of active hackers in the military or reserve? The number of network computers? Operating systems? Companies specialized in cryptography? Virus developers? Viruses in reserve? The number of dormant Trojan horses? This type of accounting for intimidation purposes will undoubtedly be on the agenda soon. The virus as weapon will be at the forefront.

7.6. Understanding the possible strategies of attackers

7.6.1. *Use of information warfare*

Information warfare can be used to:

– corrupt information content, manipulate data to make it inaccurate and insignificant and destroy knowledge;

– deceive the enemy by distorting information, by creating false knowledge and by adding information to show a situation that is different from reality;

– delay the flow of information, delay the acquisition and distribution of new knowledge. The information is intercepted and detained for a time. The objective is to deprive the adversary of information that would be useful, to prevent the acquisition and distribution of new knowledge;

– reduce the capability of producing and/or processing information. This process is a combination of (acquisition) blocking and corruption;

– permanently reduce the capability of producing and processing enemy information. We use the term "deteriorate";

– destroy information or information processing systems before it can be transmitted.

7.6.2. *Stigmergy*

The theory of stigmergy was introduced in 1959 [GRA 59] to attempt to model the communication methods and behavior of termites. How are such creatures able to work together to build the structures of a very complex architecture? The notion of stigmergy represents a social environment in which the agents act interdependently to affect their environment instead of directly communicating together. There is no point-point communication; the signals have to be able to be read and written by all. The web (sites, Internet, blogs) can also be considered as a stigmergic environment, but not the television media, radio, telephone or email.

The players leave "marks" in their environment, these marks then influence the action of other players. The conditions of the environment influence the behavior of all the players in the system.

Now, connect this theory to our area of interest, network attacks. One or more attacks, according to their importance (relative, because they are a function of the victim's perception), will generate a secure response from the victim, who will make some targets difficult, if not impossible, to reach. This reaction launches a signal to "choose another target".

Following an attack, it is described by the media and on Internet sites. This information is a signal to other attackers: "how to attack", "how are attacks interpreted", "what physical and psychological impact did the attack have".

There is a direct relation between an act committed and the resulting behavior, in reaction, of the victim. The signal then is "if we use these methods in an attack, the probability of obtaining such a result is...".

Launching different forms of attacks against a target will lead to as many different responses, and the combination will deliver new signals: "which attack is the most efficient"; "security flaws are at such a location".

The impact of attacks and all signals can be markers influencing the attitude of other players.

In cyberspace, preparing attacks can adopt this mode of communication and organization. Not communicating directly leaves fewer tracks, is less, or not detectable; the coordination of attackers is ensured by the visible results in modifications of the environment[70].

7.6.3. *Swarming*

The term "swarming" appears in the context of the netwar and cyberwar concepts. It represents the concept of a simultaneous attack against a single target, conducted by several small-sized units ("swarm" units) coordinating their action while remaining in constant communication. This permanent connection relies on the Internet and mobile telephony for knowledge sharing. The objective is to disorganize the enemy by a sudden attack (the element of surprise). Not only can the victim not predict the moment of attack, but he cannot predict the force of the attack, the composition of the attacker, which is decided in real time, or even at the last moment. Once the attack is carried out, assailants can leave quickly.

It is not Boyd's "loop" (OODA) that is in play this time, but instead "locate, converge, attack, disperse" (LCAD).

Swarming[71] and netwar can be expressed in the field of military warfare, but not only in that field. Several individuals or groups can communicate, organize, decide on a common action and share information in real time using methods of communication such as websites, blogs, chats, SMS or cell phones, to carry out their action such as, for example, organizing a demonstration, for political purposes, or as opposition, or another form of expression for people to quickly group at a given location and then disperse just as quickly.

Improvised swarming actions can, of course, be carried out in a social or cultural context, for fun and with very little consequence. But in the context of a real act of aggression, in a conflict or a war, swarm unit assailants must conduct their communications over secure systems. Wireless communications and the anonymous character of communications make it possible to coordinate actions on the operations field.

These maneuvers are intended to cut the enemy off from his communications and sources of supply, to have a negative impact on the morale of the adversary, to make any defense coordination very difficult (where to allocate resources) thus increasing the element of surprise. To ensure success:

---

70. See also [AJIT 06].
71. See also [HEN 04], [ARQ 00] and [AJI 06].

– the attackers must be unattainable; leaving no evidence behind, or appearing and leaving without the adversary having time to react. Tools for anonymity over the Internet contribute to make this attacker unattainable;

– the attackers must remain out of reach with long range fire power. Since networks have no borders, it is possible to reach a target that is very far, while remaining out of reach, especially from justice;

– the attackers must have an advantage over the situation, i.e. have more information on their adversary than the enemy has on them. The Internet is obviously the best tool to help in collecting information (intelligence) and in sharing it (encrypted communications). The advantage can also simply come from the initiative, since the adversary is then restricted to an attitude of reaction.

"Swarming" type tactics have been used successfully over time, but communication technologies and networks increase their relevance:

– the first type of swarming seen in history is the use of archers on horseback, such as the Huns and Mongolians, in Central Asian countries;

– one of the first Western armies to confront these tactics was the army of Alexander the Great;

– the Crusaders were conquered by this technique in 1097 in Dorylaeum, by the Turks;

– we can also cite: the victorious attacks of the Mongolians during their invasion of Europe between 1237 and 1241; the victory of North American Indians in 1791 during the Battle of St. Clair; the Napoleonic maneuvers at Ulm in 1805; and the German navy's tactics during the Battle of the Atlantic (1939–1945)[72];

– guerillas use the technique of swarming as an important element of their tactics.

7.6.4. *Open source models as a guerilla warfare model*

The "globalguerrillas" website posted an article on 24 September 2004 called "The Bazaar's Open Source Platform". In it, it established an interesting parallel between the operation of an open source software community and the dynamics of guerilla warfare groups in Iraq. The similarities are reported here (see Table 7.1) for the purpose of reflection. They can help in understanding the tactics or strategies used by hackers that can be taken as guerilla warfare actions.

---

72. All these examples are taken from the S. Edwards' book, *Swarming on the Battlefield: Past Present and Future*, Rand Corp., Santa Monica, 2000. Complete text available on the Rand Corporation website: http://www.rand.org/pubs/monograph_reports/MR1100/index.html.

Guerilla warfare	The open-source software world
Put in practice, test, try quickly and often, try new forms of attacks against different types of targets, do not wait for a perfect plan.	The versions are published without waiting for a definitive, perfect and finished version. It is the basic principle of how this community operates; versions to improve, nothing is cast in stone.
Take advantage of a large number of allies (individuals, groups, networks) to hope to resolve difficult problems. There is always one for whom the solution will seem obvious or more accessible.	Development relies on the community; among them are probably developers able to develop what others cannot do. Sharing skills.
When a solution to a difficult problem is found (how to reach a specific target for example) it must be reproduced.	A solution to a difficult problem is adopted by the community.
The other guerilla groups seem the best allies (allies of circumstance?)	Co-developers are the best partners.
The simpler the solution to an attack, the best chance it has of being adopted.	The simpler the technical solution, the more it has unanimous support in the developer/user community
The aggregation of small groups, of small individual actions, can have an impact that is similar to the action of greater forces conducted at one time (but we must not make this an absolute).	The aggregation of developments carried out by isolated individuals leads to the achievement of important projects, equal to (if not superior) to projects developed by large corporations. There again, this must not be viewed as an absolute. Large groups have a specific power that communities of isolated individuals do not have.
Capability to quickly innovate, making defense difficult.	Capability of quickly innovating, dependent on budgets and planning.

Table 7.1. *Similarities between guerilla and open-source world*

7.6.5. *Psychological maneuvers or how to lie on a grand scale*

Could the propagation of rumors through urban legends, hoaxes or the questioning of official interpretations of historical events not constitute an offensive information operation?

Remember first that misinformation consists of propagating false information to influence opinion and weaken an adversary (decrease his offensive and defensive capabilities). Propaganda is used to influence populations; it is a form of control of perception. Other forms of manipulation, of perception, are psychological operations in warfare and in publicity. Propaganda is one of the elements of information warfare. "Propaganda" has always been a well-known method, practiced efficiently, in different, more or less evolved, forms. It has contributed to circulate myths about invincibility, violence, power and barbarism. Propaganda was used more recently during the wars of the 20th Century and during the Cold War. Serbian television stations were bombarded during the Kosovo campaign to prevent them from broadcasting propaganda to the population and to foreign countries. Examples abound because it is a common element to all wars. Finally, deceit is the act of deliberately misleading. The term also means the method used for this intention. Today, other terms circulate in cyberspace, including "hoax", "urban legend" and "rumor".

The hoax is information that is deliberately false, with the intention of deceiving. The urban legend is a story that we believe, but that is generally false. The rumor is anecdotal; it can be true or false. We could add the category of questioning official versions (notably conspiracy theory).

Techniques of mind manipulation are within reach. Over the Internet, a rumor, or any information could, if posted at the right place, quickly inflate and sometimes grow to unpredictable proportions. The objective is to play on credibility.

Hoaxes and urban legends are often seen as pleasant and inconsequential texts. That they can be entertaining is not an issue. But that they are inconsequential is not so certain.

The abundance of false information, which Internet users get used to seeing, tends to reduce their vigilance (the phenomenon of familiarization).

Manipulation of information, images, sound and video can be anything but pleasant and inconsequential. Take the example of the sequence of images called "Iranian punishment for stealing". Several websites broadcast a series of pictures showing a child lying down on the ground, his arm outstretched over a folded blanket. The wheel of a vehicle comes nearer, and rolls over the arm. The child's face shows pain.

The titles and comments accompanying this series of images set the scene:

– a market in Iran;

– the child is a thief;

– justice required that his arm be run over as punishment.

According to the text, we are in the Muslim world and the first objective of this presentation is to show the cruelty of Muslim justice. In the international context of these last few years, the message is clear-cut; it demonizes an enemy.

In order to work, the rumor[73] needs three players in the communication circuit:

– the storyteller, starting the rumor;

– the victim, target of the rumor; and

– an essential link for the rumor to reach its target, because it does not happen automatically, is the category of "gullible people", the weapon of the storyteller, amplifying the strike against the target;

– there can be a fourth category of players: collateral victims (family, associates, friends, group corporations, social groups, ethnic group).

An example of a rumor is the situation where 147 Japanese teens committed suicide following the announcement of the delay in distributing the Dead or Alive computer game. On the basis of a translation error, the French press and media made the headlines of what they thought was information (the French daily, *Libération*, on 1 November 2004; television channel *France2* in a news bulletin on 21 November 2004).

Urban legends are a modern version of the rumor. Although amusing, entertaining, surprising, false and unverified, these 20th, and especially 21st, Century, tales mainly seen over the Internet, and often accompanied by pictures and sometimes used by duped media, can or could become weapons of propaganda or misinformation, instruments at the service of information operations intended to feed theories (plots, threats), feed conflicts (hate for a country, a race, an ethnic group or a religion) or contribute to propagating ideas or ideologies.

The urban legend can remain entertaining and only deceive gullible fools: the person holding a giant cat[74], the man who caught a catfish bigger than his boat[75], or the giant shark attacking a helicopter[76].

The urban legend can create a false representation of reality and develop doubt in some people. For example, by eating Japanese food, our brain can be devoured by

---

73. On the theme of "rumor" see [FRO 02].
74. http://urbanlegends.about.com/library/n_2004_giant_cat.htm.
75. http://urbanlegends.about.com/library/n_2004_catfish.htm.
76. http://urbanlegends.about.com/library/blsharkattack.htm.

worms and we can die[77], the Chinese restaurant serving mice[78], or the Taiwanese eating babies[79].

What will these tales become in the minds of people?

– will they prevent some consumers from going to a restaurant or from buying certain types of products?

– will they contribute to the development of negative ideas (xenophobia, racism) against some populations (they will poison us with their food; foreigners are cruel; the foreigner is a threat to our health, or our culture; he is different, inhuman and cannibalistic). Racism and hate between people is fed by these tales;

– with they maintain xenophobia, as well as technophobia, demonstrating the dangers of technologies (as for example the false test consisting of cooking an egg by placing it between cell phones to prove the danger of the waves transmitted[80]).

7.6.5.1. *Rumor and conspiracy theory*

The Zionist conspiracy was, and continues to be, the cement of the Nazi ideology. Today, because of the scope of the audience offered by the Internet, conspiracy theories can prosper more quickly and more widely. It is not so much the speed of transmission of information that is important as the possibility of infecting the vectors of content all over the world more inexpensively, for example by Internet sites, blogs, chats, newsgroups and email. The Internet reflects the ideology of those feeding it and those looking at it. Legal regulation (laws against cyber criminality, the conviction of some categories of contents) on the Internet cannot pretend to control content and activities by itself. As soon as a site is taken down on a continent, it can come back up on another.

Conspiracy theories are multiplying over the Internet:

– questioning of the official version of the J.F. Kennedy assassination. The videos of the attempts are dissected, cut into slices, shown in slow motion and from different angles. Texts claiming the quality of "analyses" or "investigations" provide "previously unpublished" information, or reinterpret the facts. Images are enlarged, and we look at every detail to find the truth, "the other truth", the one that the plot hid. Because, of course, truth is elsewhere. And if "they" hid the truth from us, it is because there was a conspiracy;

---

77. http://urbanlegends.about.com/library/bl-brainworms.htm.
78. http://urbanlegends.about.com/library/bl_rats_chinese_restaurant.htm.
79. http://urbanlegends.about.com/library/bl_eating_babies2.htm.
80. http://urbanlegends.about.com/library/bl_cook_egg_cell_phones.htm.

– questioning of the official version of the 9-11 attempts in New York. Here again, text, images, videos and audio recordings introduce new interpretations of the events:

- the towers were not attacked by commercial airplanes, but by missiles and military aircraft;

- the images broadcast on television are not reality: the airplane could not reach the tower with the curve of its trajectory; the airplane is in shadow whereas it had the sun lighting it;

- the images were created by movie studios;

- no airplane crashed in the Pentagon;

- there were no civilian victims in the so-called commercial airplanes;

- the towers did not collapse because of the impact of the airplanes. The towers were mined beforehand and when they collapsed, the towers fell like any building under demolition, straight down;

- a neighboring tower collapsed while never being hit by suicide airplanes. If it fell, it is because it was mined.

The theory fed by all these websites is the "American government's plot against its own people":

- the attempts were not organized or carried out by Islamist terrorists;

- the United States (G. Bush) organized these attacks;

- the objective was to provoke a catastrophe in public opinion to justify the war in Iraq;

- Al-Qaeda is an excuse. Ben Laden is not a criminal, and neither are the Islamists;

- the American government is a criminal government serving its own interests;

- the plot was instigated by the military–industrial complex that needed a mobilizing and expensive war to sell its products;

- the towers held secrets that needed to be destroyed;

- the gold reserves of the United States were under the Towers.

To demonstrate the validity of the theory, for the supporters of the conspiracy theory, irrefutable proof must be found:

– one of the techniques is the reference to declarations generally attributed to public people, politicians, and personalities repeating the theory in public;

– the analysis of images and the demonstration of their reasoning is a second instrument:

- the smallest sound, pixel, or image distortion is presented as proof, as truth, interpreted in such a way that it serves the interests of the theory, for example, on this image are we seeing the blast of an explosion, whilst on another we see nothing (which quickly becomes suspicious or, on the contrary, revealing);

- since everyone sees what they want to see on pixelated images, distorted by the different processes that files go through (coding, decoding, compressions, decompressions, or even manipulations and editing), it is not surprising that some could officially recognize the image of the devil, and others the image of God in the smoke from the fire of the twin towers. These visions can feed propaganda and foster beliefs;

– the reference to classified official texts leaked to defenders of truth;

– the alignment of different information for the players in the event that would enhance the theory:

- Ben Laden is not the enemy of Americans;

- the military carried out flight simulation tests;

- catastrophe scenarios were already developed predicting that planes would crash into New York's towers;

– testimony supports this theory from firefighters, employees working in the towers, or scientific experts, maintaining that the laws of physics made it impossible for the towers to collapse the way they did;

– the use of poor quality images is a possible technique. Associating a specific message with a low definition image in which we can see everything or nothing, especially anything we want to.

The simple work of journalistic investigation? A totally objective investigation? Who manipulates whom? How can we differentiate between what might be truth and what might be deception? It is so easy to lie, doctor, falsify or modify. Even the pictures of my trip to Thailand could deceive, be partially true, or completely true. The major difference between my personal photographs and pictures that a government or media would manipulate is in their impact.

Urban legends, rumors, misinformation and revisionism are tools for feeding hate between men, provoking conflicts, crises and for creating the wars of tomorrow.

This use of information and cyberspace, when it targets destabilization, crisis or conflict, is one of the forms that information warfare can take.

7.6.6. *The role of Internet sites in information warfare*

A website can be perceived as part of a game, a pawn, a tool at the service of strategic or tactical objectives. It is an element of information warfare for the following components:

– Computer Network Attacks. A website can be a target or a weapon (hiding viruses);

– Psyops/propaganda/deception[81]. Through the manipulation of content, wanting to influence the psyche of the adversary, promote ideas, denounce and distribute false information;

– Intelligence. A website can contain information useful to intelligence, delivering some information and hiding others. Some sites are real sources of information. We must collect, analyze and interpret. Data mining is used in this complex task. But we must also use the expertise of specialists to understand the results, and interpreters to read content.

7.6.7. *Using blogs?*

Can the military or other "aggressors" efficiently use blogs as a tool of influence? What is the value of blogs as targets of military influence operations? What is the value of blogs as support for intelligence operations? How much influence can blogs have on targets that we want to hit in this way?

The answers to each of these questions seem to converge. The effects are probably proportional to the popularity of the blog, as long as we can measure its popularity. There are many unknowns and uncontrollable variables.

Regardless of their use, regardless of the authors, blogs and the blogosphere remain defined by a certain number of constant variables that must be considered carefully. The influence of blogs can be directly affected by the structure of the blogosphere at a given moment:

– there is great imbalance in terms of popularity between websites/blogs. Very few are very popular, and most of them are not popular, or remain confidential;

– the "snowball" effect. The most popular websites and blogs always have more visitors, are more quoted, more referenced and linked. Even if popular sites see their popularity increase, the phenomenon only increases the gap. There are very few

---

81. Deceiving, abusing and misleading.

blogs that go from anonymous to high popularity. Creating a new blog and quickly having a following and significant impact is extremely difficult;

– the most linked websites and blogs are the most influential;

– conducting an influence action type information operation would therefore assume:

- favoring popular blogs;

- ignoring unpopular blogs;

- developing tools to measure the influence of a website/blog, a step that may be revealed as tricky: what criteria should be used to measure it? The number of visitors? The number of links or quotations?

– how can we not get lost in the mass?! 75,000 new blogs are created each day according to a study by Technorati.com (April 2006), including close to 10% of splogs (spam blogs)[82];

– a blog, as a website, can be influential, as long as the targeted population is a big user of the Internet. If that is not the case, any mass influence operation by this method is useless. Similarly, is it useless to hope to gain intelligence from a too limited or confidential blogosphere, as with countries with low Internet penetration, where only minority fringes of the population can access and express themselves?

7.6.8. *Website defacement and semantic attacks*

These two methods of attack can serve the interests of psychological operations.

Website defacement shows the vulnerability of a website to attacks, erase the content of one or more pages and replace it by other content. This new content can, amongst other things, be a slogan, a claim, a warning, a call, and have an ideological or political character. It is intended to affect opinion, or broadcast and propagate an idea.

Semantic attacks are more harmful. After an intrusion in a system, the attacker does not erase all content, but simply modifies a few words, a few lines, changing the meaning and range of messages.[83] The objective is to disseminate false information.

---

82. According to D. Kesmodel, *Splogs' Roil Web, and some Blame Google*, The Wall Street Journal Online, October 19, 2005.
83. See *Yahoo! News hacked*, by Kevin Poulsen, SecurityFocus, 18 September 2001, http://www.securityfocus.com/news/254.

Specific contexts seem particularly favorable to this category of attacks. These are situations of crisis and conflict between nations. For example Israel/Lebanon (there was a new wave of attacks against Israeli sites in 2006), the Arab world/Israel, India/Kashmir, China/United States, China/Taiwan.

7.6.8.1. *Motivations behind website defacements*

There are many levels of motivations:

– website defacements almost always involve the mark of their authors (as a code name). They want to be known and recognized;

– the technical achievement still remains one of the motivations of these actions. Accumulating the largest number of defacements, for fun, to demonstrate capability, the power of nuisance;

– to deliver an ideological, political and philosophical message, attracting attention to a cause, denouncing an act or enemy.

7.6.8.2. *Variable modus operandi*

Attack tactics and strategies in the case of website defacements can combine different forms, and follow specific tempos.

Prior to any attack, hackers will prepare the field, which means identifying vulnerabilities, identifying victims (a simple search on Google for example can provide necessary information), grouping techniques to exploit these flaws, and launching the attack:

– an all-encompassing attack or opportunistic attack where hackers do not target a specific enemy. Exploiting known and published flaws, their attacks can hit all vulnerable targets, made vulnerable notably because of the non-installation of security patches (updates);

– an attack against preferred targets. Some attackers prefer to target government websites, and others prefer corporations. The choice may be a function of the message to be transmitted;

– the attack launched by rookie hackers who will use simple techniques, that they may not even master (script kiddies). The simplicity of the attack does not mean that the damage will be less significant. If the attack is simple, it is because it is a possible option. This flaw in the website under attack is mainly the lack of corrective updates;

– an attack launched by seasoned hackers. It can control one or more websites leaving systems administrators facing very difficult problems to solve;

– the choice of the depth of the attack, for example modifying a page, modifying two pages, modifying content, attacking forums, blogs, and erasing files;

– the isolated attack. The hacker only launches an attack against one or more websites and the hostile act is not followed by other acts of the same nature against the same targets;

– attack by consecutive waves. One or more websites can be caught in a wave of attacks over a period that can be long or short, and can be disruptive for several weeks. This configuration can occur when an attacked site is restored, when a systems administrator intervenes to reestablish the site's operation. The hackers can then launch new attacks to control the situation until the capabilities of the systems administrator are saturated. The scenario can be as follows, built in several waves[84]:

- first wave: home page and forum defacement;

- second wave: manipulation of the website configuration;

- third wave: user database defaced or erased;

- fourth wave: control of the administrator account, modification of all user names in the forum, defacement of new pages;

- fifth wave: defacement of new pages and forum. Attack against blog databases;

- sixth wave: hackers wait for the site to restart following the intervention of a systems administrator, and launch another attack. Persistence with a website can become a confrontation between an administrator and hackers;

– the attack uses flaws and can rely on relatively simple techniques;

– the massive attack. A single attack targets hundreds or thousands of sites simultaneously. The fact that sites are hosted on shared servers can make the operation of hackers easier. Tools are installed on the server, which can serve to attack several sites hosted on it;

– the attack transformed into a duel between hackers and systems administrators. At each attack, the administrator restores and attempts to take security measures, and at each restoration, the hacker launches a new attack, so as to challenge him. The idea, for the hacker, of technical accomplishment still remains here.

7.6.8.3. *The players*

The http://www.zone-h.org/component/option,com_topatt/Itemid,48/ website introduces a list of the 50 most active hackers on the planet. The first one, iskorpitx, had defaced 187,926 sites (as of 23 May 2007).

---

84. This configuration was described in a report published by www.SecuriTeam.com and www.BeyondSecurity.com explaining the *modus operandi* of hackers from the Team Evil group against the Israeli site www.zionismontheweb.org.

When we observe the situation in terms of website defacements in different countries, we notice that a few hackers, most often in small groups, sign their work, and represent a high percentage of the attacks recorded.

7.6.9. *What is cyber terrorism?*

To speak of cyber terrorism establishes a link between "terrorism" and "cyber attacks" (representing attacks against information systems by computer methods). Can information warfare be used by or against terrorist organizations?

As if it was an obvious relationship, terrorism and cyber attacks, terrorism and the Internet, are now associated, leading to the concept of cyber terrorism.

7.6.9.1. *What is terrorism?*

Speaking of a terrorist act in the information sphere, on networks (Internet, telephony) supposes a definition of the concept of "terrorism", to escape from intuitive approaches. But, this concept does not have a single definition.

There are, however, a number of truisms that exist in discussing terrorism:

– terrorism is the weapon of the poor. This idea is supported by the assessment of the existence of terrorist pockets in countries said to be poor, from the third world, and because they support causes that are not those of industrialized nations;

– terrorists want to be seen and heard; killing is not their major objective. In this regard, terrorism is also presented as a symbolic act of communication, an attempt to communicate a message through the use of orchestrated violence;

– international terrorism is an alternative to conventional warfare. In this configuration, terrorism is the fight of one nation against another. The terrorists are well financed, supported by paying nations who sometimes provide them protected shelter where they can prepare new offensives;

– terrorism works in networks, and is organized in large conglomerates;

– to operate, terrorism needs significant financial means;

– terrorism is a vague term;

– security agencies are also taken by surprise by terrorist attacks;

– terrorism is based on the motivation of individuals, for example their psychological motivation (dissatisfaction, finding a meaning to life, becoming a "believer" in a cause), belonging to a group that is trying to maintain legitimacy by demanding unanimity, and becoming intolerant to others, the cultural motivation that comes from the feeling of threat to the survival of an ethnic group;

– terrorism targets and modes of attack are limitless, because terrorism does not recognize innocents (no regrettable collateral damage). The target is then chosen according to the interest that it represents for the cause and according to its accessibility;

– acts of terrorism rarely come from improvisation but from preparation, location, training and information. In 1998 the IRA constituted data banks from information stolen in Ireland, France and the United States. In order to steal data, it is not always necessary to use complex or discrete hacking techniques. Just calling on sympathizers, employees of companies managing large databases (telecommunications companies, travel agencies, electoral registers) who can steal personal information databases (phone numbers and coordinates) may be enough. From this information, the IRA defined its targets and identified the names of police officers. Intelligence is therefore vital to terrorism, regardless of its form;

– the major players in terrorism, beside C2s (thinking heads), are the terrorist-soldiers, those who will give to the cause and complete the act, the ones who can handle a weapon and munitions, the sympathizers who will contribute to the cause, the dormant units, infiltrated as close as possible to potential targets and who can suddenly strike given an order. These dormant units can exist for the preparation of physical attacks as well as cyberspace attacks. Recruitment is therefore the other vital side of the organization;

– the terrorist movement needs support structures. If they are not provided by a government, they are provided by sympathizers who were forced to help terrorists, for example provide logistics to terrorists and intelligence, broadcast propaganda, recruit and finance;

– when a CNA follows a deadly attack, those who speak (experts, journalists, government) quickly tend to connect the two events. The W32.Nimda.1@mm worm that activated a few days after 11 September 2001 was presented as a terrorist product. Both facts are connected[85]. A single-seater plane hits a building in the United States. Right away, the press speaks of attacks and terrorism. A company is affected psychologically following a crime carried out by a physical attack. A trauma leaves tracks, changes the manner in which we see things, during the following days, weeks, or even months and years. But it is always risky to establish a relation *a priori*, without any verification, on the spot, between two or more events. Proof of the weakness of the link is that it only relies on assessments that have no significant argument value. An event *must* be connected to a first event, because it happens the same day, week, less than one month after, or on the anniversary date; it seems that the relative temporal proximity often serves as an

---

85. Jane's Intelligence Review, 25 September 2001.

explanation to those who absolutely want to create a relation between two facts, as if the simplest simultaneous occurrence of both facts was enough to link them. But this paranoia is the product of the impact of terrorist actions on the psyche of individuals. This "psychological warfare" is efficient since it destabilizes good reasoning and maintains the feeling of a permanent threat. In December 2002, the owner of a cyber cafe in Kolkata, India, alerted the authorities because he found, by coincidence, a message on a computer containing the names of four known buildings with a date and time for each. Immediately, the preparation of an attack was presumed. Terrorism is so ubiquitous in our society that vigilance is permanent. Each person is concerned about everything. In this particular case, there was no relation with terrorism. But was exchanging significant files with names and precise information enough to be suspicious? Everything can become suspicious, the simplest word or behavior;

– it is undeniable, on the other hand, that links exist between political or diplomatic events and cyber attacks. In these cases, CNAs take the form of demonstrations or even ideological matches and are claimed by their authors, completely different from the appearance of a virus on networks, when we do not really know where it comes from, who launched it or why. These confrontations through networks generally oppose two camps (for example, China/USA, China/Japan, Israel/Palestine, India/Kashmir). Ideologies with marked differences, and their sympathizers, get involved in these fights, playing as a global amplifier of tensions that for some would otherwise have been limited to a restricted regional audience.

To summarize, the components of terrorism that Shitanshu Mishra, a researcher at the Institute for Defense Studies and Analyses (India), proposes to represent in the form of a wheel that he calls the chakra of terrorism (or 'T' Chakra) [MIS 03], i.e. the wheel of terrorism, are:

– a strong leadership, in the middle of the wheel;

– a C2, in the middle of the wheel;

– on the outside, the organization, motivation, recruitment and training, weapons/munitions, targets, information collection (intelligence), movements, bases, support structure, publicity (propaganda) and finances.

In the United States, terrorism is defined by the Council on Foreign Relations (US State Department) as "violence against non combatants in order to influence public opinion":

– the objective is the sensitivity of public opinion (destabilizing, creating the feeling of fear);

– the method is violence;

– the target of this violence is the civilian population.

According to the definition of terrorism proposed by the Counterterrorist Center of the CIA, the acts are:

– premeditated;

– political;

– aimed at civilian targets (which is simplistic because in Iraq we always speak of terrorist attacks against the military);

– conducted by ad hoc groups, i.e. not part of the regular national military.

7.6.9.2. *What is cyber terrorism?*

What would be the definition of cyber terrorism? In order for there to be cyber terrorism, there must be a conjunction between terrorism and attacks against/in cyberspace.

Note that if cyber terrorism (as terrorism) is conducted by ad hoc groups, this is not the case with cyber warfare or information warfare, which are, theoretically at least, attacks orchestrated by government agents (military, intelligence agents).

The American intelligence authorities consider the first known case of cyber terrorism to be an attack launched by the Tamil guerillas against the Sri Lankan government's embassy information systems in 1998, sending several thousands of emails with the message "We are the Black Tigers of the Internet and we are conducting this action to paralyze your communications" [DEN 98].

The Federal Bureau of Investigation (FBI), USA, defines cyber terrorism as "premeditated, politically motivated attacks against information, computer systems, computer programs and data which results in violence against non-combatant targets by sub-national groups or clandestine agents"[86].

The FBI definition only retains the notions of attack and violent use of cyberspace as weapon or target. But cyber terrorism cannot be summarized in these attacks. The use of ICTs to organize movement (C2, logistics, transmission of orders, intelligence and financial operations) can be qualified as cyber terrorism since it is the use of cyberspace for the purposes of terrorism. The controlled use by terrorists of methods of communication (Internet, radio and broadcasting) makes it possible to broadcast information, messages, commands, and to maintain the morale of supporters, spread propaganda, broadcast false information, and launch calls for

---

86. www.bitpipe.com/rlist/term/Cyberterrorism.html.

financial donations. Al Qaeda is known for its websites (www.mojahedoon.net). The presence of terrorist groups is actually strong over the Internet:

– Middle East, Far East: Al Qaeda, Hamas, Lebanese Hezbollah, Al Gama'a al Islamiyya, Palestine's PLO, Palestinian Islamic Jihad, DHKP/C (Turkey), PKK (Kurdish labor party), Islamic Movement of Uzbekistan (IMU);

– Latin America: Tupak-Amaru (MRTA) (Peru), Shining Path (Sendero Luminoso), The National Liberation Army of Colombia (ELN-Colombia), Colombian Revolutionary Armed Forces (FARC), Zapatista National Liberation Army (ELNZ);

– Asia: LTTE (Liberation Tigers of Tamil Eelam), Japanese Red Army (JRA);

– Europe: ETA, etc.

These English websites target an international audience including political, international organizations, journalists and populations. The websites of terrorist organizations are the showcase of ideologies and demands. We often find a history of the movement, texts and images dedicated to the glory of leaders, ideological propaganda supporting the movement, information on the last events, the last glorious facts of partisans (victories won), and especially the denunciation of crimes perpetrated by enemies, or details of prisoners of conscience, because it is better, in the eyes of the international opinion, to look like (or attempt to look like) a victim than a glorious executioner. As a victim, using violence is then legitimate, because it is the only option left by the oppressor. Terror then becomes the only weapon of the weak. Chechen websites are one example among many; a series of images of the victims of Russian barbarism, texts of ideological reflection, a calendar of recent events, or even videos of successful attacks or the capture of prisoners. The websites of organizations qualified as terrorist are now one of the major vectors of psychological operations that they conduct on international opinion. And it is precisely to counter these psychological operations that the websites are the permanent subject of attacks from hackers with opposing ideology (whether from isolated hackers, or (not quite) hiding the hand of the government, as is the case between Russians and Chechens, for example). A Cat and mouse game is engaged over the Internet. Websites change addresses, are defaced and come back, have mirror sites. Information warfare is one of the contexts in which nations and terrorist organizations carry out their confrontation.

Where is the boundary between hacking and cyber terrorism because, in the end, both use the same techniques? In reality, the difference could be difficult to establish. What looks more like the propagation of a virus than another virus propagation? What is the difference between a virus launched by an isolated hacker and a virus launched by a terrorist? Both can bring the stock market or a corporation to its knees, or hit sensitive infrastructure systems. Will the simple hacker caught by police have to demonstrate that he had no connection with any terrorist organization?

How do we define DoS type attacks launched by Palestinian teens against computers held by Hezbollah or Hamas[87]?

How can we categorize "hacktivism"[88] characterized by politically motivated cyber attacks (the conjunction of political activism and hacking, where hacking serves ideologies or political causes), premeditated, carried out by ad hoc groups (site defacement and DoS type actions, as well as, mainly, the creation of false enemy websites[89]), or by sympathizers to a cause? All these points describe terrorism as described above. Hacktivism is not an attempt at causing serious damage and its targets are not (always) civilian. Its attacks are formalized by site defacements, intrusions, flooding and propagation of viruses. Would the difference between cyber terrorism and hacktivism, then, only be the degree of "violence"?

Why do we need all these distinctions (terrorist, hacktivist, hackers, etc.)? To propose technical measures for different protection? No. To prevent attacks? Maybe. That would imply having a precise and accurate vision of ideological spheres of influence, political evolutions, and information from intelligence departments to establish security strategies based on the level of risks: all of which is difficult to achieve. Do we need the distinctions to propose different legal treatment, or to sanction differently according to motivation or the target hit?

In order for terrorism and cyberspace to converge:

– the target must be networked and highly dependent on information systems. Without this main condition, there cannot be effective attack;

– the attacker must be networked to conduct semantic attacks, or he must have access to the physical core of systems to carry out a physical attack (bombs and lasers);

– the attackers must have the skills to carry out network attacks. When they do not have them, they can acquire them by recruiting hackers who will work for them, either for payment or because of ideological conviction. In this configuration, it is not obvious that the operation will be more economical financially than the installation of a homemade bomb in a subway;

---

87. See the article *Islamic groups "attack" Israeli web sites*, by D. Kraft, 10 November 2003. http://www.landfied.com/isn/mail-archive/2000/Oct/0137.html.
88. See [AND 05].
89. A popular example concerns an Amnesty International pseudo-site.

– the degree of violence must be significant to be able to interest terrorists and influence public opinion, if that is really the objective of terrorist attacks. When will the attack against a computer system have the power of impact of a bomb exploding in a subway, in a public place or an airport? The lethal weapon triggers a visual and emotional shock amplified by the images broadcast by the media and the Internet (referencing videos of hostage decapitation, videos of the planes crashing in the New York towers, or images of the dead in the streets of Iraq towns). Can a cyber attack have the same power, the same psychological and physical impact?;

- a successful attack must be broadcast on a large scale;

- the attack must have the ability to instantly create a feeling of fear in the population. When a bomb explodes, nobody knows where the second one is, or when it will explode, and it takes a long time to move beyond that feeling, even though it is trendy to speak of the virtues of resilience. This permanent feeling of fear takes a while to develop, because even though our societies are completely dependent on information systems, they are nonetheless a defined space. When a presumed bomb is supposed to explode, all places and moments become the subject of collective fear. The analogy between "terrorism" and "cyber terrorism" can therefore not be total, because this extreme physical then psychological character (physical heartbreak for victims, heartbreak for families affected and for societies) seems hard to reconstruct after a network attack.

In a more general way, what can be called cyber terrorism is the presence of terrorists in cyberspace: their use of methods of communication (Internet network, telephony) to recruit, organize, communicate safely, finance, collect information, broadcast propaganda, plan, launch operations, and remain in the background, anonymous during the preparation of their actions and create a networks of relations.

7.6.9.3. *Relations between fighting against terrorism and cyber attacks?*

Is it possible to establish a connection between terrorism and cyber attacks without cyber attacks being qualified as "cyber-terrorism"? This is the question raised in a study published by the Institute for Security Technology Studies of Dartmouth College on 22 September 2001 [VAT 01]. Did the policy of retaliation for terrorist acts of September 11 (2001) by the United States and their allies lead to a new wave of cyberspace attacks? Establishing a connection between a political conflict and "attacks" against information systems is not new. Antecedents demonstrated the existence of this relation, but not the link with terrorism, for example the China–USA crisis when a Chinese fighter aircraft collided with an American surveillance plane (April, 2001), or when NATO bombarded targets in former Yugoslavia in Kosovo and Serbia (Spring, 2000).

Among the potential sources of cyber attacks, the report identifies terrorist groups, terrorism sympathizers, anti-American hackers, and those in search of a thrill.

Their actions, called cyber attacks, mainly cover site defacements, DoS attacks, the use of worms, viruses, the exploitation of vulnerabilities, and intrusions in systems in order to corrupt sensitive data. Against these "threats" the countermeasures are the same whether the attack has a link with terrorism or not. We speak of technical measures, human measures, and quick information from authorities in order to carry out future investigations.

7.6.10. *Use of web applications by insurgents*

The use of forums by Iraqi insurgents was recently the subject of a publication called "Cyber Mobilization: A Growing Counterinsurgency Campaign" [THO 06]. According to this article, the doctrine of insurgents is based on two types of offensive actions, armed conflict and mobilization of the masses. In Iraq, the main weapon of insurgents for armed conflict is IED (Improvised Explosive Device). To mobilize the masses and carry out cognitive activities, the insurgents learned to use to their advantage a more high-tech weapon, cyberspace, that they use to plan, identify targets, train, recruit and influence sympathizers. "Cyber mobilization" through the Internet and mobile telephony must therefore be one of the targets of counterinsurgency actions conducted by coalition forces.

The Internet and mobile telephony have been used as tools for mobilizing crowds or groups for a long time, making it possible to arrange meetings in locations announced by email or SMS. Events are announced online only. We need only look at recent events organized by MySpace, for example. Communication tools no longer only communicate point-point; they have become a lever, a power intensifier at the service of organizers of movements involving a larger number of people. Mobilizing is "recruiting" participants in large numbers to carry out an action. We must first win their support to our cause, which is the role of psychological operations (propaganda, promises) and make them act, which is easier when they rally to the ideology. The first phase can be carried out through Internet sites, forums, blogs, chats and virtual communities. The action can also be carried out through instructions, orders, calls, pictures of targets, plans, all types of information on the enemy, distribution of combat manuals (how to carry out a kidnapping, how to make a bomb, how to kill a person) through websites and especially through dynamic applications such forums, blogs, and mobile telephony, SMS and email.

Iraqi insurgents have used these mobilization tools, such as online information, propaganda, broadcasting of ideology, extremist religious teaching (to this day, there are over 4,000 extremist Islamist websites), manipulation of public opinion, mobilization of marksmen, recruitment of candidates for suicide missions, and for the immortalization of their sacrifices.

The insurgents use websites to broadcast information and propaganda. Images and testimonials are put up faster than broadcasts from Americans and their allies.

How can we counter the impact of these Internet sites? One of the keys seems to be speed. We must react very quickly to a situation by providing the population with information before the insurgents do, who always present the facts to their advantage, even if they are detrimental to the truth. The insurgents in Iraq conduct a physical attack and an information operation over the Internet quickly follows. From culprits, they turn into victims. Speed, plus the absence of direct confrontation, as well as the element of surprise (surprise attacks, sniper strikes, homemade bombs, are all unexpected and difficult to control) disrupt the OODA loop of the Americans. The insurgents do not operate on the same OODA base; they operate on a PAIR loop (Physical Action – Information – Response). The scenarios imposed by the quick surprise actions of the insurgents prevent the coalition troops from closing the loop; they are limited to deciding and acting (DA), not able to observe and orientate. Recognizing an efficient PAIR loop is also recognizing the failure of the Americans in controlling information, as well as failure in lack of reactivity and the refusal to adopt similar methods as the insurgents, refusing to fight against them on an equal footing.

Insurgent websites, with information that can be relayed by Islamist websites all over the world, compete against official information agencies. The objective of these insurgent sites seems to be to rally believers to their cause, not to convince the world of political projects. The challenge is great for Western forces unaccustomed and unprepared for these methods of occupation of cyberspace by insurgents. Counterinsurgency measures in the information space must be implemented to face the challenges of this virtual warfare arena (a concept introduced by the British expert, John Mackinley [JM05]). This arena can operate on a deeper level. Insurrection grows like a virus and acts intuitively, which may require the reorganization of security structures and consideration of a new *modus operandi*.

The analysis of the *modus operandi* proposed by Timothy L. Thomas[90] raises some questions:

– is it realistic to speak of insurgent doctrine?

---

90. See [THO 00], [THO 01], [THO 03] and [THO 04].

– is the Internet really the most efficient weapon of modern extremists?

– should we only see advantages in the form of battle adopted by the insurgents? They may have been holding the coalition forces in check for years, but at what price in human lives? The losses are disproportionate. The flexibility of the organization and the mobilizing power of the Internet alone cannot explain the resistance;

– can coalition forces not use their control of networks to paralyze the most popular websites? Defacements, viral attacks and DoSs are all techniques relatively simple to implement to take down the servers and websites hosting such content. Why is no action taken?

– even though it appears that the Insurgents do not seem to use viral attack type CNAs against the information systems of the United States, preferring to use ICTs for communication, mobilization and manipulation, what is preventing their adversaries from adopting very aggressive CNA actions?

– coalition forces may find it more advantageous to let these sites survive, because they also represent a great source of intelligence.

7.6.11. *Questioning the relations between political context and cyber attacks*

Many political crisis situations are represented on the field of confrontations in computer networks.

When tensions between nations or communities are heightened by an event serving as a trigger, cyber attacks immediately increase between the parties in conflict. The following events occur:

– a crisis situation exists for years, such as for example the conflict between Pakistan and India over Kashmir, the Israel–Palestinian conflict, the ideological conflict between China and the United States, the war in the former Yugoslavia, etc;

– in this context, an event occurs, brutally exaggerating the existing tensions or the conflict. The Indian army carries out an intrusion in Kashmir, the Israeli army kills Palestinians, Palestinians explode bombs killing Israelis, a Chinese fighter aircraft collides with an American surveillance place, NATO bombards targets in Kosovo and Serbia;

– Indian, Pakistani, American, Chinese, Israeli, Palestinian hackers or pro-Indian or pro-Pakistani hackers (who we will call sympathizers) attack the websites of the designated enemy and/or allies/sympathizers;

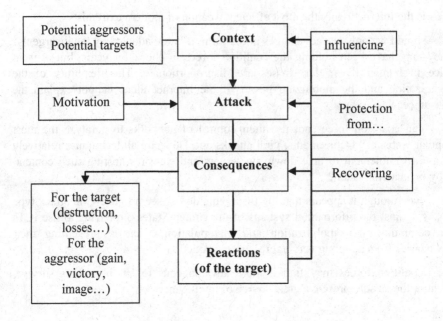

Figure 7.6. *Context – Attack – Consequences – Reactions cycle*

– the attacks are motivated by politics and ideology. They are not gratuitous, fitting in to a well-defined context;

– "sympathizers" sharing the same ideals, made up of foreign hackers or hacker groups or a diaspora, can lend a hand in these confrontations, as the cooperation is made easier by communication networks (via the Internet). In the case of NATO bombings in Kosovo, the "sympathizers" were Serbian, Russian and Chinese. The attackers of this coalition of sympathizers of common causes did not attack NATO's C2 systems but did disrupt its efforts in its strategy of using the Internet for propaganda purposes to accelerate the end of the Milosevic regime (one of the American sites attacked listed atrocities perpetrated by Milosevic to justify the bombings [PRI 04]). Other examples include when Pakistani or pro-Pakistani (or so-called Pakistanis) attack Indian and American websites, or when Israelis (or pro-Israelis or would-be Israelis) attack Hezbollah websites and anti-Israeli hackers respond on the same playing field by network attacks (e.g. Knesset, Israeli defense forces and Bank of Israel website attacks);

– we also find "mercenary" hackers, selling their skills to one party or another. Nations are suspected of using hackers all over the world, recruited for their needs and paying them for their services;

– the attacks can be developed and follow a strategy such as first attacking official sites of the government, then attacking economic interests, communications infrastructures (servers, ISPs), and attacking foreign targets to expand the conflict[91];

– modes of operations are always the same: DoS, DDoS attacks, saturation of servers, viruses, worms, Trojan horses, intrusions, theft or distortion of data, and site defacements;

– the attacks launched by belligerents against one another also involve allies/sympathizers, but their actions also have consequences for third parties (other countries) whose networks or computers are used as gateways, for rebound attacks. The resources of "neutral" countries can also be hit. This was reported in an article published on the Zataz.com website on 19 May 2001[92], according to which Korea served as a gateway during the attacks between China and the United States in April 2001;

– hacker attacks can be publicly condemned by their governments, but few actually convict them (there have been no arrests or convictions in China for network attacks against American interests). Without condemning them, or even recognizing them through silence, governments tolerate, or even approve of, these actions.

---

91. This would be one of the strategies followed by the Palestinians in their "cyber Jihad" according to Michael A. Vatis in [VAT 01].
92. Quoted (in French) on http://strategique.free.fr/archives/textes/ca/archives_ca_14.htm "Chine/USA, c'est la Corée qui trinque".

Chapter 8

An Information Warfare Law?

The views expressed by victimized governments attract our attention. They speak of "culprits" and "attacks" involving the Chinese "army" or Russian "government" that would affect the American "Department of Defense" or German "government services". The reactions involve "intelligence services" when we speak of "espionage", and we use "NATO" when we suspect that the aggression is conducted by a government.

The events of 2007 lead us to one question: should we place them in the context of "information warfare"?

Up to this point, we have been careful not to use the term "cyber criminality". The broadcasting of illicit content (pedophilia, content attacking individual rights, etc.), intrusion in information systems, distortion of data, data theft, site defacement, virus propagation and fraud (spam, phishing, Nigerian scams, identity theft) are all part of cyber criminality, and can be dealt with by a government's criminal laws, by the European convention against cyber criminality, or by international legal cooperation.

But when a State attacks another State, even though it might use methods, techniques, tools or even players involved in "traditional" cyber criminality, it appears difficult to speak only of cyber criminality. The attack of one government by another has a political, strategic, diplomatic, military and security dimension that a criminal act from a delinquent, or even an international criminal organization, mainly aiming at financial gain, does not.

It is therefore necessary to establish a distinction between "cyber crimes" and "use of force/armed attack". This distinction will at least make it possible to adapt the level of response and the mode of reaction to aggressive acts, and to adapt international positioning and methods used to ensure the victim's security.

The first problem is the ability to make the distinction between these two levels of attack. This is not always easy because technologies and techniques are often the same, the targets can be the same, a "cyber offense" can prepare or support an act of war, the cyber criminal can be the armed side of the war, and because cyber criminality can serve information warfare by, for example, contributing to the destabilization of a target (whether that be a country, an economy, the operation of a player's information systems, etc.)

Fighting a war is using force to impose our will on the enemy. But the use of this force is supported by law in order to channel man's animal instinct, so that not everything is allowed in war. Can law be used for the new forms of warfare, those we call "cyberwar", "fourth generation wars", "network warfare" and "information warfare"? We can clearly see the efforts from governments to have laws to manage illicit acts in cyberspace, such as the European convention on cyber criminality or national laws to regulate information systems players to fight against computer delinquency, against system intrusion, data distortion, information theft and the production and distribution of computer viruses. But this legal context is a solution in the civilian sector and in a context of peace. Would it bring a solution to an act of aggression, through networks, by one government against another? Would the perpetrators be judged as criminals (in the same way as terrorists or insurgents not recognized as war combatants), or could international law invoke the United Nations charter or other international conventions surrounding warfare? Could the UN Security Council have to assess whether an act of aggression had taken place in a case where the critical information systems of a country were paralyzed following an attack by hackers?

8.1. Warfare and the law

The laws of warfare strictly condition the right to use force. This part of the law is called *jus ad bellum* (laws of war), and includes all legal standards regulating the legality of use of force by governments. Once hostilities are declared, other rules affect the belligerents, and other laws protect civilian and military combatants; this part of the law is called *jus in bello* (laws during war). This expression designates the legal framework handling what is accepted or not during hostilities.

Jus ad bellum mandates fundamental principles: to have the right to use force, there has to be a just objective, legally constituted authority and the solution must be the last recourse. The *jus ad bellum* recognize the right to self-defense.

Jus in bello is the group of restraints involving war players. The war being fought must be just, the immunity of non combatants must be ensured, the war must be proportional to objectives, collateral damages are acceptable but they must be limited, the attacker must discriminate, targeting national assets is prohibited (objects vital to the survival of the civilian population and the environment).

Laws of warfare protect against acts of force which would be criminal acts, such as murder and aggression, if they were committed during times of peace. Not respecting the laws of war is a war crime. Because of the limits they impose, these laws are a guide to the selection of methods, weapons and targets.

Laws of war were codified as international laws for international armed conflicts: *jus ad bellum* (The United Nations charter) and *jus in bello* (the Hague convention (how to engage in and conduct warfare) and the Geneva conventions (how to protect combatants and non combatants)).

8.2. Engaging in and conducting a war

The United Nations charter condemns the use of force (Article 2) and regulates its use under the control of the Security Council:

– Chapter I, Article 2, paragraph 3: all Members shall settle their international disputes by peaceful means in such a manner that international peace and security, and justice, are not endangered. (Does a hacker attack threaten international security? Is a psychological operation conducted in time of peace considered a peaceful operation?);

– Chapter I, Article 2, paragraph 4: all Members shall refrain in their international relations from the threat or use of force against the territorial integrity or political independence of any state, or in another manner inconsistent with the purposes of the United Nations. (The charter condemns the use of force. Are a network attack, blinding of a satellite by a laser and paralysis of infrastructures by a viral "attack" included in use of force[1]?);

---

1. Technology, Policy, Law, and Ethics Regarding U.S. Acquisition and Use of Cyberattack Capabilities. William A. Owens, Kenneth W. Dam, and Herbert S. Lin, editors, Committee on Offensive Information Warfare, National Research Council, 2009.

– Chapter VII, Article 39: the Security Council shall determine the existence of any threat to the peace, breach of the peace, or act of aggression and shall make recommendations, or decide what measures shall be taken in accordance with Articles 41 and 42, to maintain or restore international peace and security. (An act of aggression can be assessed by the Security Council. The council has not yet assessed information warfare type aggressions);

– Chapter VII, Article 51: nothing in the present Charter shall impair the inherent right of individual or collective self-defense if an armed attack occurs against a Member of the United Nations, until the Security Council has taken measures necessary to maintain international peace and security. The use of force is therefore condemned except in cases of self-defense or following the decisions of the Security Council. The nations then have a legitimate monopoly to violence, a consequence of the principle of sovereignty. Nongovernmental actions trigger the right to self-defense, such as invoked by the Security Council following the attacks of 11 September 2001 to support American retaliation. Self-defense is authorized *a priori* when there is an attack from one government to another. Several ambiguities remain involving self-defense. Can it be by anticipation (preemptive) or can it only be carried out after the fact (retaliation, reaction)? Can a hostile intention justify a self-defense attack? In this case, what is a hostile intention, what must be the degree of threat for a step to be crossed toward legitimacy of an action of force? Is saturation by network attack (of the methods of communication of a nation), or a virus attack, an event that speak of hostile action?

8.3. Protecting combatants and non-combatants

Protocol I (1977) of the Geneva Convention relates to the protection of armed conflict victims. Methods of enemy destruction have no limits, so the object of these conventions is to limit war cruelty. Could this protocol be expanded to "victims" of information warfare? The essence of Protocol I has the following points:

– Title I, Article 1, paragraph 2: in cases not covered by this Protocol or by other international agreements, civilians and combatants remain under the protection or authority of principles of international law derived from established custom, from the principles of humanity and from dictates of public conscience. (The Article lays down the bases of respectful humanitarian rights of an individual, regardless of the nature and conditions in which a conflict evolves. It is the famous Martens clause, from the Hague convention of 1899/1907. According to this clause[2], a principle

---

2. Frederic de Martens was a Russian delegate in the Peace conference of 1899 which proposed that any person (population and belligerent) remains "under the protection and the control of the principles of people's rights, as they result from established uses, principles of humanity and requirements of public conscience". This clause appeared for the first time in the introduction of the Hague Convention II in 1899.

widely accepted by humanitarian rights organizations, everything that happens during an armed conflict is subject to the application of humanitarian rights principles;

– Title III, Section I ("Methods and Means of Warfare"), Article 35: the belligerents cannot use any other method of warfare. In any armed conflict, the right of the Parties to the conflict to choose methods or means of warfare is not unlimited;

– Article 37 prohibits the use of treachery with the intent to kill, wound, or capture the adversary, such as for example the feigning of civilian, non-combatant status (Paragraph C). (But the anonymity behind which cyberspace players can hide can make this treachery possible);

– if treachery is prohibited, war ruse remains authorized (Article 37 al. 2). Ruses of war are not prohibited. Such ruses are acts which are intended to mislead an adversary or to induce him to act recklessly but which infringe no rule or international law applicable in armed conflict, and which are not perfidious because they do not invite the confidence of an adversary with respect to protection under that law. The following are examples of such ruses: the use of camouflage, decoys, mock operations and misinformation. Military deception, counter-intelligence operations, psychological operations and the creation and broadcasting of false information are all components of information warfare that could be covered by Article 37;

– barriers are placed against psychological operations by Article 40, which stipulates that it is prohibited to order that there shall be no survivors, to threaten an adversary therewith or to conduct hostilities on that basis;

– populations and civilian assets must be the subject of a specific protection according to the terms of Title IV of the Protocol;

– Article 48 specifies that in order to ensure respect for and protection of the civilian population and civilian objects, the Parties to the conflict shall at all times distinguish between the civilian population and combatants, and between civilian objects and military objectives, and accordingly shall direct their operations only against military objectives. (Can computer network operations make this distinction? The interconnection of civilian and military infrastructures makes the task very difficult. When the American military used civilian satellites to transmit their communications during the Gulf War, would the enemies have had the right to destroy those satellites?);

– civilians are the subject of a specific protection (Article 51). The civilian population and individual civilians shall enjoy general protection against dangers arising from military operations. The civilian population as such, as well as individual civilians, shall not be the object of attack;

– the attacks must categorize targets: indiscriminate attacks are prohibited (Article 51, paragraph 4);

– conducting attacks against the civilian population is banned (Article 51). By civilian population, people and assets are included. The targets must be limited to military objectives. But what is a military objective? Is a civilian building in which the military take position a military or civilian target? Is a civilian communication infrastructure used by the military during a conflict a military or a civilian target? Even though Article 52 specifies that the destruction of an asset must offer a precise military advantage, categorization remains difficult. Can a population that supports war methods and offers shelter to its combatants be a military objective?

– the attack must offer a defined and precise military advantage;

– it is prohibited to threaten violence with the goal of terrorizing populations (Article 51): propaganda and psyops must be strictly restricted;

– attacks without categorization are prohibited (Article 51): methods must discern and not direct attacks anywhere; they must be precise;

– the principle of proportionality: violence must be proportional (Article 51). An attack must be proportional to the military advantage expected. But this advantage is often difficult to evaluate in advance. Precision guided weapons follow this principle, by limiting the risks of collateral damages;

– cultural assets and sites of religious significance must be protected. In terms of the protection of cultural property, the Statute of the International Criminal Court (ICC: 17 July 1998) added new Articles (8, 2, b, ix and 8, 2, e, iv) declaring any deliberate attack against religious, educational, art and scientific buildings to be a war crime. (Could some Internet spaces come under the protection of these articles?);

– Article 57 mandates taking precautions before launching an attack, to verify that there really is a military objective. But because of the speed of execution of the OODA loop, in a combat situation, it is not always possible to "verify" the military nature of the objective.

8.4. The challenges of information warfare for international law

When Estonia was the victim of cyberspace attacks, it did not limit its reaction to returning its systems to normal and then possibly filing a complaint to be handled as an act of ordinary cyber crime. Instead, it raised the problem on the political stage and requested help from the international community. What could we do faced with a wave of attacks without a name? Does international law make it possible for a country to prove that it was attacked by another nation and then to carry out actions of retaliation, or to get gangster states removed from the international scene?

"Information warfare" components create challenges to international law:

– the paradox of information operations (which are simultaneously methods of attack, tools of defense and weapons of retaliation) must be examined with precision;

– international law must define that an act of aggression in cyberspace is not just an act of cyber criminality;

– waves, signals and networks know no national territory or national sovereignty. In cyberspace, how can we preserve the principle of sovereignty (one of the fundamental principles of international law since the treaty of Westphalia in 1648) which recognizes that each nation has exclusive authority within its borders?

– a cyber attack can be an act of war before war, an act of war during wartime, or a criminal act in time of peace;

– is humanitarian law adapted to the protection of non combatant targets from cyber attacks? Should we consider the application of humanitarian law in this context?

– during a conflict between two states, the territory of neutral nations is supposedly impregnable by belligerent forces. And yet a network attack can use resources from neutral countries. Can this utilization without authorization be considered as an act of war against a neutral country?

– can a country, victim of an attack that has "gone through" a neutral nation, launch a legitimate attack against this "neutral" country because it did not take appropriate measures to prevent its infrastructures being used as a means of attack against its will?

– how can we reaffirm or reinforce the terms of humanitarian law conventions? The definitions of fourth generation war and those of information warfare converge toward two major points: the target is the human mind and its psychology, and there is no longer – or less and less – a boundary between civilian and military worlds. Each individual is a potential target, or a soldier or potential weapon. War objectives no longer come down to confronting armies, or weakening military forces. Civilians can be the subject of attacks;

– when military communications use civilian infrastructures (for example commercial communication satellites or the Internet) during a conflict, is the attack against these civilian infrastructures an infringement of the laws of warfare?

– the transition of defensive to offensive operations can be subtle, and the resources are the same. When does transition occur, from a technical and thus from a legal standpoint?

– we must be able to bring legal protection to victim states, even in the absence of identification of actual authors;

– we must be able to carry out international investigations;

– we must be able to provide the means to respond to these attacks;

– we must define what a cyber attack is: when is it an act of war, when is it a criminal act, when is an information operation a legitimate preemptive weapon? What are the rules regulating cyber attacks, protecting targets/victims?

– these questions go beyond a simple analogy with the laws against cyber criminality, surrounding and sanctioning unauthorized access to information systems and to information, or attacks against the integrity of data and against systems operation;

– we should redefine "military objectives" and the status of dual use objects (servers, satellites, etc.)[3].

How, for example, should we assess the events of 2007: as acts of cyber criminality or acts of "war"? If we choose the first response, the role of the police is central, and the individual penal laws of nations will apply to the offenders. If we opt for the second solution, international law will need to launch a process involving governments at a political and military level.

But what attitude should be adopted? Repressive? Aggressive? How do we fend off and anticipate the next attempted aggression? It is the paradigm of security that must be reevaluated, because we can no longer want to place illusory defences (new policies of security, new software security applications, new protocols, new regulations…) on top of fallible defences (the internet, the basis of cyberspace, was not created with a secure foundation, and any new security protection we might develop today or in the future will be built on that insecure and fragile base).

The concept of information management and systems must be rethought, and collective or cooperative security must be organized. From a strictly technical standpoint, responses seem fragile. Technical, political and legal approaches must be combined. International law must surround these acts in a more precise way and we should not be limited to recourse through conventions on cyber criminality which relate to a situation that is very different from that of conflicts between nations. And since it often appears that conflicts in cyberspace are simply the extension of the tangible world, laws and policies have a major role in the control of events.

---

3. For more in-depth information on the legal dimension, see [SCH 99], [BAY 01], [TAI 06].

Conclusion

Defining information warfare is not an easy task. For some, it is simply different packaging for the theories and methods of conventional wars. For others, information warfare consists only of using hacking methods in crises or conflicts between nations or groups to serve political or private interests. Others see it as the extension of electronic warfare, widening the control of the electromagnetic spectrum to all information from a conflict, incorporating information control. Still, others expand the war perimeter well beyond military questions and include all forms of action for destabilizing a nation through aggressions against its economy and vital infrastructures. One of the reasons for the problem in defining precisely the concept of "information warfare" is probably due to the diversity of the players involved: governments, political blocks, corporations, citizens and the military. This problem of finding a definition is revealed by the different approaches taken by the broad range of sources which, each with their point of view and specific interests, adopt the one that is most appropriate at the time. Even the different departments of the American military have their own definitions that evolve through doctrines formulated over time.

Myths also come into play. Information warfare is a clean and smooth war guaranteeing the end of physical and kinetic violence. There will be no more bombs, dead and wounded. In the future, wars will only be conducted through computers and networks in cyberspace. Computer warfare is getting closer, and the Estonian conflict of April 2007 was only the beginning. But, for now, information warfare is only a complementary method of warfare and not a substitute.

The second myth often encountered involves the invincibility of those who control information. Even though the objective is to control the OODA loop, it does not guarantee the final success of a war, especially today, as wars do not really have a beginning or an end.

Another misconception is the greater efficiency of an information warfare attack. How could an attack against computer networks be more powerful, more dissuasive or more efficient than a kinetic attack against enemy armies? Bombings don't always win against the resistance of enemies (the phenomenon of resilience in part explains this capacity to endure violence). Would psychological attacks or computer virus attacks succeed against this resistance?

The fourth misconception is that technological superiority ensures superiority of methods necessary to information warfare, and because of this, final victory is achieved. If that was the case, the situation in Iraq would have been taken care of a long time ago by the Americans.

The last myth is the real threat of a computer Pearl Harbor. This idea, dating from the 1990s, suggests that an attack would happen soon, from an unknown source, and be carried out through networks to destroy the whole communications infrastructure of a country, rendering it completely helpless. This does not take into account the strong interdependence that connects global communication infrastructures today. For example, remember that, in March 2003, the US Air Force had to reject an attack plan against Iraqi financial computer systems because the banking network of that country was connected to a financial communication network in France. An attack against Iraqi networks could have interrupted banking machines in Europe[1].

Regardless of the problems over definitions of information warfare, a consensus seems to be emerging on its objective: the exploitation of information to obtain an advantage over the adversary. Another consensus involves the extension of these practices in peacetime, beyond times of crisis or conflict.

To summarize the approaches, we could, then, define information warfare as the aggressive/defensive use of information space components (which are information and information systems) to reach/protect the sovereignty of a nation through actions conducted in times of peace, crisis or conflict[2]. The concept is then centered on its political and military dimensions, and a connection of dependence is established between the notions of information space and sovereignty – which comes down to saying that an aggressive/defensive action conducted in the information space is not always an information warfare operation: some acts are simply part of cyber criminality or delinquency.

---

1. Charles R. Smith, *Cyber War Against Iraq*, www.newsmax.com, 13 March 2003.
2. Daniel Ventre, "Guerre de l'information: la prolifération des capacités?" *Défense et Sécurité Internationale Review* (*DSI*), No. 38, June 2008. pp. 30–35.

Generally, we speak of information warfare when:

– information in its digital form is used as a weapon and/or as a target;

– information systems are taken as vectors for attacks and as targets;

– cyberspace is taken as a space used for violence;

– there are (geo)political, (geo)strategic, military and sovereignty stakes in play. In this way, cyber criminality is theoretically placed outside the scope of information warfare.

Information warfare is also the reflection of all our fantasies, dreams and wishful thinking. Not least of which, the dream of invisibility, is formalized by the possibility of acting in cyberspace by masking our identity, by remaining elusive, untraceable and unidentifiable. Attackers use this capacity.

Transparency would be another dream, consisting of having the ability to read man's thoughts, to see everything, understand everything and see beyond the horizon without being seen. Information control and dominance enables us to achieve this power.

The weapon of information is the weapon of the weak against the powerful. It could be victorious in asymmetrical situations, in situations of inferiority of numbers because, in the digital space, there is no longer any real notion of superiority and inferiority; each is practically equal. The other virtue of the information space is the power of communication given to the weak. If a weak player is attacked, he can announce it to the world in a few minutes, mobilize international public opinion, play on his weakness, rally the world to his cause and tip the scales to his advantage. The powerful is then perceived as the bully, the weak as the innocent little lamb, even though he may not be.

Information warfare is the pursuit of the dream of invincibility, of absolute supremacy, of world domination and of superiority acquired by controlling information. In the 1980s, the doctrine of the American Department of Defense considered the Internet as a technology that was invulnerable to a nuclear attack. Information technologies were considered technologies of invincibility.

The goal of information control was to ensure absolute precision, only aiming at and striking predefined targets, and being first in confrontations. It would also ensure precision in all circumstances (day, night, combat), anywhere (seeing beyond the horizon). It would also allow precision in the knowledge of our opponent and ourselves, and in processing information and the resulting vision of the world.

Speed and efficiency, two major operational qualities, had to be developed and multiplied with the use of ICTs. The idea is to communicate faster and better, capturing and processing information in real time.

Information warfare can also be perceived as a clumsy operation consisting of wanting to transform a potentially weak, unfinished, prototype (the Internet, TCP/IP protocol, etc.) into a weapon, which is supposed to be strong and without weakness.

Information warfare (let us call it information operations, or to limit it even more, computer warfare, or cyberwar, because of the predominant role that CNO type operations play in cyberspace today) as we know it, is the subject of unanswered questions:

– How can we use NICTs for aggressive/defensive purposes in an efficient way?

– Can NICTs really revolutionize the art of war?

– Information warfare is a group of aggressive/defensive operations conducted in a space that nobody knows who it belongs to. Who do the networks, systems and information space belong to? Where are the borders? Is it a space without right to sovereignty?

The lack of answers to these questions may be explained by the lack of originality or invention that the people debating this subject for many years have displayed. Even though we add new facts to the analyses each year (new "attacks", new apparent balances, new methods of action, new enemies or new threats), we have to admit that themes are slow in developing, and the human mind seems to be carried by a line of thought from which it cannot escape, which is unfortunate when dealing with a subject that is said to be so revolutionary. In fact, the themes are part of all the analyses proposed for over 15 years, such as, for example:

– the vulnerability of modern societies linked to information systems;

– the vulnerability of players in defense and sensitive infrastructures because of their connections with the Internet;

– many countries (>120?) have acquired cyber attack capabilities;

– the problems with implementing efficient defensive/reactive measures;

– the vulnerability of information systems (American and others) against cyber attacks.

These paths of reflection were raised in the middle of the 1990s in reports from the Rand Corporation, the American Congress, in the media and during American Senate hearings in 2000. They were brought up as sources of challenges for the security of cyberspace in the 1990s; they remain open today in 2009.

The same limitations seem to be in place today. For example, since 2007, it seems impossible to discuss information warfare or cyber security without referring to Estonia. This extreme focus, which may be wrong, on the Estonian situation is clearly an intellectual easy way out, but the risk is that the debates will always return to a single course. We must get away from the Estonian debate.

Do our minds have a hard time renewing themselves? Maybe more so than we think. Here is a short quotation:

"Telegraphy and wireless telephony were used from one corner of Europe to the other and so easy that the poorest man could talk, when he wanted and how he wanted, to a man located anywhere on the globe. [...] It was the lifting of borders. Critical hour indeed! [...] The French Republic, the German Republic [...] Switzerland even and Belgium, each expressed, by unanimous vote from their parliament and in huge meetings, the solemn resolution of defending against any foreign aggression the national territory and national industry. Tough laws were announced [...] regulating severely the use of the wireless telegraph [...] Our borders are defended by electricity. The federation is surrounded by a zone of thunder. A simple man wearing glasses is sitting somewhere in front of his keyboard. He is our only soldier. He has only to touch a key to destroy an army of 500,000 men". We recognize contemporary themes; the global dissemination of a communication technology, the concern that it raises from governments, the feeling of threat against security and national defense, the resulting authoritative reactions and regulation, and finally the image of absolute power in the hands of a single man as powerful as a whole army, able to destroy an adversary in one fell swoop, in an image of the Apocalypse, recalling the catastrophic predictions of an electronic Pearl Harbor type war. But these lines are not from the 21st Century. They were written in 1905 by Anatole France, in a book titled "Sur la pierre blanche".

Information warfare is part of the modern wars of the end of the 20th and the beginning of the 21st Century, but it also fits into an older awareness. Is this war so different from the ones of the past?

If we ignore the technical and technological methods available to belligerents today, we could say it is not. The objective of war is always to conquer an adversary, to impose our will. War remains the promulgation, through other methods, of political objectives.

But, if war is different today, it is because of technology which makes information the major player in conflicts. Information is a weapon, an objective and a target. It has forced us to rethink the concept of conflict space. The technologies using it make it possible to see better and faster (technologies enable us today to see what was invisible, beyond the horizon, at night and through cloud), to acquire superiority in all spaces (ground, air, sea, cognitive space), to engage more precisely and to reduce the lethality of operations. Information has made it possible to expand the field of players involved in wars. Whereas before, threats were unique, identified and the armies fought in a battlefield in an ordered way; today the risks are more numerous, threat outlines are more vague and the battlefields are greatly expanded. Reaction delays are shorter. Whereas before, information may have been scarce, penalizing the decision of commands, today too much information may be a greater risk. Finally, information is omnipresent, even sometimes where it should not be. Combatants are observed, we can find their trace during and after network attacks, they can be filmed in action and videos can be made public over the Internet.

Information warfare shares a common point with all forms of war, however: it is the expression of violence. And in order to be efficient, this violence must be channeled and directed. Gratuitous attacks are of no interest to the attacker, even though the ease and low cost of acquiring information "weapons" can open up possibilities to warriors in training.

Information warfare satisfies many characteristics of war in general and draws on its objectives. It can be, or contribute towards, the expression of a solidarity, maintaining or reinforcing the social adhesion of a group (groups of hackers who get together around an interest of common targets illustrate this adhesion). War is the extension of policy, a group attacking another group fights to protect or increase its economic and social future. It is the fight to maintain or acquire a space (information space is the object of this war), for domination, to impose a will or to decide who is the strongest. If we accept the idea that war is part of human nature, then information warfare is only one of its forms; it is a new form, perhaps, more evolved from a technological standpoint, less lethal but still aggressive towards man, and certainly not the last.

Bibliography

[AJI 06] AJITH A., CRINA G., VITORINO R., *Swarm Intelligence in Data Mining*, Springer, Studies in Computational Intelligence, vol. 34, XVIII, p. 267, ISBN 978-540-34955-6, 2006.

[AJIT 06] AJITH A., CRINA G., VITORINO R., "Stigmergic optimization", Springer, *Studies in Computational Intelligence*, vol. 31, p. 299, 2006.

[AND 05] ANDERSON K.E., *Hacktivism and Politically Motivated Computer Crime*, Network Risk Management, LLC, Draft Publication, 13 June 2005.

[ARQ 93] ARQUILLA J., RONFELDT D., "Cyberwar is coming!", Comparative Strategy, vol. 12, No. 2, Summer 1993.

[ARQ 97] ARQUILLA J., RONFELDT D., *In Athena's Camp: Preparing for Conflict in the Information Age,* Rand Corporation, Santa Monica, 1997.

[ARQ 99] ARQUILLA J., RONFELDT D., *The Emergence of Noopolitik: Toward an American Information Strategy*, Rand Corporation, Santa Monica, 1999.

[ARQ 00] ARQUILLA J., RONFELDT D., *Swarming and The Future of Conflict*, Rand Corporation, Santa Monica, 2000.

[ARQ 01] ARQUILLA J., RONFELDT D., *Networks and Netwars. The Future of Terror, crime and militancy*, Rand Corporation, Santa Monica, 2001.

[ASH 02] ASHRAF T.M., "Doctrinal reawakening of the Indian armed forces", *Pakistan Air Force Military Review*, November/December 2002.

[BAK 01] BAKSHI, P. (LT. COM.), "Security implications of a wired India: challenges ahead", *Strategic Analysis*, April 2001.

[BAY 01] BAYLES W.J., *The Ethics of Computer Network Attack*, Parameters, pp. 44–58, http://www.iwar.org.uk/iwar/resources/ethics-of-cna/bayles.htm, Spring 2001.

[BIL 04] BILLO C.G., CHANG W., *Cyber Warfare, An Analysis of the Means and Motivations of Selected Nation States*, Institute for Security Technology Studies, Dartmouth College, December 2004, 142 pp. http://www.ists.dartmouth.edu/docs/cyberwarfare.pdf

[CAM 92] CAMPEN A.D., *The First Information War: The Story of Computers and Intelligence Systems in the Persian Gulf War*, AFCEA International Press, 1992.

[CAM 96] CAMPEN A.D., *Cyberwar*, Washington DC, AFCEA Press, 1996.

[CASS 93] CASSIDY R., *Russia in Afghanistan and Chechnya: Military Strategic Culture and the Paradoxes of Asymmetric Conflict*, Strategic Studies Institute, U.S. Army War College, February 1993.

[CHE 07] CHENG A., *La pensée en Chine aujourd'hui*, Folio essais, Gallimard, 2007.

[CHO 02] CHOMSKY N., *Propaganda*, Du Félin Editions, 2002.

[CLI 07] CLIFF R., BURLES M., CHASE M.S., EATON D. and POLLPETER K.L,. *Entering the Dragon's Lair: Chinese Anti-access Strategies and Their Implications for the United States*. RAND Project Air Force, 155 pp., 2007. http://www.rand.org/pubs/monographs/2007/RAND_MG524.pdf.

[DAI 00] DAI Q., *Innovating and Developing Views of Information Operations*, Zhongguo Junshi Kexue, Beijing, April 2000.

[DEN 98] DENNING D., *Information Warfare and Security*, Addison Wesley Longman Inc., 1998.

[DUN 96] DUNNINGAN J.F., *Digital Soldier: The Evolution of High-Tech Weaponry and Tomorrow's Brave New Battlefield*, St. James Press, New York, 1996, First Edition, 309 pp.

[FIT 92] FITZGERALD M.C.., *The New Revolution in Russian Military Affairs*, Royal United Services Institute for Defence Studies, London, 1994.

[FIT 94] FITZGERALD M.C., "Russian views on electronic signals and information warfare", in *American Intelligence Journal*, Signals Intelligence & Information War, Spring/Summer 1994 (Vol. 15, No. 1), USA.

[FRO 02] FROISSARD P., *La Rumeur – Histoire et Fantasmes,* Belin Editions, October 2002.

[GRA 59] GRASSE P.P., "La reconstruction du nid et les coordinations interindividuelles chez *Bellicosi-termes natalensis* et Cubitermes sp. La théorie de la stigmergie: Essai d'interprétation des termites constructeurs", in *Insectes Sociaux*, Vol. 4, No. 1, pp. 41–83, 1959, France.

[GRI 06] GRIFFITH S.B., *Sun Tzu – The Art of War*, Evergreen, Taschen GmbH, 2006.

[HEN 04] HENROTIN J., "Airborne Dragon (Kurdistan, mars–avril 2003) et le potentiel conceptuel du swarming", *Cahiers du RMES* (*Réseau Multidisciplinaire d'Etudes Stratégiques*), No. 1, July 2004, France. http://www.rmes.be/1_JH2.pdf.

[HUS 05] HUSAIN Z., PATHAK A.K., VYAS R., "Management of information warfare: emerging paradigm", *International Journal of Information Technology and Management*, vol. 4, No. 1, p. 67, 2005.

[JOH 02] JOHNSTON A.L., *Toward Contextualizing the Concept of a Shashoujian (Assassin's Mace),* Government Department, Harvard University, August 2002.

[LEI 98] LEI Y., *New Breakthrough in the Study of Information Warfare*, Jiefangjun Bao, July 1998.

[LIB 96] LIBICKI M., *What is Information Warfare?*, National Defense University Press, Washington DC, 1996.

[LIB 07] LIBICKI M., *Conquest in Cyberspace. National Security and Information Warfare*, Cambridge University Press, 2007.

[LIM 02] LIM T.W., *Analysis of China's Strategic Power*, Singapore Institute of International Affairs (SIAA), 8 December 2002.

[LIN 89] LIND W.S., NIGHTENGALE K., SCHMITT J.F., SUTTON J.W., WILSON G.I., "The changing face of war: Into the fourth generation", *Marine Corps Gazette*, October 1989, Pages 22–26, USA.

[MAC 05] MACKINLEY J., *Defeating Complex Insurgency*, The Royal United Services Institute, Whitehall Paper 64, 2005.

[MED 07] MEDEIROS E.S., "China's international behavior: activism, opportunism and diversification", *Joint Force Quarterly*, issue 47, 4th quarter, 2007, pages 34–41. USA. Available at http://www.ndu.edu/inss/Press/jfq_pages/editions/i47/8.pdf.

[MIS 03] MISHRA S., "Exploitation of information and communication technology by terrorist organizations: strategic analysis", in *Institute for Defense Studies and Analysis*, vol. 27, No. 3, pp. 439–462, July–September 2003.

[MU 98] MULVENON J., YANG R.H., *The People's Liberation Army in the Information Age*, Rand Corporation, Santa Monica, 1998.

[NIU 00] NIU L., LI J., XU D., *On Information Warfare Stratagems*, Beijing Zhongguo Junshi Kexue, Beijing, April 2000.

[POL 05] POLLPETER K.L., "The Chinese vision of space military operations", in *China's Revolution in Doctrinal Affairs,* Mulvenon J. & Finkelstein D. (Eds), pp. 329–369. Center for Naval Analysis, Alexandria, 2005. http://www.defensegroupinc.com/cira/pdf/doctrinebook.pdf

[PRI 04] PRICHARD J.J. and MACDONALD L.E., "Cyber Terrorism: A Study of the Extent of Coverage in Computer Security Textbooks", *Journal of Information Technology Education*, Bryant University, Smithfield, RI, USA, 2004.

[QIA 99] QIAO L., WANG X., *Unrestricted Warfare*. PLA Literature and Arts Publishing House, Beijing, China, February 1999, 228 pages. Full text available at http://www.terrorism.com/documents/TRC-Analysis/unrestricted.pdf.

[SCH 94] SCHWARTAU W., *Information Warfare – Chaos on the Electronic Superhighway*, New York, Thunder's Mouth, Press, 1994 (1st edition).

[SCH 99] SCHMIDT M.N., "Computer network attack and the use of force in international law: thoughts on a normative framework", *Colombia Journal of Transnational Law*, vol. 37, 1999.

[SCH 02] SCHMIDT M.N., *Wired Warfare: Computer Network Attack and jus in bello,* RICR, vol. 84, No. 846, pp. 365–399, www.icrc.org/Web/eng/siteeng0.nsf/3e02cd6224ce0af61256, June 2002.

[SCH 05] SCHWARTAU W., *Information Security*, Rodney Carlisle (Ed.), Encyclopedia of Intelligence and Couterintelligence, 2005.

[SHA 98] SHALAMANOV V., *Process-oriented Model of Information Warfare*, Information and Security, vol. 1, No. 2, pp. 59–66, 1998.

[SHE 99] SHEN W., *Checking Information Warfare-Epoch Mission of Intellectual Military*, Jiefangjun Bao, February 1999.

[SUN 95] SUN Z., *Strategies to Minimize the High-Technology Edge of the Enemy*, Xiandai Bingqi, No. 8, pp. 10–11, August 1995.

[TAI 06] TAIPALE K.A., *Deconstructing Information Warfare*, Center for Advanced Studies in Science and Techology Policy, presentation for the Committee on Policy Consequences and Legal/Ethical Implications of Offensive Information Warfare, Washington DC., October 2006.

[TAK 04] TAKAHASHI S., "The Japanese perception of the information technology-revolution in military affairs: toward a defensive information-based transformation", in Emily O. Goldman and Thomas G. Mahnken. (eds.), *The Information Revolution in Military Affairs in Asia*, NY, Palgrave Macmillan, 2004.

[THR 96] THRASHER R.D., *Information Warfare Delphi: Raw Results*, Naval Postgraduate School, Monterey, California, USA, June 1996, 56 pages. http://www.iwar.org.uk/iwar/resources/usnavy/delphi.pdf.

[THO 98A] THOMAS T.L., "Dialectical versus empirical thinking; ten key elements of the Russian understanding of information operations", *The Journal of Slavic Military Studies*, http://leav-www.army.mil/fmso/documents/dialect.htm, 1998.

[THO 98B] Thomas T.L., "The mind has no firewall", *Parameters*, 28 no. 1 (Spring 1998), pp. 84–92.

[THO 00] THOMAS T.L., "The Russian view of information war", in *The Russian Armed Forces at the Dawn of the Millennium*, Michael H. Critcher (Ed.), December 2000.

[THO 01] THOMAS T.L., "47 China's electronic strategies", *Military Review*, May–June 2001.

[THO 03] THOMAS T.L., "Like adding wings to the tiger: Chinese information war theory and practice", *Military Intelligence Professional Bulletin*, July 2003.

298   Information Warfare

[THO 04] THOMAS T.L., *Dragon Bytes, Chinese Information War Theory and Practice*, Fort Leavenworth, KS: Foreign Military Studies Office, 2004.

[THO 06] Thomas T.L., "Cyber mobilization, a growing counterinsurgency campaign", in *Iosphere*, Summer 2006, pp. 23–28, Joint Information Operations Center. http://fmso.leavenworth.army.mil/documents/cyber-mobilization.pdf.

[TOF 80] TOFFLER A., TOFFLER H., *The Third Wave*, New York, Bantam, 1980.

[TOF 93A] TOFFLER A., *Powershift: Knowledge, Wealth and Violence at The Edge of the 21st Century*, Bantam Books, 1991.

[TOF 93B] TOFFLER A., TOFFLER H., *War and Anti-war: Survival at the Dawn of the 21st Century*, Little, Brown and Company, 1993, 302 pages.

[VAT 01] VATIS M.A., *Cyber attacks during the war on terrorism – A predictive analysis*. Institute for Security Technology Studies, Dartmouth College, USA. 22 September 2001, 30pp. http://www.dtic.mil/cgi-bin/Get TRDoc?AD=ADA395300

[YOS 01] YOSHIHARA T., *Chinese Information Warfare: A Phantom Menace or Emerging Threat?*, www.iwar.org.uk/iwar/resources/china/iw/chininfo.pdf, November 2001.

[WAN 95] WANG P., *Meeting the Challenge of Information Warfare*, Zhongguo Junshi Kexue, Beijing, February 1995.

[WAN 97] WANG B., *A Preliminary Analysis of Information Warfare*, Zhongguo Junshi Kexue, Beijing, pages 102–111, November 1997.

[WAN 99] WANG B., *New Military Revolution in the World, Subduing Enemy Force without Battle, Informationized Warfare*, Zhongguo Junshi Kexue, Beijing, May 1999.

[WAN 00] WANG B., *The Current Revolution in Military Affairs and its Impact on Asia–Pacific*, Zhongguo Junshi Kexue, Beijing, April 2000.

[WEN 00] WEN J., *Revealing Secrets of Beijing's 998 State Security Project*, Tai Yang Pao, June 2000.

[WOO 95] WOOD R., The Foundation of Information Warfare, Research Report, Maxwell AFB, Air War College, 1995.

[XIE 99] XIE G., *Wars under High Tech*, Beijing Renmin Ribao, December 1999.

[YUA 99] YUAN B., *On IW, Digital Battlefields*, Zhongguo Junshi Kexue, Beijing, February 1999.

[YUS 97] YUSOPOV R.M., *Information Security is the Foundation of National Security*, Vooruzheniye, Politika, Konversiya, March–April 1997, No. 3–4, pp. 35–38.

Index